D0368640

POPULATION AND DEVELOPMENT IN RURAL EGYPT

POPULATION AND DEVELOPMENT IN RURAL EGYPT

Allen C. Kelley
Atef M. Khalifa
M. Nabil El-Khorazaty

Duke Press Policy Studies
Studies in Social and Economic Demography
Durham, N. C. 1982

Printed in the United
States of America

Library of Congress Cataloging in Publication Data

Kelley, Allen C.
Population and development in rural Egypt.

(Studies in social and economic demography) (Duke Press policy studies)
Includes bibliographical references and index.
1. Egypt--Population, Rural. 2. Egypt--Rural conditions. I. Khalifa, Atef M. II. El-Khorazaty, M. Nabil, 1943- . III. Title. IV. Series. V. Series: Duke Press policy studies.
HB2541.7.A3K44 304.6'0962 82-2425
ISBN 0-8223-0475-9 AACR2

The Egyptians...obtain the fruits of the field with less trouble than any other people in the world.

Herodotus, Persian Wars, II, 14.

CONTENTS

TABLES AND FIGURES

TABLES

FIGURES

PREFACE

Egypt, like most countries in the Third World, faces a "population problem": record growth rates, Malthusian pressures in rural areas where arable land and water are already scarce, expanding and crowded cities, high dependency burdens, and rising underemployment. While the government of Egypt has actively attempted to curb these population pressures for about two decades, the results of this effort--especially the spread of family planning in rural areas--have been disappointing. Alternative strategies for coping with the burgeoning population have thus been sought.

One such strategy, the "development approach" to population policy, emphasizes the upgrading of the living standards of the population (health, education, nutrition, work opportunities) with the expectation that, at some stage, population growth will automatically decline. After all, this is what has happened in developed countries during their own "demographic transition." In contrast, a second strategy is represented by the "family planning" approach, which emphasizes the provision of information and training about, and the distribution of low-cost services for, family size control. There has been considerable debate in Egypt about the relative efficacy of the development *versus* the family planning approach to population policy. Although this debate has in the past taken the form of an either/or confrontation, this is, fortunately, no longer the case. Analysts and policymakers are now attempting to identify an optimal format to *combine* development programs with family planning so that development and population goals will be mutually reinforcing. The Population and Development Project (PDP), designed and implemented by the Population and Family Planning Board (PFPB) in 1977, represents one possible prototype of an integrated response to the population problem.

In an attempt to provide quantitative evidence of the relationships among economic, social, and demographic change, and to gain information on the effectiveness of alternative population policies, several major data collection efforts have been carried out in Egypt. The present study analyzes one of these data sets, the 1979 Rural Fertility Survey (RFS), financed by the UNFPA with a grant to the PFPB. A wide variety of issues are treated, ranging from the determinants of fertility, mortality, age at first marriage, and workforce participation, to the nature of contraceptive knowledge, approval, and use. Moreover, community-level and household-level data have been combined in our search for findings relevant to the formulation and appraisal of population and development policies. (Indeed, an early evaluation of the PDP is undertaken.)

The analysis has been carried out using an eclectic research strategy that has employed several different statistical techniques to evaluate hypotheses drawn from the disciplines of economics, demography, and sociology. While the resulting study might be classified by some as "academic" in its attempt to be rigorous and objective in standards of research, at every stage we have also attempted to formulate questions and present materials in a way that may be useful to policymakers. This has been accomplished by relegating technical detail to appendixes and designated sections of the book, by summarizing the research findings in an introductory chapter, and by offering guarded policy suggestions when appropriate. This attempt to strike a compromise between the esoteric nature of academic research, on the one hand, and the pragmatic need of policymakers for simple, bottom-line answers to complex questions, on the other hand, has sometimes led to tough research choices regarding subject matter, modeling approaches, and statistical techniques. The dimensions of some of these choices are outlined in a concluding chapter, which also provides an agenda of research themes that merit particular attention in Egyptian demography. We hope our study contributes to and stimulates this research effort.

It is amazing how the number of debts mounts as one undertakes research. We would like to acknowledge some of those individuals who were helpful to the completion of this book: for sponsorship, research colleagueship, and data collection in Egypt--M. Mohmoud, H. Rashad, H. A. Sayed, and researchers at the office of Monitoring and Evaluation and the departments of Statistics, and Population and Development of the PFPB; for programming and data preparation--Hong-Sik Ahn, Silvia Pantelas, Stan Paskoff, Robert Schmidt, and Becky Teeter; for editorial assistance and manuscript preparation--John Menepace, Martha Rappaport, and Reynolds Smith; for providing substantive research suggestions and assistance on various parts of the manuscript--James Abernathy, Aris Anada, Rakesh K. Bhala, Abraham David, Janet Griffith, Elizabeth Heilman, Beverly Jones, H. Gregg Lewis, Josephine Mauskopf, George Myers, Babu Shah, Laura Slobey, George Tauchen, Shuiliang Tung, T. Dudley Wallace, and Laurie Zivetz; and for financial support--the Integrated Population and Development Planning Program of the Research Triangle Institute (US Agency for International Development contract AID/DSPE-C-0062). Five individuals must be singled out for special thanks: Dale Horne and Brian A. Kelley for their tireless assistance and creative input into manuscript preparation; Bryan Boulier for his extensive suggestions on various aspects of modeling and analysis; A. Bindary for promoting the analysis of the PFPB data sets; and, most of all, James C. Knowles for his valuable suggestions on research design and analysis and his encouragement at every stage of the project.

A.C.K.
A.M.K.
M.N.K.
February 1982

POPULATION AND DEVELOPMENT IN RURAL EGYPT

1. DEMOGRAPHIC CHANGE AND SOCIOECONOMIC DEVELOPMENT IN RURAL EGYPT: FINDINGS AND POLICY

1.1 INTRODUCTION

1.1.1 Approaches to Population Policy in Egypt

Egypt is in the midst of a period of economic and social transformation, the pace of which has seldom been equaled in the nation's long history. In contrast to its earlier agricultural development, Egypt's present course is marked by dramatic urbanization and industrialization. Indeed, the pace of urbanization has been much more rapid than in most other Third World nations. Moreover, the two principal cities in Egypt, Cairo and Alexandria, have attained sizes of world rank, and in the year 2000, Cairo's population is expected to exceed fifteen million.

Yet rapid economic and social change in Egypt has not occurred without problems. Conspicuous among these are the large size and growth rate of the population. Currently at forty-four million, the population is expanding at a record rate of 3 percent per annum. This rate is not only a problem in and of itself, but is also the root from which many other problems stem. For example, population in rural areas is pressing against increasingly scarce land and water resources and is stimulating migration to the cities. In a nation where desert comprises almost all of the countryside, Malthusian population pressures could soon pose a serious constraint on urban, as well as rural development. Thus, the identification of the determinants of rapid population growth, and the relationships between population growth and economic and social progress, constitute crucial areas of study which could have significant bearing on government policies and ultimately, of course, on the lives of the Egyptian people.

Leaders in Egypt are not unaware of the consequences of rapid population growth, although the exigent need to reduce it is yet to be made a top priority. Even though this country has, for almost two decades, had a national policy of limiting population through programs that provide family planning services, the results of this effort have fallen short of expectations, particularly in rural areas. Contraceptive prevalence rates in rural Egypt are still quite low. Moreover, skeptical observers have been quick to point out that in the recent past, increases in the rate of contraceptive use have occurred when fertility rates and, hence, population growth rates have been rising. While such simple correlations cannot and should not be taken as indicating causation or be interpreted with confidence, they have certainly provided an impetus to identify population strategies that do not rely exclusively on family planning.

One possibility lies in the "development approach" to population policy, which emphasizes efforts to upgrade living standards by reducing mortality rates, improving health and education, and providing increased economic opportunities, particularly to women. The expectation is that, at some stage, population growth in Egypt will decline automatically with improvements in economic and social conditions, since this pattern has been observed in many other countries. However, a disconcerting trend appears to exist in Egypt: in the last several years increases in the population growth rate (including the fertility rate) have occurred simultaneously with improvements in economic and social conditions. Again, simple correlations are misleading, but they do cast some doubt on the utility of relying exclusively on a strategy of awaiting socioeconomic development and modernization to curb population.

There has been considerable debate in Egypt over how much emphasis should be attached to the family planning approach versus the development approach to population policy. Unfortunately, much of this dialogue has been cast in an either/or framework. However, the pendulum is now swinging to a more balanced perspective where the joint use--and even the integration--of these two approaches is in vogue.[1] This is our position as well. Increased emphasis on family planning can indeed provide desired effects, but when coupled with targeted development programs, family planning is likely to realize even greater success in meeting population goals. Likewise, development efforts targeted to curb population growth will be most effective if they are integrated with effective family planning programs. We will argue below that at present this balanced approach to population policy represents the optimal strategy for rural Egypt.

In an attempt to provide quantitative evidence on the relationships among economic, social, and demographic change, several major data collection efforts have been carried out for both the urban and rural areas of Egypt. Though many research papers based on these data have been written, they have for the most part been descriptive, and cautious in providing explanatory and prescriptive results useful for policy formulation. The time is ripe to use this household survey data to identify some of the underlying relationships between family size determination and economic and social conditions, with the specific objective of providing policy recommendations that are consistent with national population and socioeconomic objectives. This is the purpose of the present study.

1.1.2 Research Themes

Our focus will be on rural Egypt, and we will analyze the results of the 1979 Rural Fertility Survey (RFS) conducted by the Population and Family Planning Board.[2] (Details of the sample design are outlined in chapter 4, section 4.3.1.) While the study will concentrate on the total rural area, Upper and Lower Egypt will at times be examined separately. Even though we are somewhat skeptical about the value of the classification of Egypt into Upper and Lower areas, the results will serve to illustrate the potential importance of considering specific geographic areas and policies.[3] Our study will also be confined to the single-period RFS data. We will not examine the time-dimensioned, retrospective data, since they were not in a form suitable for analysis at the time of the present research.

Four research themes are considered, each of which is useful in appraising current population programs.

1. *The identification of the determinants of desired family size.* How are the determinants of desired family size related to actual family size? What groups of Egyptians are able to attain their desired family sizes? What groups fail to achieve or exceed their desires, and why? What will be the likely impacts of socioeconomic development and family planning activities on reconciling the differences between

desired and actual family size?

2. *The identification of the determinants of children ever born and child deaths.* How will development in general, and government programs in particular, affect these determinants and, in turn, the rate of population growth?
3. *The identification of the determinants of knowledge, approval, and use of modern contraceptives.* How will government programs affect these determinants? What groups should be targeted for family planning programs?
4. *The identification of the likely outcomes of two alternative (although not mutually exclusive) strategies for effecting demographic change in rural Egypt: (a) a major upgrading of education services, and (b) a set of programs which integrate family planning and development approaches to population policy, as exemplified by the Population and Development Project (PDP).* What are the techniques and data required to evaluate the usefulness of such population strategies?

This is an ambitious list of research questions. We do not claim to confront each of these issues with equal success. Limitations of both data and social science theory pose serious research constraints. Nevertheless, our research findings permit us to reject several commonly held beliefs regarding population and development in Egypt. Moreover, they enable us to offer guarded conclusions from which some policy implications logically follow. Finally, our research identifies important areas requiring further inquiry, preferably with expanded data bases.

The first three research themes are common to the literature on population, but the fourth is not. Egyptian population policy toward rural areas has recently changed from an almost exclusive emphasis on family planning to an orientation in which family planning is considered as one important (possibly still the key) element in an integrated program of population and development. The newness of this policy necessitates considerable experimentation in programming, and also merits evaluation. An example of this policy is the PDP, which was initiated, designed, and implemented by the Population and Family Planning Board since 1977. We have elected to examine the PDP in some detail, not only because it represents current and, possibly, future directions of Egyptian population programming (and, therefore, deserves a careful documentation for a baseline picture), but also because it establishes a demanding requirement for analysis and evaluation, one which social scientists must be willing and able to meet.

1.1.3 Orientation and Organization of the Study

It is tempting in a study such as this to present the results to an audience of social scientists familiar with the requisite methodologies, theories, and statistical tools. But such an exposition would not be as accessible to individuals whose training is in other areas, many of whom are in a position to influence population and development policies. We take seriously the need to present our findings to decision-makers and have organized our writing to this end. Thus, the remainder of the present chapter will provide a summary of the key findings and the policies that follow from them. (To streamline this exposition, numerical results and statistical techniques relating to the research findings are suppressed, although section numbers directing the reader to the detailed analyses in subsequent portions of the book are provided in brackets for reference.) Additionally, the major research themes in our study are analyzed twice: once using familiar tabular techniques (chapters 5, 7, and 9), and once more using less familiar multivariate statistical models (chapters 6, 8, and 10). Those chapters that employ the more complex methodologies begin by presenting the key findings and conclusions, and then take up the analyses, with most of the detailed statistical results relegated to appendixes.

The salient features concerning population and economic change in Egypt over the last two decades are presented in chapter 2. Chapter 3 follows with the theoretical framework used to guide our empirical analysis. Our general approach to research is eclectic: we draw upon economic, demographic, and sociological theories, and we use a variety of statistical methodologies. In chapter 4 the data used to test the various models are described. This chapter provides both a quantitative and a qualitative picture of contemporary rural Egyptian society. The detailed statistical analyses of the determinants of children ever born, child deaths, desired family size, and knowledge, approval, and use of contraceptive methods are presented in chapters 5 through 8.

Throughout the study our emphasis is on the positive, as distinct from the normative, aspects of population. We do not promote family planning, nor do we assert what the size of the Egyptian family *should* be. Rather, we attempt to assess what rural Egyptian household behavior *will* be in response to changes in the social and economic environments. Similarly, in the context of policymaking, we attempt to assess what the demographic outcomes *will* be if alternative population and socioeconomic policies are pursued. These perspectives are important to chapters 9 and 10, which examine, respectively, the impacts of education and the Population and Development Project (PDP) on rural demographic change. Since the PDP exemplifies a unified population-development strategy, the assessment of it must be based on an integrated analysis of socioeconomic and demographic variables. While our results in chapter 10 are preliminary, the methodology presented should be useful for evaluating population policies in the future, and especially those policies based on an integrated framework of family planning and economic and social change.

1.2 MAIN RESULTS

The main research findings can be readily summarized by considering four broad questions about rural Egypt that follow from the research themes discussed above: (1) Why are families so large? (2) How will socioeconomic development affect population growth? (3) Why are contraceptive prevalence rates so low? and (4) What is the likely impact of programs that integrate family planning and socioeconomic development? Before these questions are examined, however, it is useful to consider some salient facts about the rural Egyptian population. These features constitute the backdrop for our study, and although an attempt is made in this chapter to minimize the number of detailed statistical results presented, some familiarity with the quantitative dimensions of the rural Egyptian household is essential.

1.2.1 Overview of the Rural Population

Table 1.1 provides information derived from the RFS on key attributes of the total rural population, of Upper and Lower Egypt separately, and of women who have largely completed their childbearing years (aged 45-49). Our discussion will focus on this latter group.

In rural Egypt the completed family size (5.2 children) derives

Table 1.1 Attributes of Rural Egyptian Households

Household Attribute	All Households			Ever-married Women		
	Upper	Lower	Total	Upper	Lower	Total
Children Ever Born	4.2	4.4	4.3	7.5	7.4	7.5
Child Deaths	1.2	.9	1.0	2.7	1.9	2.3
Surviving Children	3.0	3.5	3.3	4.8	5.5	5.2
Desired Number of Children	5.0	3.8	4.3	5.5	4.2	4.8
Age at First Marriage (years)	16.8	17.1	16.9	16.6	16.9	16.8
% AFM less than 16	38.7	32.1	35.2	44.3	38.7	41.3
% Husbands Illiterate	67.7	57.9	62.6	74.0	73.0	73.4
% Wives Illiterate	80.5	73.1	76.6	82.9	77.4	80.0
% Current Using Modern Contraceptives	5.1	18.6	12.2	5.1	18.6	12.3
% Ever Used Modern Contraceptives	11.9	34.2	23.7	14.3	40.2	28.1
% Wives Ever Worked[a]	13.0	28.4	21.1	11.4	30.6	21.6
No. of Personal Assets[b]	.7	1.2	.9	.7	1.2	1.0
No. of Real Assets[b]	1.5	1.8	1.6	1.5	1.8	1.7
% with Electricity	32.6	52.7	43.1	33.7	56.8	46.0
Total Households	1819	2011	3830	175	199	374

[a] Wives ever worked represents women who at some stage have worked inside or outside the household in "nontraditional" housework activities.

[b] Personal assets include refrigerators, stoves, radios, televisions, sewing machines, clocks, and tape recorders. Real assets include farm land, construction land, agricultural machinery, buildings, and animals.

from high numbers of births (7.5) and high numbers of deaths (2.3) per family. For the total rural area, the number of surviving children on the average slightly exceeds the desired number (4.8).

Social and economic conditions are at a low level, with approximately 75 percent of all parents being illiterate, and with relatively few households reporting ownership of more than three personal and real assets.[4] Electrification is moderately widespread (46 percent). Although 28.1 percent of ever-married women aged 45-49 have at one time used a modern contraceptive method, current contraceptive use is low (12.3 percent). These results for the total rural area derive from quite different conditions in Upper and Lower Egypt. In Upper Egypt (comprising about 43 percent of the total rural population) poverty is greater, illiteracy is more prevalent, and modernization in the form of women working outside the home or employing modern contraceptives is less advanced than in Lower Egypt.

It is of considerable interest to note that approximately the same number of children are born to women in Upper and Lower Egypt in spite of the higher child mortality and the greater desire for children in Upper Egypt. This suggests that the greater poverty in Upper Egypt may be associated with lower rates of natural fertility (lower fecundity and greater sterility), or that natural fertility is itself a constraint on completed family size. Indeed, on average there is an excess demand for children in Upper Egypt; that is, the desired number of children (5.5) exceeds the number of surviving children (4.8) by .7. The opposite is the case in Lower Egypt where there is an excess supply of children; that is, the desired number of children (4.2) is exceeded by the number of surviving children (5.5) by 1.3. These findings may be important in explaining the different contraceptive prevalence rates in Upper and Lower Egypt (current prevalence rates are 5.1 and 18.6 percent, respectively). Writers have also emphasized the more conservative and traditional behavior of Upper Egyptians in their attitudes toward contraception in general and in their use of modern contraceptives in particular.

Finally, for rural Egypt as a whole, desired family size (4.8) is less than the number of surviving children (5.2) by .4, a result suggesting that there is significant scope for family planning.

1.2.2 Why are Families so Large in Rural Egypt?

This question can be answered at two levels. First, from the perspective of the rural Egyptian household, families may not be all that large. Though the number of children born to an average woman by the end of her childbearing age is 7.5--which, when considered alone, seems large--an average of 2.3 of her children die. If, in fact, the household strives for at least two surviving sons to support it in old age and to provide a means of transmitting the family's name and assets to the next generation,[5] then 5.2 surviving children (at age 45-49) may not be excessive. This figure will surely decrease by the age of the parents' retirement, providing an even closer approximation to the two-son norm. High fertility rates might therefore be attributed, in part, to high rates of mortality, and the rural Egyptian household may be fairly close to its optimum family size.

A second approach to explaining large families in Egypt is to consider three contrasting views, each of which commands considerable support among analysts of Egyptian demography. The three differ markedly in their implications for population policy. They are:

1. *Irrational behavior:* family size is determined outside a framework of rational choice; the number of children is "up to God," and the number of surviving children is, thus, the by-product of sexual activity and mortality.[6]
2. *Rational behavior with overproduction:* family size is determined by rational choice; parents weigh the benefits and costs (broadly viewed) of children and attempt to attain a family size goal. However, most families exceed that goal due to a lack of knowledge or the high cost or the improper use of contraception. Large families are, therefore, explained by the presence of unplanned children.
3. *Rational behavior:* family size is determined by rational choice, and, while there may be some overproduction of children, large families are explained to a great extent by the relatively high benefits and the low costs of children.

While there are elements of truth in each of these views, the weight of the evidence appears to support the third view as the best description of Egyptian behavior. The research findings presented below are generally consistent with the conclusion that factors which raise the costs of children or diminish their value to the household will result in smaller family sizes (at least in the intermediate to long run). The most convincing feature of this evidence is the fact that highly consistent results are amassed from several different measures and types of behavior: from knowledge, approval, and use of contraceptives, from statements about desired family size, and from measures of children ever born and the couple's response to child mortality.

The view that large families are explained *primarily* by the overproduction of children is not convincing as the dominant description of rural Egyptian behavior. It is true that a sizeable proportion of the households that have completed their childbearing indicate that they have more children than they desire. Yet some 59 percent either have the number of children they desire or seek to expand their families, and for the entire rural area the average number of children desired is still high (4.8). Furthermore, among those families who appear to have an excess number of children, current contraceptive prevalence rates are low. Of course, the latter result might be explained by an insufficient amount of resources devoted to family planning programs or a less than fully effective use of the resources that have been committed.[7] But further analysis of the household data reveals that even traditional means of contraception are little used by those couples who appear to possess an excess supply of surviving children. Thus, while the overproduction of children does indeed account for a portion of the large family size in rural Egypt, it does not appear to represent the dominant explanation.

The rationality framework appears to constitute the best model within which to analyze the behavior of the rural Egyptian household. Children are highly valued in rural Egypt, and their costs are low. To a significant extent, large families are explained by this fact, and consequently research must be directed toward identifying the benefits and costs of children and the household's response to changes in these determinants. Nevertheless, as noted above, large families are also explained in part by the overproduction of children, and as a result research must be directed to the determinants and efficacy of family planning as well. Having said this, we hasten to point out that the demographic situation varies enormously by region. Large numbers of households are quite receptive to family planning; others would seek ways to augment their fertility. This heterogeneity of the rural Egyptian population represents a critically important demographic dimension and should be kept in mind in formulating Egyptian population policy.

A final observation on the behavior of the rural Egyptian household is appropriate at this point. While we have portrayed a sizeable portion of the rural population as attempting to attain a desired family size and as making this family size assessment by weighing the costs and benefits of children, we have been vague on the details of this choice.[8] The benefits of children are very broad:

children provide happiness to parents, they assist in household chores and on the farm, they help care for parents in old age, and beyond these economic advantages, according to Islamic teachings, they are a gift from God. Children also require resources in their upbringing (food, clothing, housing, etc.) and they demand the time of parents (especially the mother) in care. We do not envision households as making fine-tuned calculations about these various benefits and costs; they do not determine with precision an optimal family size. However, in the abstract there may be such an optimum, and changes in the costs and benefits of children may, as a result, alter the family size goal. In time, household responses to those changing costs and benefits of children will show up in altered fertility rates and in the use of contraception.

1.2.3 What is the Impact of Socioeconomic Development on Rural Population Growth?

To answer this question it is necessary to examine at the household level the impact of improvements in socioeconomic conditions on four determinants of completed family size: (1) family size goals, (2) child deaths, (3) use of modern contraceptives, and (4) children ever born. In the present study, several measures of household socioeconomic status are investigated, including the education of the husband and the wife, the number of personal assets owned (consumer goods such as radios, TV, tape recorders, sewing machines, and stoves), the number of real assets owned (producer goods such as farm tools, animals, land, and buildings), and the presence of electricity (a proxy for income and wealth). Below, we present first a summary of the main empirical relationships between various measures of socioeconomic change and the components of population change. These findings are then integrated through a discussion of the likely impacts of development on rural population growth.

A Synopsis of the Research Findings. The major research results pertain to desired number of children (DNC), child deaths (CD), use of contraceptive methods (UCM), and children ever born (CEB).

Desired number of children declines with socioeconomic development [7.4, 8.2.3]. In particular:

1. DNC declines with increases in male and female education

(the latter has the greatest deterring impact),
2. DNC declines with increases in age at first marriage,
3. DNC declines with the ownership of personal assets and electricity, and
4. DNC is invariant to the ownership of real assets.

Child deaths, in contrast, are largely independent of these household attributes [5.2, 6.2.3]. Thus:

1. CD are largely uninfluenced by male and female education or asset ownership, although
2. CD are somewhat lower for households with electricity.

Use of contraceptive methods increases with socioeconomic development; moreover, the form of that development may be important [7.3, 8.2.1]. In particular:

1. UCM increases with male and female education,
2. UCM increases with personal asset ownership and with electricity, but
3. UCM decreases with real asset ownership.

Children ever born derive largely from the net impact of these three influences [5.1, 6.2.1]; i.e., family size goals, child deaths, and contraceptive use. Somewhat surprisingly:

1. CEB are largely unrelated to male and female education after controlling for age at first marriage and other intervening influences.
2. CEB are uninfluenced by wealth ownership in the form of personal assets, but
3. CEB increase with wealth ownership in the form of real assets and electricity.

At first glance these various findings pose several apparent inconsistencies and paradoxes.

1. Family size goals decline and contraceptive use increases with education, yet children ever born reveal no apparent relationship to education levels.
2. Family size goals decline with one form of wealth (personal assets), yet are unrelated to another form of wealth (real assets).
3. Contraceptive use increases in households with relatively

high levels of personal assets, yet declines in households with relatively high levels of real assets.

4. Family size goals decline with development in general, yet children ever born may increase with development.

Are these apparent paradoxes the result of spurious statistical findings, or can they be reconciled within a framework of consistent and rational decision-making behavior? Three factors provide the necessary reconcilation.

First, significant numbers of rural Egyptian households with women aged 35-49 years apparently have an "excess demand" for children; that is, they desire *more* children than they are able to attain. For these households, improved socioeconomic conditions may result in little change in or even expanded family sizes [7.4, 8.2.3]. (Approximately 30 percent of households with women aged 35-49 years may be in this situation.) Moreover, the absolute size of the excess demand for children in these households is large: an excess demand of 3.1 children on average. On the other hand, the excess demand group is approximately offset by its counterpart (around 40 percent of the rural population) where there is an "excess supply" of children; that is, households which desire *fewer* children (2.9 children on average) than they have attained. For these households, improved socioeconomic conditions will likely result in reduced family sizes. Since the impact of socioeconomic development may operate in opposite directions for these two groups of households, the *net* impact of development on children ever born may be slight, although it may be larger for each group considered separately. (It is important to note that while the groups with an excess demand and excess supply of children may be broadly offsetting for rural Egypt as a whole, their relative sizes are quite different by region. In Upper and Lower Egypt, the proportion of the families who seek additional children are 42 and 21 percent, respectively. The corresponding figures for families who have an excess supply of children are 30 and 52 percent, respectively. Thus, socioeconomic development is more likely to have a larger deterring impact on population growth in Lower than in Upper Egypt, at least in the short-to-intermediate run.)

A second factor relevant to reconciling the apparent paradoxes in the research findings pertains to the interpretation of the different impacts of personal assets and real assets on household behavior. It may be hypothesized that owning personal assets is likely to be *competitive* with children; that is, fewer personal assets can be afforded in large families. In contrast, real assets may be *complementary* with children; that is, land, tools, and animals make children more productive on the farm. The finding that households with relatively large stocks of real assets elect to use contraceptive methods to a lesser degree than households with few real assets is thus not too surprising. Many of these households would seek additional children. Moreover, the finding that personal assets have a negative impact on family size goals, while real assets do not, can now be interpreted.

A third factor relevant to explaining the results pertains to the impact of education. While contraceptive use increases and family size goals decline with increased education, CEB is little influenced by this variable. This set of results could be explained in part by the different responses to education by the excess supply and excess demand groups discussed above. However, it could also be the result of our inability to measure accurately the full range of educational impacts. There is little measured variation in the educational characteristics of rural Egyptians. Most are either illiterate or have had only small amounts of formal education. (Only 4 percent of the sample had at least a primary certificate.) The statistical analysis must of necessity be confined to the boundaries of these data and cannot be extrapolated with much confidence beyond this range. We must therefore be somewhat cautious in basing firm conclusions on our results relating to education.

In sum, given the finding that many Egyptian households have more children than they desire, while other households have fewer children than they desire, and given the evaluation of the different impacts of household assets on behavior, the results presented above can be reconciled in a framework of rational choice. Moreover, the results derive from several different measures of behavior and their internal consistency thus provides added credibility to the research findings taken as a whole.

Additional Findings. An assessment of the impact of socioeconomic development on population growth necessitates an examination of several other factors. These relate the impact of infant and child mortality on fertility and the impact of education on female employment.

While our research has not identified specific household attributes that are strongly correlated with infant and child deaths, mortality rates are related to, and will decline with, the increased availability of community-level services: pure water, sanitation, medical facilities, and the like. Hence, it is relevant to assess the impact of reduced mortality on fertility, which may include a tendency of households to "hoard" children in expectation of deaths, and to replace children who have died [6.2.3, 10.7]. In the short-to-intermediate run it is possible that reductions in child mortality will result in increased rates of rural population growth. On the one hand, some families presently seek more children than they can attain, and reductions in child mortality will facilitate their attainment of higher family size goals. On the other hand, it may take time for households to recognize that the community mortality rate has declined and to adjust their fertility downward in response to this trend.

Another relationship between socioeconomic development and population growth lies in the impact of female education on workforce participation in nonhousework activities,[9] as well as the impact of this workforce activity on desired family size. It is commonly believed that one of the impacts of providing increased education to women is to raise their employment opportunities and the value of their time outside the home. This, in turn, is supposed to lead to an increase in the costs of raising children, thereby reducing their demand. In rural Egypt this influence is likely to be small, since: (1) the educational status of women has little influence on their likelihood of entering the workforce [6.2.2]; (2) working outside the home does reduce the desired number of children [7.4, 8.2.3]; but (3) children ever born are uninfluenced by female workforce status [5.1, 6.2.1].

Taken together, these findings downplay the quantitative importance of possible family size reductions deriving from a changing employment structure for women, although the impact still diminishes family size goals. It may be that the opportunities presently available for rural Egyptian women to work in nonhousehold activities are so limited that our statistical analysis is unable to measure this impact. Our results should be treated as quite tentative on these issues.

While the overall impact of socioeconomic development on population growth in rural Egypt is difficult to assess, our forecast is that such development may not reduce population growth in the near future and that it may even result in increased growth. Much depends upon the *form* (real versus personal wealth accumulation) of that development, as well as its distribution (Upper versus Lower Egypt).[10] This conclusion gains further support by our analysis of various community-level indices of development, where for the total rural area it is found that: (1) higher levels of socioeconomic development in general are associated with an increase in the number of children ever born and a decrease in the number of child deaths [10.7]; and (2) agricultural mechanization is associated with a reduction in the desired number of children, an increase in contraceptive use, and a reduction in the number of children ever born [10.7]. The conclusion is further reinforced by findings which show that: (1) in Upper Egypt real asset accumulation (in the form of buildings, land, tools and animals) reveals no significant impact on desired family size or use of modern contraceptives [8.2.1, 8.2.3]; whereas (2) in Lower Egypt, real asset accumulation is associated with larger desired family size and reduced use of modern contraceptives [8.2.1, 8.2.3].[11] In Upper Egypt, families are more likely to desire more children than they can attain and, as a result, are less influenced by real asset accumulation. In Lower Egypt, the opposite is likely to be the case. Thus, the *level, form,* and *distribution* of development can have an impact on the relationships between socioeconomic change and population growth, something that should be specifically taken into account in Egyptian policymaking. These issues will be examined in greater detail below.

The Pattern of Development and Population Change. A final and important dimension to the relationships between Egyptian population growth and rural development pertains to the pattern of change over time. Figure 1.1 presents a pattern of population growth and development which has been widely found using data on aggregate births and deaths for a number of developed and presently developing countries. This pattern is also consistent with the findings of the present study, which are based on household-level data. There are several components of this pattern: stage I where

Figure 1.1 The Demographic Transition

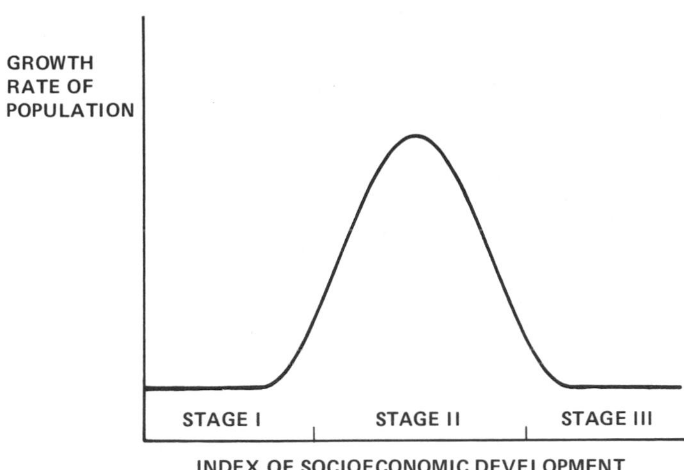

population growth is low and relatively constant; stage II where it increases, reaches a peak or plateau, and declines; and stage III where it is low and relatively constant. Stages I and III differ from each other in that the former derives from high birth and death rates, and the later from low rates. Much of the discussion of this pattern, referred to in the literature as the "Demographic Transition,"[12] has centered around the nebulous concept of "modernization" and its impacts on fertility and mortality. Our results for rural Egypt permit us to be more specific about empirically measured modernization attributes that relate to population change.

Rural Egypt is at present in stage II of the demographic transition. With further reductions in the infant and child mortality rates, it is possible that population growth will rise further. The timing of this event, the length of the population-growth plateau, and the pace at which population will then decline constitute key issues in projecting the course of Egypt. Our research provides some results relevant to speculating about these matters. In particular, there appears to be a "threshold" level of development in rural Egypt beyond which increasing socioeconomic progress will result in a fairly rapid decline in the rate of population growth. Three empirical research findings support this interpretation.[13] The first relates to what we label as the *compositional* effects of socioeconomic development on population growth. Here we wish to contrast one group of rural Egyptians in which development will have a negative impact on completed family size (i.e., those with unplanned children and who are using modern contraceptive techniques with increasing prevalence and effectiveness) with another group in which socioeconomic development may result in a negligible or even a positive impact on completed family size (i.e., those who seek more children and for whom education and income may facilitate that goal). The composition or weight of these two groups in the total rural population could be important to determining the pattern of stage II in figure 1.1.[14] One might speculate that rural Egypt is at present close to a "switching point" in its demographic transition.[15] That is, the group of rural Egyptians (around 31 percent of ever-married women aged 35-49) who have an excess demand for children (3.1 children on average) is now approximately (or somewhat more than) offset by the group of rural Egyptians (41 percent) with an excess supply of children (2.9 children on average). The distribution of the benefits of socioeconomic change between these two groups could be important in determining whether population growth rises, stabilizes, or declines with development.

The second empirical result relating to the pattern of aggregate population growth rates concerns what we label as the *nonlinear* effects of socioeconomic development on household behavior. Here we emphasize that the underlying determinants of family size may not vary evenly (or proportionately) with changes in the household's level of prosperity. In fact, several research findings reveal diminishing impacts of some attributes of socioeconomic change on the components of population growth. For example:

1. The impact of education on knowledge, approval, and use of modern contraceptives, though positive at all levels, becomes less significant at higher levels of education [7.2, 7.3].
2. Knowledge, approval, and use of modern contraceptives are also most sensitive to changes from absolute poverty to relatively low levels of real and personal asset holdings [7.2, 7.3].
3. Family size desires are affected most by small amounts of education, and while the relationship is inverse throughout,

the impact diminishes with higher levels of education [7.4]. These results suggest not only that modest doses of development may at some stage result in relatively large impacts on population growth, but also that the incremental doses thereafter will result in lesser, yet still deterring, effects. Referring back to figure 1.1, the research results further imply that the length of the growth-rate plateau may be shortened and the rate of decline may be hastened if Egypt is increasingly successful in providing basic education and minimum standards of economic well-being to the mass of the rural populace.

The third empirical finding relevant to explaining the pattern in figure 1.1 concerns the determinants and impact of changes in infant and child mortality. As death rates decline significantly from their present high levels in rural Egypt, the impact on population growth may be notable. We have speculated above that the impact may be positive in the short run. This could well bring rural Egypt to a peak rate of population growth. Once households perceive the lower death rates and adjust their fertility to them, and once there are smaller numbers of Egyptians who desire more children than they can produce--a trend that usually occurs with reductions in the infant and child death rates--the impact of development on reducing population growth may be relatively large.

In sum, rural Egypt may not have yet reached the level of development where increases in prosperity will result in significantly reduced rates of population growth. But once a set of socioeconomic preconditions is reached, not only will the population growth rate decline, but also the rate of decline may be fairly rapid.

What remains to be confronted is whether a major push in the area of family planning is likely to have a significant impact on reducing the rate of rural population growth in rural Egypt. Equally important is how could, and how should such a family planning program relate to national socioeconomic development? These are the subjects of the next two sections.

1.2.4 Why are Contraceptive Prevalence Rates So Low in Rural Egypt?

There are two common responses to this question. First, it is often argued that prevalence rates are low because insufficient funds have been committed to family planning programs, or because these programs could be implemented with greater efficiency. These allegations cannot be refuted since additional spending or better deployment of available funds on family planning programs would almost certainly have a positive impact on knowledge, approval, and use of contraceptives. However, the central issue is not whether such an allocation of resources would have a positive impact, but whether it would have a greater impact on population reduction and contraceptive use than alternative and/or complementary population programs.

Second, other observers allege that low contraceptive prevalence rates are the result of a low demand for family planning, as distinct from an insufficient supply of contraceptive services. In particular, low contraceptive prevalence rates derive from the desire for large families. Furthermore, socioeconomic change--particularly when it raises the costs and reduces the benefits of children--is said to be a prerequisite to decreases in family size aspirations and to be commensurate with an increase in the demand for family planning.

While there is substantial merit to both positions, our research provides some support to the view that it is necessary to alter those socioeconomic factors that determine family size aspirations and, thus, the demand for family planning. In fact, a population policy that coordinates, and possibly even integrates, specific fertility depressing socioeconomic development strategies with strong and targeted family planning programs appears to merit considerable support.

Some Salient Facts About Current Contraceptive Prevalence Rates. An analysis of family planning in rural Egypt should begin by reviewing some key features about contraceptive prevalence rates. First, the current contraceptive prevalence rate of modern methods for rural Egypt is 12.2 percent. In Upper and Lower Egypt, the rate is 5.1 and 18.6 percent, respectively. For all methods, modern and traditional, the rates are 15.0, 8.1, and 21.1 percent for total, Upper, and Lower Egypt, respectively. Second, for women approaching the end of their childbearing years (aged 35- 44)--a prime group for using modern contraceptives--the prevalence rates for total, Upper and Lower Egypt are 17.4, 3.0, and 29.7 percent, respectively. Third, if the 35-44 aged group is further divided between those who have an excess supply of children (where the stated desired number of children is less than the number of surviving children), and those who have an excess demand for children (where the stated desired number of children is greater than the number of surviving children), rural prevalence rates are, respectively, 29.7 and 3.0 percent for total rural Egypt; 13.1 and 1.5 percent for Upper Egypt; and 38.8 and 6.1 percent for Lower Egypt.

These results are consistent with those of several other studies revealing low contraceptive prevalence rates in rural Egypt. However, our most interesting research finding pertains to the enormous variation in contraceptive prevalence rates between regions and groups of individuals. These rates are five to ten times higher in Lower Egypt than in Upper Egypt. They are, moreover, five to ten times higher for those households with an excess supply of children than for those with an excess demand for children, and this finding is invariant to region.

What accounts for such a wide variance in prevalence rates? It cannot be explained solely, or possibly even in large part, by differential levels of family planning services provided in each region, or to different groups. Indeed, comparisons of per capita availability of doctors in family planning centers, family planning extension workers (Raiyda Riyfia), and family planning centers in Upper and Lower Egypt reveal a broadly comparable distribution of services between the two areas.[16] It has also been observed that 98 percent of the population is within five kilometers of a family planning service.[17] Major differences in contraceptive prevalence rates are therefore significantly influenced by variations in the demand for family planning from one region to another and from one group to another.

Determinants of Knowledge, Approval, and Use of Contraceptives. An effective family planning program depends on knowledge of family planning methods, on approval of these methods, and on use of one or more techniques.

Knowledge. Knowledge of at least one family planning method is high in rural Egypt (89.0 percent) [7.2]. Consequently, knowledge of contraceptive devices does not appear to represent a constraint on the use of family planning. Moreover, increases in the knowledge of family planning are most substantial as spouses obtain a limited amount of education, wives participate in nonhousework activities, and households accumulate a small holding of household wealth [7.2]. It is the impoverished and illiterate rural Egyptians who possess somewhat lower levels of contraceptive knowledge. But this group also has large family size aspirations, and many desire more children than they can attain. It is therefore probable that the "need to know," that is, the demand for family planning services, in large part explains variations in knowledge rates of modern contraception.

Approval. Family planning approval by females is 57.4 percent, and by males is 47.0 percent [7.2]. Increases in approval are greatest as households move from the extremely poor and illiterate categories to a situation with limited amounts of education and assets; the impact on approval of yet additional increases in education and wealth is somewhat less [7.2]. These results are consistent with those on knowledge of modern contraceptives.

Use. The results on contraceptive use may be summarized by six major findings. First, 27.9 percent of the rural women have ever used a family planning method, and 23.7 percent have ever used a modern contraceptive method. The two rates are 17.3 and 11.9 percent for Upper Egypt and 38.2 and 34.2 percent for Lower Egypt, respectively [7.3]. Second, 15.0 percent of ever-married women are currently using a contraceptive method, whether modern or traditional, and 12.2 percent are currently using a modern method. The two rates are 8.1 and 5.1 percent for Upper Egypt and 21.1 and 18.6 percent for Lower Egypt, respectively [7.3]. Third, for those women who have used a contraceptive method, the pill is the method most frequently used (22.6 percent); this is followed by prolonged breastfeeding [7.3]. Fourth, increases in contraceptive use are greatest as households move from the illiterate to the some-education categories; larger doses of education have smaller incremental effects on use [7.3, 8.2.1]. Fifth, contraceptive use is negatively related to real asset ownership, but is positively related to use of electricity or ownership of personal assets [7.3, 8.2.1]. Sixth, the contraceptive continuation rate, measured as a ratio of current to ever use of modern methods, is low in rural Egypt (.52). The ratio for Upper and Lower Egypt is .43 and .54, respectively, showing higher discontinuation rates for Upper than for Lower Egypt [7.3].

The fifth result is of considerable interest. It is consistent with the hypothesis that contraceptive use responds to variations in the relative demands for (i.e., changes in the benefits and costs of) children. As noted above, while children are likely to be competitive with the ownership of personal assets, they may be complementary to the ownership of real assets. In this case, the availability of productive capital would increase the value of children on the farm.

The impact of education on contraceptive use is equally interesting. While overall contraceptive use rates are low, they almost double when moving from couples in the illiterate category to couples with some education (less than primary certificate); they increase only modestly thereafter. This result has significant implications for development policy directed toward population control. Specifically, if the government is considering how to allocate its educational resources, then a policy of providing widespread, but modest levels of education may have a greater impact on contraceptive use than a policy of distributing higher levels of education to a smaller group of households. On the other hand, the impact of such a policy on population reduction (as distinct from contraceptive use) is still uncertain, since modest increases in the levels of education may also enable the very poor and illiterate to match their number of surviving children with their already-large family size desires.

Summary of Contraceptive Prevalence Rates. In rural Egypt knowledge of contraception is widespread, approval is moderate, and use is low. Neither knowledge nor approval of contraceptives appears to represent the major barrier to current use. While limited improvements in living conditions may augment both knowledge and approval rates, this impact alone is not likely to account for large increases in family planning use. As indicated above, there is accumulating evidence that the demand for children (their benefits and costs) is central in determining family planning use. This conclusion is supported by comparisons between the impact of real assets and the impact of personal assets on family size desires and contraceptive use. It also accounts for a notable portion of the differences in contraceptive use between Upper and Lower Egypt, since here our research has been able to partially control for variations in the supply of family planning services. And finally, it is important to an explanation of the enormous differences in contraceptive use between those households with an excess supply of children and those with an excess demand. These three results, taken together, provide considerable support for population policies that attempt to integrate targeted development strategies with an active and equally targeted family planning program. It is to this topic to which we next turn.

1.2.5 What Is the Likely Impact of Integrated Population and Development Programs? Preliminary Results From The PDP

Population policy in rural Egypt has evolved from its early exclusive emphasis on family planning to its present state, in which policymakers emphasize the importance of integrating population and development planning. This more comprehensive approach to population policy is exemplified by the Population and Development Project (PDP) implemented by the Population and Family Planning Board. Initiated in 1977, the PDP is a community-based program designed to reduce population growth and improve population characteristics through the manipulation of socioeconomic variables at the local level. While the PDP provides improved family planning delivery systems, it also stimulates socioeconomic development in general and, in particular, those specific activities that are thought to have a deterring impact on population growth. The PDP is more than a program of rural socioeconomic development. It introduces the population issue and family planning into all developmental activities with which it is involved. These activities include, for example, expanded education facilities, transportation and communication systems, health and sanitation services, employment opportunities (especially for women), village cottage industries, and agricultural mechanization. Before PDP funding is provided to any of these activities, local government leaders and volunteers, organized to provide substantial local resources of money and time, set targets and programs for population growth reduction.

The PDP represents a format for integrating population and development policies and strategies in rural Egypt. Our research findings provide some support to the efficacy of this approach. Yet there exist two principal difficulties in evaluating the PDP. First, the program had only been in operation for an average of ten months in the villages sampled at the time of the RFS, and the per capita level of PDP programming was low. Second, the available data are not ideal even for an early evaluation. It would have been desirable to have data on *changes* in demographic responses that occurred since the beginning of the PDP, and further it would have been useful to have community-level information on all RFS villages, not just those in the PDP. Nevertheless, we have been able to provide an early and quite tentative exploration of the possible impacts of the PDP. In addition, our analysis provides a baseline picture of the socioeconomic-demographic relationships prevailing at the early stages of PDP programming that should be helpful in future evaluation efforts. Without considering the research design in detail (this is done in chapter 10), what are our key findings?

The Impacts of the PDP. The statistical results [10.6] show that PDP programs are associated with: (1) increases in prevalence rates of modern contraceptive methods and decreases in discontinuation rates; (2) decreases in child deaths; (3) increases in female workforce participation; and (4) decreases in the desired number of children. We also found that PDP villages have a higher mean children ever born (CEB) than non-PDP villages. However, we cannot infer that PDP programs increase CEB, since it is unlikely that the PDP, operating for an average of only ten months, could have already exerted a direct impact on CEB. On the other hand, when such an impact is ultimately measured, it is possible that the impact will be positive for a period of time. PDP programs will increase community-level wealth which, given our previous results, may exert a short-run positive impact on CEB. This is particularly the case if the accumulation of community-level wealth is in a form that makes children more productive on the farm, and/or if its distribution and format increase the capacity of very poor families to realize their family size goals (which, in some instances, exceed the number of surviving children).

The PDP programs are associated with a reduction in child deaths, although here, too, it is problematical whether the decline is due to the PDP. The results pertinent to workforce participation and family size goals show PDP to have a fertility depressing impact. Finally, while the data show contraceptive use to be greater in PDP villages, there is no significant difference in the *ratio* of current to ever use of modern contraceptive methods (a measure of the discontinuation rate) in PDP and non-PDP villages. However, this same ratio was computed using data collected twenty months later from the 1980 Contraceptive Prevalence Survey, and here PDP villages clearly showed a higher proportion of use of modern contraceptives [10.6].

These various findings apply to all of rural Egypt. An examination of the impacts of PDP programs by region provides additional results of considerable interest. Specifically, in Lower Egypt, PDP is associated with increases in contraceptive use and reductions in desired number of children; it is unrelated to the number of children ever born. On the other hand, in Upper Egypt, PDP is unrelated to contraceptive use and desired number of children; it is positively associated with the number of children ever born.[18] These findings are consistent with the hypothesis, advanced in the previous sections, that some families, especially those in Upper Egypt, may desire more children than they can obtain. While it is too early to justify the result showing a positive impact of the PDP on CEB in Upper Egypt, still there is no statistically significant association between the PDP and contraceptive use and family size goals in this region.

In sum, the short-run impacts of the PDP remain abstruse. The PDP represents a package of wide-ranging activities designed to meet several objectives, only one of which is the reduction in population growth rates. In some instances PDP activities may have no impact on population growth or may even increase it in the short run. However, such an increase may also constitute a necessary prerequisite to establishing the conditions for fertility reduction in the intermediate to long run. In this sense, the PDP may be viewed as a way to shorten the period of rising population growth rates which are a part of the demographic transition, and to facilitate the rate of reduction from high growth rates once a trend of declining births has been established.

Demographic Change and Development in Rural Egypt. Quite apart from an evaluation of the PDP, the availability of community-level data permits a further examination of the impacts of the community-level development and complements the findings presented above which focus exclusively on the household-level data. The PDP is a program directed towards community development, and it is designed to affect household behavior through changes in community and environmental conditions. The community-level variables collected for PDP villages have been compiled into indices of various specific activities (e.g., urban transportation and communication services, agricultural mechanization, education services, health services), as well as a single composite index of "socioeconomic development." The statistical analysis using these various compiled indices of socioeconomic change provides the following results [10.7]:

1. Children ever born may increase in the short run with socioeconomic development in general, but will likely decrease with the provision of mechanized agriculture and urban transportation and communication services.
2. Child deaths will decrease with socioeconomic development and with the provision of educational services.
3. Desired number of children will decrease with the provision of educational services and the expansion of mechanized agriculture.
4. Contraceptive use will increase with the provision of agricultural mechanization and educational services.

These findings suggest that, while general socioeconomic development could have a short-run positive impact on population growth, the quantitative importance or the likely occurrence of this impact depends significantly on the *form* of that development.

1.3 POPULATION POLICY

Several conclusions concerning the expected impacts of various government programs designed to reduce population growth in rural Egypt are provided by our research. Though these results may not be wholly optimistic, we feel they are realistic, and they point to policy strategies that are broadly consistent with the current population objectives of the government.

There are two major policy conclusions that can be drawn from our analysis, and these form the basis for many of our subsequent recommendations:

1. Population policies should coordinate and/or integrate specific development strategies with active and targeted family

planning programs.

2. Different segments of the rural Egyptian populace will respond quite differently to various population programs, and consequently there can be no single policy that is "right" for everyone. Some variation in population programming across groups of people and by region may, therefore, be merited.

A strong family planning program should constitute a key component of population policy. However, major increases in family planning programs alone are not likely to elicit increases in contraceptive use as significant as one would find if such efforts were coupled with complementary development programs. This is because the demand for modern contraceptives differs from one segment of the population to the next and from one region to the other. As noted above, while an excess supply of children exists in rural Egypt on average--a result which bodes well for the potential impact of family planning--approximately one-third of the women who have largely completed their child bearing years have an excess demand for children. The very poor and illiterate tend to be in this latter category. Upper Egypt is characterized by the excess demand state, whereas Lower Egypt is characterized by the excess supply state.[19]

The implications of these variations in the demand for birth control techniques take on added significance when the following generalization is considered: rural Egyptians are quite rational in their decision-making. The stereotypes that portray most rural peasants as largely fatalistic and even irrational in their approach to life are not consistent with our research findings. Indeed, those rural Egyptians who indicate that they have more children than they desire are, in fact, more knowledgeable about contraceptives, approve of them with greater prevalence, and are much more likely to use contraceptives than their counterparts--those rural Egyptians who have an excess demand for children. For the latter group there is little incentive to acquire and use contraceptive devices.

Given the significant variations in the need for and receptivity to family planning programs, one might then ask: How can the demand for contraceptive techniques be increased among those segments of the populace in rural Egypt in which prevalence is low? Our research indicates that in the long run socioeconomic development will increase the demand for birth control devices if such development reduces the benefit-cost ratio of children. The research provides some examples which may satisfy this criterion: provision of agricultural technologies and institutional arrangments which are competitive with childrearing, and construction of communication and transportation systems to make urban centers more accessible to rural residents.

While in the long run socioeconomic development will increase the demand for contraceptive methods, in the short run there may be little change (or possibly even an increase) in completed family size. The principal reason derives from the heterogeneity of the population. Many have an excess supply of children and attempt family planning; others have an excess demand and do not. The latter group is disproportionately represented by the very poor and illiterate. To the extent that socioeconomic change benefits this group in particular, then some "undesired" or disappointing short-run demographic outcomes may emerge.

Having said this, we should note that the possible fertility stimulating effects of socioeconomic development in the short run might be attenuated through two policies. First, family planning programs could be more closely targeted toward those groups in which the excess supply of children is greatest. Providing all rural Egyptians with broadly comparable family planning services could represent an inefficient allocation of resources. It might be more appropriate, for example, to orient family planning resources toward "high receptivity groups," to work closely with these groups to insure more effective use of modern contraceptives; and at the same time to alter the form of the family planning program for "low receptivity groups" to focus on the building of knowledge about modern contraceptives and on changing attitudes toward family planning in general. This is not to say that there should be significantly different levels of government spending per capita on population programs between, say, Upper and Lower Egypt. Rather, it suggests that the nature of specific programs should differ between these regions. For those groups that seek additional children, some socioeconomic change may represent a prerequisite to a significant increase in the demand for birth control. Moreover, development programs should be of the form that are most likely to reduce the benefit-cost ratio of children as quickly as possible. In contrast, for those groups who have an excess number of children or who have met their family size goals (both groups combined represent the majority of the rural population), family planning programs should be strong and focus on more effective use of contraceptives.

A second method of minimizing the potential short-run fertility stimulating effects of socioeconomic development relates to policies that cope with the reduction of infant and child mortality. The infant and child mortality rate is high in rural Egypt.[20] Socioeconomic change which reduces that rate--a national goal that is intrisically desirable--could, for a period of time, result in larger completed family sizes. This is because reductions in mortality rates are unlikely to be taken into account immediately by households when making decisions regarding childbearing. Special policies could be implemented to minimize the number of couples who overshoot their completed family size goals in the period when mortality rates decline. For instance, public health programs to reduce child mortality could be coördinated with intensive efforts to educate parents on the family size implications of these programs. Moreover, family planning efforts could be especially productive if coordinated or integrated with programs which strive to reduce child mortality.

The research results, taken in their entirety, point to the wisdom of coordinating and integrating family planning with programs of socioeconomic development targeted, at least in part, to achieve lower rates of population growth. Furthermore, our results demonstrating different demographic characteristics and responses from one segment of the rural population to another and one region of rural Egypt to another support a "staged population strategy" whereby initial, basic inputs (health and education) are put in place, followed by other elements which will alter the benefit-cost ratio of children and simultaneously lower the costs of attaining a family size goal. Of course, staging would not be necessary if resources were unlimited--but obviously they are not. As an example of such a staged strategy, in Upper Egypt (where many couples have an excess demand for children) programs could focus on developing the preconditions for family planning by providing basic health care to reduce child mortality, augmenting basic education programs, and establishing strong informative programs aimed at increasing knowledge of and shifting attitudes toward family planning. In Lower

Egypt (where couples are likely to be in a state of excess supply), increased attention could be devoted not only to reducing child mortality and augmenting basic education, but also to developing employment opportunities for women which are competitive with childrearing, stimulating access to towns in rural areas where urban light industry is more prevalent, stimulating consumption patterns which compete with children, and targeting active family planning programs to those specific groups most affected by this socio-economic change.

The Population and Development Project represents a prototype for a program which coordinates family planning with targeted development programming. Though it is still at its early stages, the PDP appears to offer promising strategies for rural Egypt in the years to come.

2. EGYPTIAN POPULATION: CHARACTERISTICS AND POLICY

2.1 TRENDS IN POPULATION AND SOCIOECONOMIC STRUCTURE

The documented demographic history of Egypt spans fifty-three centuries, with census data available as early as 3340 B.C. While many censuses were taken during the era of the pharaohs, they were conducted for specific purposes, such as war and taxes, and resulted in population estimates that fluctuated widely. The first census in modern times occurred in 1800, when Egypt's population was found to be 2.5 million. This estimate was followed by a mid-century count of 4.5 million and a series of regular censuses starting in 1882.

Table 2.1 shows that the rate of natural increase has been accelerating since 1937. This growth has resulted from a birth rate fluctuating around 40 per thousand, and a sharp decline in the death rate. Medical advances and improved health conditions lowered the recorded death rate from 28 per thousand in 1945 to 14 per thousand in the early 1960s. However, infant mortality rates, estimated by the National Academy of Sciences,[1] were 246 per thousand live births in 1945, 168 in 1960, and 116 in 1976.

In mid 1981 Egypt's population stood at 43.6 million, based on an estimated crude birth rate of 40.9 per thousand and an estimated crude death rate of 11 per thousand. The annual rate of natural increase approached 3 percent, a record high in Egypt's recent history.[2] This rate has resulted in an age structure where about 45 percent of the population is below 15 years of age. The resulting dependency ratio is approximately unity, one of the highest in the world. A further implication of the high population growth rate is noteworthy: around 1.4 million additional Egyptians will be added to the population in 1982. Although it took 63 years, from

Table 2.1 Egyptian Population: 1882-1976

Year	Population (000)	Annual Average Growth Rate
1882	6,810	-
1897	9,747	2.42
1907	11,287	1.48
1917	12,751	1.26
1927	14,218	1.09
1937	15,933	1.14
1947	19,022	1.78
1960	26,085	2.38
1966	30,076	2.54
1976	38,228	2.71

Source: CAPMAS. *Statistical Yearbook.* Cairo: Central Agency for Public Mobilization and Statistics, Selected Years.

1897 to 1960, for Egypt's population to increase by 16 million, an increase of comparable magnitude was attained in only 20 years, from 1960 to 1980.

Egypt appears to be moving through the stage of the demographic transition in which the population growth rate approaches a peak.[3] In time the next stage will ensue, and one may then expect a decline in the birth rate and a resulting reduction in the natural rate of increase. When the present stage will end, and how quickly the next stage will occur, are currently two of the most researched topics in Egyptian demography.

In this context it is worth noting that Egypt witnessed a downward movement in fertility between the mid 1960s and mid 1970s. On the other hand, the last few years have revealed a "baby boom," and Egypt presently appears to be reversing that downward trend. While the recorded crude birth rates fell steadily from more than 41 per thousand in the mid 1960s to 34.4 in 1972, they have since increased gradually to exceed 40 per thousand in 1980. A recent study by the National Academy of Sciences[4] has shown that, assuming underregistration of births at the same level as for the previous years, the birth rate is estimated to be just above 40 in 1977 and 1978 and about 44 in 1979.

The problem of high growth rates is complicated further by an uneven population distribution. Ninety-nine percent of the population lives on only 3.5 percent of the total land area, resulting in an effective average density of about 1000 persons per square kilometer.

The distribution of population is characterized also by an increase in the proportion of the population living in urban settings. The percentage of the total population living in urban areas increased from 37 in 1960 to 44 in 1976. Urban growth is greatly influenced by rural-to-urban migration and has resulted in overcrowding of urban areas such as Cairo and Alexandria.[5] By January 1981, Greater Cairo's population had reached 7,570,000, which approaches one-fifth of the total population of Egypt. (Alexandria, the second most populated city in Egypt, reached a figure of about 2,555,000.[6]) The population density within Cairo has concurrently increased to about 26,148 persons per square kilometer. There is also a great disparity in density among the districts of Cairo--from a high of 110,333 to around 7,000 persons per square kilometer.

Egypt not only exhibits rural/urban disparities in population density, but also manifests differences in fertility between rural and urban settings. These rural/urban fertility differences (based on data covering the period 1930-1976) may be classified into three stages.[7] The first stage covers the period up to the early 1940s, when fertility measured by the crude birth rate (CBR) or the general fertility rate (GFR) was reported to be higher in rural areas than in urban areas (rates for both areas were relatively high, ranging between 40 and 51 for the CBR and between 170 and 240 for the GFR). The second stage extended for the next twenty years, up to the early 1960s, and showed the rural fertility level to be below the urban level.[8] During this period urban fertility gradually increased and peaked during 1950-1955, when the CBR registered a value of at least 50 per thousand, with a value of 51.8 for the year 1951. Urban and rural fertility then declined since the early 1960s to the early 1970s. However, the rate of decline was higher in urban areas so that a third stage beginning in the early 1960s showed rural fertility again surpassing urban fertility. This last stage is expected to continue through the 1980s. Estimated infant mortality rates in 1946-1947 were about 187 per thousand live births in Cairo and Alexandria, 204 in Lower Egypt and 259 in Upper Egypt. The three numbers were 109, 99, and 145, respectively, for 1975-1976.[9]

Against the backdrop of historical and emerging demographic trends, it becomes increasingly apparent that central to explaining the rate and timing of the next phase of the demographic transition--when fertility rates will steadily decline--will be those factors that determine the rate of urbanization, on the one hand, and, on the other, those that explain the pace of socioeconomic and population change in the rural setting. The present study focuses on demographic change in rural Egypt.

Low levels of social and economic conditions constitute yet another dimension of the demographic setting in Egypt.[10] These characteristics, in terms of health, nutrition, illiteracy, education, life expectancy, and the status of women, have been associated with low rates of labor productivity and, hence, with only moderate rates of socioeconomic development. Based on 1976 census data, (1) the illiteracy rate was 56.5 percent of the population aged 10 and over, (2) life expectancy at birth was 54 years, (3) recorded infant mortality was 83 per thousand, and (4) 9 percent of the women aged 15-59 participated in the formal labor market.

While these statistics portray a picture of poverty for the average Egyptian, economic development at the aggregate level has proceeded at a respectable pace over the 1970s. Table 2.2 presents data on Egyptian economic performance for the period 1960-1977.[11] Here it is seen that in the 1970s, output growth per capita exceeded 4 percent, a rate faster than that experienced in most developing countries. The gross national product has grown in recent years at a rate of at least 8 percent annually. In terms of the changing structure of production, the shift of output and labor force away from agriculture has been relatively slow. On the other hand, while agriculture has been a relatively lagging sector in output growth, the margin between agricultural output growth and population growth is still large by comparison with many developing countries.

High rates of population growth are pressing on the scarce endowments of natural resources, water, and land. As a result, the rate of economic growth, and especially that in the rural areas, may be losing ground to the requirements of simply maintaining the population at existing standards of living. While national policies promoting socioeconomic development will continue to be actively pursued, it is becoming increasingly important to consider the

Table 2.2 Indices of Egyptian Economic Change: 1960-1977

Variable	Egypt			Developing Countries		
	1960	1970	1977	1960	1970	1977
Growth Rates (Percentage)						
Gross Domestic Product		5.2	6.4		6.0	5.7
Agriculture		2.9	3.6		3.0	2.7
Manufacturing		4.7	6.7		7.5	7.4
Population		2.3	2.1		2.4	2.5
GDP/Population		2.9	4.3		3.6	3.2
Shares (Percentage)						
Agriculture/GDP	29.9	29.4	30.2	30.1	22.7	19.4
Manufacturing/GDP	20.1	22.0	23.5	18.6	20.2	21.5
Urban/Total Population	38.0	42.3	43.9	21.2	26.4	29.3
Ag. Labor/Total Labor	58.4	54.4	51.0	62.0	53.9	49.4
Mfg. Labor/Total Labor	12.2	18.8	26.0	11.0	13.2	15.3

Source: World Tables: 1980 (Baltimore: Johns Hopkins University Press for the World Bank, 1980). Cols. 1-5, pp. 74-75, 372-375; cols. 6-7, pp. 390-393; col. 8, pp. 436-439; cols. 9-10, pp. 460-463.

conditions under which fertility rates will begin to decline and, equally important, the likely effectiveness of policies that have, as their aim, the acceleration in the reduction of population growth rates. Indeed, the prospect for lowering population growth will itself depend to a significant extent--although in complex ways--on the pace and pattern of socioeconomic change.

2.2 POPULATION POLICY: A HISTORICAL OVERVIEW[12]

Though population growth rates began to accelerate in the 1930s, relatively little attention was focused on the potential consequences of this trend until the mid 1950s. However, over this twenty-year period there occurred a series of events that began to raise the public's consciousness toward population issues. For example, religious leaders issued statements that Islamic teachings permitted the use of family planning methods. University seminars were also conducted on the consequences of large families, and the mass media began to expound the population problem as a pressing issue of the time. Political leaders, however, remained relatively silent until 1954, when the Association for Population Matters was established. The efforts of this organization, later known as the Egyptian Family Planning Association (EFPA), were modest.

In the 1960s, the government's interest in population increased notably. The Egyptian Charter (1962) emphasized the seriousness of the population problem and the need to pursue possible avenues for its solution. The Supreme Council for Family Planning, established in 1965, was assigned the responsibility to devise policies for curbing the population growth rate. Chaired by the Prime Minister, and with a membership including eight cabinet members, the Council outlined a program which assigned family planning responsibilities to all health units and extended the availability of modern family planning methods. Serving the Supreme Council, the Family Planning Board acted as a technical secretariat responsible for coordinating, monitoring, and evaluating family planning activities. In 1973 the Council's name was changed to the Supreme Council for Population and Family Planning (SCPFP) and the Family Planning Board's name was changed to the Population and Family Planning Board (PFPB). The Minister of Health was appointed as Chairman of the Council in 1978.

While at present the government's commitment to resolving the population problem is relatively strong, it has yet to elevate population growth to an issue of major national concern. Thus, even though government programming affecting population growth occurs in many ministries, these programs are as yet not coordinated or even evaluated as a coherent population plan of action. Whether such coordination is in fact desirable and, if so, whether a feasible format can be devised in which coordination can take place, is one of the questions that may be illuminated by some of the results described in this book. In particular, our research attempts to isolate, however tentatively, some of the ways in which economic and social change affect both family planning activities and major demographic outcomes--births, deaths, and marriage. To set the stage for consideration of these issues, it is useful to examine in greater detail the nature and objectives of the institutions that have been responsible for population policy since the 1960s, and then to set out several research questions, the answers to which should provide useful inputs for formulating population policies in the future.

2.3 POPULATION POLICY: RECENT DIRECTIONS[13]

The evolution of recent population policy in Egypt has proceeded through three phases. The first, beginning with the establishment of the Supreme Council in 1965 and lasting until 1972, stressed traditional family planning services -- the provision of contraceptives, communication, and training activities. Though the Council held a few meetings at the beginning of this period, no significant operational activities were established. However, in 1969 the Council set a national population objective to reduce the crude birth rate by one per thousand annually, and population activities increased accordingly. Over the next three years the number of family planning centers increased by 3,000. Given the greater availability of family planning as well as the modest rate of socioeconomic development in the 1960s, a setting was created for limiting family size. In addition, the draft associated with the 1967 war caused marriage rates to decline from 10 per thousand in 1966 to 7 per thousand in 1967. The crude birth rate decreased from 41.7 per thousand in 1965 to 34.4 per thousand in 1972.

The second stage of Egyptian population policy, spanning the years 1972-1975, emphasized the need for a balance between population growth and socioeconomic development through the manipulation of socioeconomic factors. This emphasis evolved in part as a result of the deterioration of family planning activities in the early 1970s and in part due to an expansion of economic activity associated with the reduction of government restrictions and the increase in private and foreign investments. It is alleged by some that these economic and political measures, along with the 1973 war, created an atmosphere conducive to population increase.[14] In 1973 population policy was again officially promulgated, which retained the one per thousand reduction in the crude birth rate.[15] Additionally, the new policy explicitly stressed socioeconomic factors as instruments of population change. In particular, the new policy stressed that an increase in the demand for family planning services hinged critically on the rate and nature of socioeconomic change, including such measures as raising the socioeconomic standards of individuals, expanding functional education, upgrading the status of women and increasing their participation in the labor force, mechanizing agriculture, spreading cottage and agro-industries, extending social security, and reducing infant mortality. This recognition of the importance of socioeconomic factors in demographic change led to the next phase of population policymaking in Egypt.

In 1975 population policy entered its third phase, where three dimensions of the population problem--viz., growth, unbalanced spatial distribution, and unfavorable population characteristics (which impede fertility reduction) -- were simultaneously considered. Thus, while the traditional family planning approach focused only on the growth dimension of population, the new policy considered ways to upgrade the "quality" of the population (e.g., health, education), as well as its socioeconomic environment. On the one hand, structural, social and economic changes brought about through development were needed to change reproductive behavior and attitudes toward family planning. On the other hand, reduced population growth would in turn facilitate continued socioeconomic progress.

The government is presently giving new impetus to a population strategy that stresses the following three programmatic areas:

1. Upgrading family planning services integrated into relevant health and social activities.
2. Institution of community based socioeconomic programs conducive to family planning practice.
3. Strengthening population education and IEC (information, education, and communication) programs which aim at fertility behavior change, the small family norms, and contraceptive practice.[16]

Since 1977 seven actions have been taken to implement this broad population strategy:

1. Family planning services have been integrated into health services and a Family Planning Directorate has been established in the Ministry of Health.
2. Family planning methods have been made available in more than 4,400 pharmacies at nominal prices, equal to those at family planning centers. Family planning outlets number more than 8,000 across the country.
3. A new law for local government has been issued, which

transfers executive responsibilities in the population area from the president to the governors. Governors, in turn, have delegated their authority and responsibilities to local levels down to the village level. The law now stresses that family planning is the responsibility of local governments.

4. Programs have been developed to upgrade rural infrastructure (e.g, health, social services, education) and to provide electricity, safe water, transportation, and mechanization of agriculture.
5. The status of women has been elevated through measures such as allocating 30 seats to women in the National Assembly, passing a new civic law protecting women's rights, and encouraging women to participate in policy decisions and development activities at all levels.
6. Social security has been extended to cover the entire population.
7. A Higher Council for Population Communication has been established and has launched a national mass media campaign emphasizing community-based, face-to-face communication.

An important part of recent population policy has been the extensive decentralization of responsibility for population activities, and the development of incentive structures for local government and participants to establish programs for reducing population growth. For example, some local socioeconomic development activities are provided support at the national level on the basis of an assessment of their impact on population growth rates and on the basis of the local government's commitment to population activities. Similarly, local politicians are evaluated on their effectiveness in the area of population programming. Finally, there has been a shift in emphasis toward stressing and rewarding *outcomes* (reductions in fertility) as distinct from stressing intermediate *activities* (contraceptive sales).

Starting in 1977, the PFPB began to implement a program called the "Population and Development Project (PDP)." According to the National Population and Family Planning Strategy, the program is described as follows.

> Projects within this program area aim to contribute to fertility reduction through a number of interrelated projects

simultaneously attempting to: raise the quality of health/social/family planning services, improve the status of women through functional literacy programs and greater participation in waged economic activities, promote small scale and cottage industry, improve sanitation, promote mechanization of agriculture, facilitate access to urban areas, institute cultural activities, and promote information and communication through community institutions such as mosques and youth clubs, and through community outreach workers. At the same time, the activities are designed to contribute to the improvement of population characteristics and to a better spatial distribution by making the rural village a more suitable place in which to live.

An overall activity in this program area is the upgrading of the managerial capabilities of local councils and local officials who have the responsibility of designing and implementing projects in their communities as well as mobilizing community participation. A number of projects have been designed over the past few years and are now gaining momentum.

Priority will be given to projects aiming to:

- Strengthen ongoing projects.
- Expansion to nationwide coverage, including extension on a pilot scale to satellite villages and hamlets and to desert and coastal communities.
- Strengthen the components related to sanitation, upgrading the status of women, and literacy, especially women's literacy.
- A greater coordination of inputs provided by various ministries and agencies.[17]

2.4 POPULATION POLICY: THE FUTURE AND THE ROLE OF RESEARCH

Given the evolution of population policy in developing countries over the last two decades, the present Egyptian strategies appear to be relatively progressive. They stress local and individual incentive structures, they recognize and reward outcomes rather than intervening activities, and they establish population programming as a part of a broad strategy of socioeconomic development.

These important policies establish the environment and guidelines for implementing change. They delineate *what* is to be accomplished and provide the broad principles for effecting these goals. However, the difficult decisions regarding *how* these policies are to be carried out remain for the future. It is in the area of *specific* decision-making that the critical actions will be needed in the 1980s.

In population programming, as in other areas of decision-making, choices must be made to allocate scarce economic resources among desirable competing uses. In the Egyptian case, this set of choices will be much more difficult than in the typical developing country, where population programs focus almost exclusively on the dissemination of family planning methods. The broadened perspective of Egyptians in placing population programs in the context of socio-economic change is likely to necessitate much greater requirements for evaluating the likely impacts of alternative activities. It is our hope that this book will provide some data and analysis that will prove useful to this effort.

3. ANALYTICAL PERSPECTIVES ON POPULATION

3.1 INTRODUCTION

This chapter presents the analytical perspectives that guide our empirical analysis of Egyptian rural fertility. It should be noted that the authors who have adopted this framework represent several disciplines: biostatistics, demography, sociology, and economics. Each discipline has a distinct literature for its analysis of population issues. For an interdisciplinary project such as the present one to be successful, each researcher must be willing to compromise some of his discipline's prejudices with respect to the most appropriate procedures for approaching population questions and interrogating data. Fortunately, the present research falls short of a complete melding of the alternative approaches. Thus, in this book, similar questions will sometimes be addressed with alternative statistical methods. Likewise, similar results may on occasion be analyzed with slightly different interpretations. However, the overall consistency of our interpretation of Egyptian socioeconomic and demographic behavior, regardless of the approach, gives added credibility to the results.

Our theoretical approach draws most extensively upon the economics literature that has developed since the early 1960s. In the 1970s a synthesis emerged in this literature, which theretofore had been divided into two broad streams: a school that relies on the household's calculus in appraising the costs and values of children (the "new home economics") in determining family size, and a school that emphasizes factors such as natural fertility (e.g., fecundity), contraceptive efficiency and costs as being relatively important to demographic outcomes (the biological-demographic-sociological approach). In our review of the literature, and especially as it applies to the economic-demographic relationships of Africa in general and to Egypt in particular, we conclude that it is unproductive for us to enter the debate on these competing schools of thought. Both schools constitute an important part of an integrated explanation of Egyptian household demographic behavior. Moreover, given data constraints imposed by the Egyptian Rural Fertility Survey, it is still not possible to sort out conclusively the relative importance of the various factors. Thus, at points in the analysis we will emphasize one facet or the other, realizing that until further data become available and/or more sophisticated analytic techniques emerge, a satisfactory decomposition of the several key relationships will not be possible.

We begin by presenting R. A. Easterlin's framework, which synthesizes the economic and the biological-demographic-sociological approaches to the analysis of household demographic behavior. This is followed with a summary of four alternative views of the role of children in family decision-making. A formal statement of one of these views--the new home economics framework--is presented, together with several testable hypotheses. At the same time, an attempt is made to integrate these hypotheses with variants that derive from competing views of the role of children in Egyptian society. The chapter concludes with a discussion of some statistical and methodological issues on the interpretation of the Egyptian data. The impact of education on family size serves to illustrate these methodological issues.

3.2 THE EASTERLIN SYNTHESIS

While alternative views of family size determination are somewhat overlapping, it is appropriate to broadly characterize the economic approach as one which highlights the benefits and costs of children, and the biological-demographic approach as one that highlights the physiological determinants of the supply of children.

The economist has viewed children in several contexts: as a "consumer durable" (a durable good that yields direct utility over a period of time); as a "producer durable" (an asset in which investments are made and from which monetary and other returns are expected at some time in the future); and as a form of "insurance" (a contingent claim on an asset which provides a hedge against various forms of uncertainty). The principle notion underlying the economic approach is that families rationally determine their optimal number of children and the "investments" (e.g., health, education, nutrition) in these children. The household balances its subjective tastes against exogenously determined constraints (projections of life-time income, and prices and wages available in the marketplace). The goal is to maximize lifetime utility. Simply stated, a rational, cost-benefit analysis of family size constitutes a key aspect of household decision-making. This set of decisions leads to a *desired family size*, defined as the number of births desired if the cost of fertility control were zero.

Desired family size may deviate from actual family size for either of two reasons. First, the supply of surviving children may not be perfectly controllable; this supply is determined by biological and cultural factors, as well as by child mortality. On the one hand, supply is influenced by *natural fertility*, which is defined as the number of children a couple would have in the absence of voluntary birth control. Natural fertility, in turn, is related to health, nutrition, sexual habits and taboos, prevalence of breastfeeding, migration behavior, and the like. On the other hand, the supply of surviving children is determined by child mortality. Child survivorship can be extremely important to the analysis and will be examined in more detail below.

Second, the supply of children is influenced by family behavior to regulate births. Birth control techniques possess uncertainty and costs and constitute an integral part of the household's *optimal surviving children* outcome, defined as the net result of the household's desired fertility, natural fertility, child mortality, and fertility regulation. Biologists, demographers, and sociologists have emphasized the determinants of natural fertility, mortality, and fertility regulation in their analyses of optimal fertility. Economists have placed relatively greater emphasis on the determinants of desired family size. An integration of the economic and the biological-demographic-sociological frameworks has been provided by R. A. Easterlin and is displayed as figure 3.1. The vertical axis measures the number of children, and the horizontal axis represents an index of development or modernization: increasing levels of education, per capita income, health, urbanization, industrialization, and so forth.

Following Easterlin, it is useful to highlight four distinct phases of demographic behavior. Phase I, representing low levels of

Figure 3.1 Easterlin's Model of Fertility Determination

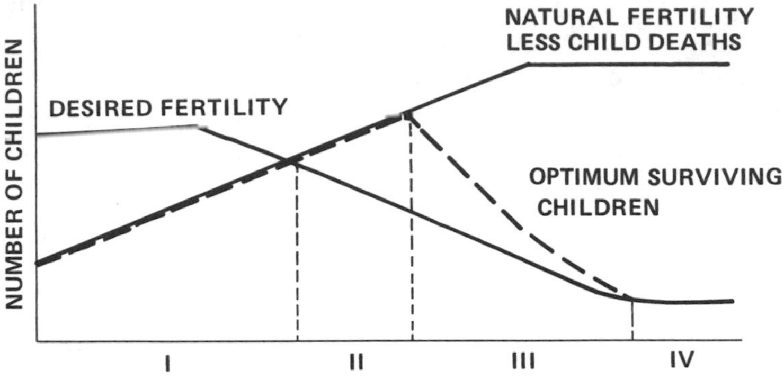

SOURCE: R. A. Easterlin [1978, p. 106, panel f].

development, is characterized by an "excess demand" for children: desired fertility exceeds natural fertility. In these societies the ability to supply children is constrained by poor health, nutrition, and high mortality, as well as cultural conditions such as sexual taboos and migrant behavior. Although natural fertility exceeds desired fertility in phase II, the optimal family size continues to follow the course of natural fertility, since the benefits of family size reduction are not sufficient to overcome the costs of fertility regulation. In phases III and IV, optimal family size is governed by the determinants of desired family size and the costs of fertility regulation, beginning in phase III with positive and declining costs of fertility regulation, and concluding in phase IV where these costs are negligible.

While the horizontal axis in figure 3.1 has been interpreted here as applying to stages of economic development, it can also apply to groups of individuals *within* a society. For example, might Upper Egypt be best represented as in phase I while Lower Egypt be characterized as in phase II or III? Might rural areas in Egypt be in the earlier stages of the transition (phases I and II) while urban centers such as Alexandria and Cairo be in phase III? Answers to these questions, which are central to the formulation of Egyptian population policies and programs, are discussed in chapters 5 through 8.

This representation of a separation of the economic and the biological-demographic-sociological schools of family size determination is not quite as clear-cut analytically as it may appear from the above presentation, and a major qualification is in order. While some of the biological-demographic-sociological factors may at first glance appear to be constraints on behavior--for example, sexual taboos due to rigid cultural norms--in fact they may change slowly over time and, themselves, be influenced by economic conditions. As a result, the distinctions between economic and other determinants of family size may rest in part on the time dimension of the analysis.

Nevertheless, we feel that the schematic representation in figure 3.1 highlights several ideas critical to the analysis of demographic behavior in developing countries in general, and in Egypt in particular. First, it underscores the need to broaden one's approach to consider not only the economist's emphasis on price and income effects, but also the biological and cultural factors relevant to fertility regulation and natural fertility (phases I and II). Second, the Easterlin framework emphasizes the need to determine at what point in time, with which groups of people, and for what reasons "supply constraints" may exist. Population policies that focus on optimal family size will differ greatly depending on the phase of demographic development. Finally, the Easterlin model stresses the importance of focusing on several dependent variables in examining household demographic outcomes: births, deaths, knowledge of and attitudes toward contraceptives and fertility regulation, natural fertility, and desired family size. The present study will utilize this broad set of perspectives to analyze Egyptian rural fertility behavior.

3.3 ALTERNATIVE VIEWS OF CHILDREN IN HOUSEHOLD DECISION-MAKING

3.3.1 Natural Fertility

Many writers have emphasized the concept of natural fertility to explain birth rates in low-income or traditional societies and, as a result, have downplayed the household's conscious decision-making to balance the benefits and costs of children. Louis Henry, in his classic article on natural fertility, defines this concept as "the fertility of a population that makes no deliberate attempt to limit births."[1] As Easterlin has noted, the concept of natural fertility is something of a misnomer since it is determined not only by biological factors (e.g., coital frequency, permanent or temporary sterility, proportion of ovulations fecundable), but also by cultural factors (e.g., traditions with respect to breastfeeding, taboo- or culturally-determined abstinence, migration patterns of spouse).[2] Contrary to popular belief, there are widespread differences in natural fertility among countries and even within countries. Even with little indication of conscious fertility regulation, completed fertility in parts of Africa is similar to the low levels in currently developed societies.[3] Natural fertility ranges from maximum rates of around thirteen live births over the reproductive period to rates as low as three or four births per married woman in other societies.

Studies on the determinants of natural fertility are inconclusive. A guarded consensus appears to be emerging that there is no significant link between food intake and childbearing, even in situations of chronic malnutrition. This conclusion is based on several research studies on low income populations in which biological results fail to confirm a correlation between nutrition and intermittent sterility in the female, delay in menarche, or the hastening of menopause.[4] If these results are general, then observed wide variations in natural marital fertility would appear to be explained more by behavioral than by biological factors.

One must be cautious, however, in inferring that economic factors--even through biological connections--are unimportant in influencing natural fertility. Instead, the relationships may be somewhat indirect: cultural and biological factors can be interdependent, and the interrelationships can in turn be strongly influenced by economic considerations. For example, cultural beliefs may result in mothers breastfeeding for extended periods of time, but this "tradition" may be due in part to economic conditions. Similarly, in some societies it is common--in part due to economic necessity--for the mother to live with her parents during "hard times," a practice that enhances better health and survival prospects for the mother and child and, at the same time, reduces marital fertility. Finally, economic conditions influence the periods of separation of husband and wife due to temporary migration of the breadwinner to towns and villages.[5]

3.3.2 Choice-Theoretic Formulations of the Demand for Children

While natural fertility and contraceptive use may be important in some instances in constraining and/or determining completed family size, the economics literature has focused on the costs and benefits of children. Three broad motivations for children have been highlighted. These are articulated well by H. Leibenstein:

> We distinguish among three types of utility to be derived from an additional birth and two types of costs. The types of utility are: (1) the utility to be derived from the child as a "consumption good," namely, as a source of personal pleasure to the parents; (2) the utility to be derived from the child as a productive agent, that is, at some point the child may be expected to enter the labor force and contribute to family income; and (3) the utility derived from the prospective child as a potential source of security, either in old age or other. The costs of having an additional child can be divided into direct and indirect costs. By direct costs we refer to the conventional current expenses of maintaining the child, such as feeding and clothing him at conventional standards until the point is reached when the child is self-supporting. By indirect costs we refer to the opportunities foregone due to the existence of an additional child. These are represented by such lost opportunities as the inability of mothers to work if they must tend to children, lost earnings during the gestation period, or the lessened mobility of parents with large family responsibilities.[6]

Although Leibenstein applied his early analysis of family size determination to the low-income setting, the basic notion of households comparing the benefits and costs of an additional child with alternative allocations of household income and wealth forms the basis of an emerging literature of rational household choice. Most of this literature has focused on children as "consumer durables," and has been articulated in a series of seminal papers by G. Becker, as well as in the writings by authors predominantly associated with the University of Chicago, Columbia University, and the National Bureau of Economic Research.[7] Empirical work evaluating this treatment of children has largely pertained to developed countries. Indeed, it is alleged by several scholars that this emphasis on children as consumer durables is more relevant to high- than low-income countries. In the brief survey that follows of alternative views of children, we will therefore begin with an examination of children as producer durables; next, as a source of security or as insurance; and finally, as consumer durables.

Children as Producer Durables. The value of children as producing agents is widely documented in historical accounts of developed countries and in contemporary descriptions of the Third World.[8] Particularly on the farm, but also to a lesser extent in cities, children contribute to the household in the areas of home production (child care, food preparation), farm labor, market activity (including the distribution of farm products), informal sector activities, and modern sector activities. Increasing evidence reveals sizable amounts of inter- and intra-family transfers of financial and real resources in extended family networks.[9] Thus, the view of children as producer durables--assets yielding a return to their parents after they account for direct and indirect costs of upbringing--possesses some appeal in the low-income setting.

On the other hand, the purely financial return from investment in children may be low. Consequently, an approach that views children solely or even primarily as producing agents is difficult to sustain.[10] Indeed, several cost-benefit analyses on the *net* flows of child-related resources to parents--resource inflows netted of all relevant childrearing costs and properly discounted to the present--calculate a negative rate of return on children. This is not to deny that over the life cycle, substantial flows of resources in kind and in cash flow from children to parents, but as yet there is little empirical evidence to indicate that as a form of pure investment, children offer a particularly attractive rate of return. Of course, fragmented and imperfect capital markets may force parents to consider relatively unattractive investments, and in many instances children, land, livestock, and consumer durables represent the only viable forms of asset accumulation for households in low-income rural areas.

The view of children as producer durables yields several hypotheses on the relationships between family size, child quality, and economic conditions in low-income countries. Other things being equal, the more useful children are as producing agents, the larger will be family sizes (1) on large versus small plots of land, (2) on land using labor-intensive versus capital-intensive techniques (mechanization), and (3) in rural versus urban areas. Furthermore, the value of education may be relatively low in rural areas. Education may not contribute notably to the child's productivity on the farm, and too much education may encourage the bright child not only to move to the city, but also to weaken kinship ties, thereby lowering future remissions of earnings to parents. Some of these hypotheses will be used in this study to guide our analysis of rural Egyptian fertility.

Children as Insurance. R. Blandy and A. Woodfield have expanded the producer durable views of children to highlight the children's roles as a form of insurance. They note:

> There is one class of financial asset which people hold willingly which yields zero or negative returns, however. These are assets held to insure against the consequences of adverse states of the world coming into existence. People everywhere willingly forgo some of their consumption levels in "good" states of the world to enhance their consumption levels in the event of "bad" states of the world coming into existence. Maslow rates such "safety needs" as second only to physiological needs in his needs hierarchy.[11]

According to Blandy and Woodfield, children are particularly attractive as insurance assets in low-income societies because (1) the environment is relatively risky (i.e., families are at the margin of subsistence and the costs of financial loss can be high, e.g., starvation and death); (2) there are few private market options for hedging against many risks (actuarial risks can be borne by insurance, but catastrophic risks due to massive crop failures cannot); (3) widespread geographical diffusion of population makes for costly collection of premia, and erratic incomes result in an unreliable flow of premium payments; and (4) children are particularly desirable insurance instruments by comparison with many fully paid-up financial policies in that the present value of children in nominal terms is roughly indexed to the rate of inflation.

The actual attractiveness of children as insurance is based on many factors, including their mortality rate, the strength of blood commitments and kinship ties, and so forth. Indeed, Blandy and Woodfield offer speculations such as "under high mortality and weak kinship ties, couples will choose to have 'lower quality' children than under low mortality and strong kinship ties, other things being equal."[12] Property and inheritance laws also play a central role in influencing the bonds between children and parents.

> They [children] become even more expensive if parents cannot enforce obligations on the part of their children to allocate part of their income during their parents' retirement. In such circumstances, parents may be able to avoid these risks by also holding an alternative asset (say, land or cash balances) which a child will inherit contingent upon income transfer from child to parent during the latter's retirement. This emphasizes one type of risk in holding children, relative to other assets.[13]

The Blandy and Woodfield paper is rich with speculations deriving from the view of children as sources of insurance and old age security. To list a few, they postulate that fertility rates will be inversely related to (1) the spread of social security programs; (2) higher income levels (which reduce the severity of the consequences of disaster); (3) lesser income inequality at any average income level for the society (by reducing the proportion of people for whom disasters have severe consequences); (4) lower risks of death and disease; (5) price stability in developing countries; and (6) inheritance taxes and the restriction of private property.[14]

Children as Consumer Durables. The most widely expounded and investigated economic framework of fertility is based on a working hypothesis that families are typically able to produce the number and quality of children they "desire." These desires are ultimately determined by the benefits and costs of children. B. Boulier and N. G. Mankiw summarize this theory in a single sentence:

> The economic model of fertility determination assumes that a couple chooses the number of births which maximizes a utility function, having surviving children and other goods as arguments, subject to a budget constraint, which equates expenditures on children and other goods to income, and a constraint that surviving children equals births times the proportion surviving.[15]

In this theory, children are primarily considered to be "consumer durables," items that yield direct utility to parents over an extended period of time.[16] The early conceptualization of this model by G.

Becker has been expanded and formalized by him and many others, but all of these frameworks stress the importance of (1) the investment in human capital (e.g., education and health), (2) a household production function highlighting the allocation of human time, and (3) a view of the family that merges consumer choice with the household production of all services, including the bearing and rearing of children.[17]

The model can be summarized as follows. The family is assumed to allocate its scarce resources so as to maximize the family's happiness or utility. In the most elementary versions of the model, only two elements enter this utility function: c is utility derived from children, and s is utility derived from all other goods and services consumed within the households. Thus, $U = U(c, s)$.

One of the important analytical extensions of the new home economics view of children beyond Leibenstein's formulation is that c and s do not contribute directly to utility, but instead must be "produced." Children and goods must be combined with other inputs--purchased goods and services and parents' time--to be transformed into a form that yields utility.[18] A household production function is required:

$$c = c(t_{m,c}, t_{f,c}, x_c; E_c) \text{ and}$$

$$s = s(t_{m,s}, t_{f,s}, x_s; E_s).$$

The t's represent the time of male (m) and female (f) adults in producing c and s; the x's represent other purchased inputs necessary to the production of c and s; E is the technology specific to household production.

The total level of the household's utility depends not only on the consumption of some c and s, but also on the amount consumed. Thus, total consumption is constrained by the household's wealth. It is also in this area where the new home economics expands upon the classical treatment of consumer demand, since "full wealth" now represents a valuation of all of the household's time (spent in both market and household production), as well as any net flows of nonearned wealth into or out of the household. Full wealth, R, is defined as:

$$R = w_{mk}t_{mk} + w_{fk}t_{fk} + V$$

where w represents wage rate, k represents alternative uses of the parents' time, ranging from market activity to home production (the mother's time in housework; the father's time in cultivating crops that are consumed at home; leisure time), and *V* represents transfers of nonearned income. (Young households may transfer assets to their parents; older households may experience a reverse flow.) The theory of consumer choice assumes that each family member allocates his or her time so as to equalize the value of that time on the margin between competing uses, and that the value of this time is equal to an exogenously given wage rate appropriate to that individual. The theory further assumes that the family allocates its total budget between competing uses so as to maximize total utility; i.e., it allocates its budget between goods and services so that the marginal value of each is equalized.[19]

Without dwelling in detail on the mathematics representing these ideas, the new home economics model reduces to a set of demand equations for child services and other goods, which have the following forms:

$$c = c(w_m, w_f, p_x, R; E_c)$$
$$s = s(w_m, w_f, p_x, R; E_s).$$

Focusing on the demand for child services, we see that family size depends on the household's "preferences" for children vis-a-vis other goods and services (a set of preferences which is unexplained by the new home economics),[20] exogenously given wage rates (w) and prices (p), the household's full wealth, and the technology for producing child services.

Several testable hypotheses follow from this framework. Since child services are relatively time intensive in production, and since more of the mother's time is used traditionally to produce c, then

1. increases in wage rates reduce the consumption of children in general, *ceteris paribus*;
2. increases in the wage rates of females have a relatively greater negative impact than do increases in the wage rates of males on the demand for children.

On the other hand, increases in wages also increase R, and since children are "normal" goods (i.e., more children are demanded at greater levels of income and wealth), there is some positive influence of wage increases on the demand for children. Indeed, it is possible that an increase in the father's wage rate will increase the demand for children, while an increase in the mother's wage will decrease the demand for children. In any case, an increase in V is expected to exert a positive influence on the demand for child services, *ceteris paribus.*

Over time children may become relatively more or less expensive to produce (the relative price of p_c may rise or fall) due to a number of factors. For example, the costs of education may rise (increased tuition, compulsory education laws), and, for this reason, fewer children may be demanded. Note, however, that the substitution of s goods for c goods depends on *relative* price changes, p_c/p_s, as well as the nature of the technologies, E_c and E_s, in the production of these goods.

There are many extensions of the new home economics model. The most important focuses on the decomposition of child services into the "quantity" and the "quality" of children. In particular, child services can be viewed as some mix of child quantity and child quality. However, if one goes further to permit differential effects of income on the demand for child quality as distinct from child quantity, the family decision-making becomes more complex.[21] There are many ways in which families might choose between child numbers and child quality. One possibility would be to assume that families strive to invest equally in each child.[22] If this were the case, and one further assumed that families tend to purchase more child quality versus child quantity as income rises (i.e., the income elasticity of child quality exceeds that of child quantity), then one could observe child numbers *decreasing* with increases in income. Indeed, government policies to cultivate this preference may already constitute an important element in family planning programs in low-income countries.

The view that equal investments are made in each child has a substantial impact on the predictions of the new home economics model, and while this assumption commands considerable *a priori* appeal, it is still a feature which requires careful scrutiny. W. C. Sanderson has vividly contrasted the difference between this conception of household behavior and demand for consumer durables in general.

> The dependence of prices on household decisions in the Becker model is the result of a specification that may be appropriate for the analysis of fertility decisions, but whose

> applicability to the demand for consumer durables is dubious. ...If we consider houses instead of children, the unusual nature of this specification becomes clear. Suppose a couple who owned a $50,000 house decided to buy a $20,000 summer cottage in the mountains. The Becker model would tell us that the summer cottage would be a source of utility, but the fact that the couple spent less on their summer cottage than on their permanent residence would be a source of disutility because their average expenditure per house would have declined. But this is clearly unrealistic.... The model when applied to children, however, seems more appropriate. It is plausible that parents could suffer some disutility from not being able to spend as much money on, say, a third child as the average amount they spent on the first two. The assumption that this is the case, however, is not derived from pure economic theory.... Rather, it is like Easterlin's assumption of changing tastes, a special assumption that is necessary to create a plausible model of fertility behavior.[23]

Early writers on fertility have also argued that the quality-quantity tradeoffs between children and other consumer durables merited special treatment.[24] The empirical evidence appears to reveal, however, that in some low-income countries families make quite different investments in children depending on the sex, health, and parity of the child.[25] This may not represent a strong qualification to the equalization-of-child-investment hypothesis when children are considered as consumer durables, but rather it may reflect that in low-income countries, children increasingly partake of producer-durable attributes where differential investments make more sense.

3.4 ALTERNATIVE ECONOMIC VIEWS OF CHILDREN: AN ECLECTIC APPROACH

This review of alternative economic views of children supports our own eclecticism with respect to the analysis and determinants of family size decisions in rural Egypt. This eclecticism takes two primary forms. First, we do not subscribe to any single predominant *economic* motivation for having children and investing in them: in rural Egypt, children are a form of insurance; they yield valuable productive services; they convey direct utility and happiness to their parents; and they are in some instances unintended by-products of sexual activity. While in lower-income societies the insurance, producer-durable, and by-product attributes of children may be relatively more important than in higher-income societies, we do not underestimate the intrinsic maternal and paternal values that Egyptians place on their offspring. This broad view of children in Egyptian society establishes the framework for our own approach to the analysis of the Egyptian Rural Fertility Survey. In particular, selected empirical findings will possess multiple interpretations, mainly because the underlying theory or the data are insufficient to offer a definitive interpretation. While tighter, and possibly more "scientifically elegant" interpretations would be possible in some instances by imposing somewhat dubious and/or restrictive assumptions about Egyptian behavior, the cost of this accomodation is excessive. We would therefore like to describe the present study of Egyptian economic-demographic relationships as guided by a broad theoretical, but somewhat unsettled literature in biology, demography, economics, and sociology. The interpretations we provide of the data are preliminary, given the present state of these various literatures.

A second manifestation of our eclecticism pertains to the weight we attach to economic versus all other motivations that determine family size. Biologists, demographers, and sociologists have been quick to point out the apparent excessive preoccupation by economists with "rational" decision-making, with cost-benefit calculations for children, with self-interest as the motivating force in resource allocation, and with maximization of material well-being as a (the?) dominating drive which guides human behavior. We are well aware of this literature, but, while we are prepared to respond to it in considerable detail, we do not feel this debate would be productive to the current research effort.[26] We simply acknowledge that the economic motivation is *not* the only factor guiding the family size decision. On the other hand, the theory of economics is sufficiently well articulated and explicit in its predictions, by comparison with alternative frameworks, that we feel considerable progress can be made at this time by emphasizing the economic paradigm. This having been said, the reader will recall that we began this chapter with the "Easterlin Synthesis," which integrates biology, demography, and sociology with economics into a single framework. We will continue to develop our analysis of Egyptian rural fertility behavior in this synthetic mode. This will be particularly apparent where we identify a group of Egyptian families who are likely "supply constrained," i.e., families who desire more children than they are able to obtain. Here the disciplines of biology and demography will be relatively important to untangling the underlying family-size relationships.

3.5 THE QUAGMIRE OF CAUSATION AND STATISTICAL INFERENCE IN POPULATION ANALYSIS: EDUCATION AS AN EXAMPLE

The determinants of human fertility are varied and complex, which makes the drawing of conclusions from limited statistical data hazardous in the absence of sophisticated theoretical and statistical analysis. While the present study attempts to draw upon much of the theoretical literature of the last two decades, it does not emphasize some of the recent advances in statistical methodology, largely because the available data do not merit the application of complex statistical techniques, which "fine tune" results.[27] Ours is therefore a preliminary statistical inquiry into the determinants of demographic behavior in rural Egypt, but one which we feel is guided by the main body of theoretical and statistical literature appropriate to the data. While we are fully aware of the difficulties involved in ferreting out empirical insights from these data, it is useful at this stage to illustrate such a difficulty as it pertains to the interpretation of the results. We have chosen the relationships between education and fertility behavior, both because the "accepted wisdom" in this area appears to be quite firm--we argue inappropriately so--and because the education variable is important to current Egyptian policy planning and to the present study.

3.5.1 Increased Education Decreases Fertility ... Or Does It?

There is probably no variable in the empirical literature on the determinants of fertility that commands wider agreement on causation than education. S. Cochrane cites several studies which summarizes the relationships.

> The inverse relationship of education to completed family size is one of the most clear-cut correlations found in the literature.[28]

With regard to educational attainment, we hypothesize that:

> The higher the educational level of the husband and wife, the lower the fertility. There is certainly overwhelming empirical evidence for this hypothesis.[29]

> ...and parental education in LDC's reduces fertility, this much is clear from both cross-national and intracountry cross-sections.[30]

Yet, Cochrane's comprehensive review of the role of education in family size determination reveals that such confidence on the direction of causation is unfounded. She concludes:

> Thc evidence seems to indicate that education may increase or decrease individual fertility. The decrease is greater for the education of women than of men and in urban than rural areas. But education is more likely to *increase* fertility in countries with the lowest level of female literacy.[31]

We conclude that the apparently pervasive evidence on the inverse correlation between education and completed family size has been exaggerated, and that further, there is little theoretical reason why a dominating inverse relationship should exist over all stages of development and across all cultures. There are in fact situations in which a positive relationship would be expected on theoretical grounds, and furthermore there are methodologies for identifying these various situations. The problem with the empirical literature is that the data available and the methodologies employed have been inadequate to confront these alternative analytical possibilities. While this data constraint will prevail in the present study as well, it is important for the interpretation of the results to understand why this is the case. (Parenthetically, it should be noted that the methodological discussion in this section applies not only to the fertility-education relationship, but to other relationships as well.)

The problems in sorting out the education-fertility relationships arise because of (1) multiple direct and indirect causal relations between the variables, and (2) the statistical difficulties of untangling the causal relationships. Consider each point in turn.

3.5.2 Multiple Impacts of Education on Fertility

T. W. Schultz summarizes well the complexity of the education and family size relationships:

> The education of parents, notably that of the mother, appears to be an omnibus. It affects the choice of mates

> in marriage. It may affect the parents' preferences for children. It assuredly affects the earnings of women who enter the labor force. It evidently affects the productivity of mothers in the work they perform in the household, including the rearing of their children. It probably affects the incidence of child mortality, and it undoubtedly affects the ability of parents to control the number of births. The task of specifying and identifying each of the attributes of parents' education in the family context is beset with analytical difficulties on a par with the difficulties that continue to plague the economic analysis of growth in coping with the advances in technology.[32]

Put simply, education directly and indirectly affects so many variables influencing completed family size that untangling the relative importance of each impact (whether positive or negative) is nearly impossible. This is a discouraging quandary if limiting family size is an objective of social policy. In that case, social science research must be able to measure the sizes of each of the negative and positive effects of education on fertility for the formulation of effective policy.

As another example of the complexity of the education-fertility relationships, consider Cochrane's rendering of the connections involved. These are illustrated diagramatically by two figures borrowed from her study. The first, reproduced below as figure 3.2, shows how some of the impacts of individual and community education on (1) literacy, (2) skills, (3) certificates, and (4) socialization influence various aspects of fertility. These latter influences can in turn be integrated into her broader framework of family size determination as displayed in figure 3.3. As one example of the interaction of these diagrams, note that individual education (1) raises the wife's earning power (figure 3.2) which increases the time costs of raising children (and thereby lowers the demand for children) and (2) increases the family income (and thereby increases the demand for children).

Since children are "time intensive" in production, and since most of the time costs are assumed by the mother, the weight of the empirical literature reveals that the *net* impact of increasing the education of mothers will be to decrease the demand for children. A *negative* relationship between education and fertility would be

Figure 3.2 Effects of Individual and Community Education

SOURCE: S. Cochrane [1979, p. 29].

anticipated, *ceteris paribus*. But other things may not be equal. Increasing the mother's education simultaneously influences other aspects of household behavior. Also, an increase in the mother's education may alter the supply of children available to the family. This supply influence may go either toward increasing or toward decreasing family size. On the one hand, education may delay marriage and reduce the period of marital fertility, it may result in more favorable attitudes toward contraception, and/or it may improve the efficiency with which contraceptives are used. These impacts of education would decrease the supply of children. On the other hand, increased education of the mother may improve her own health or the health of her child (improved knowledge of nutrition, food preparation technologies, personal hygiene and sanitation); it may reduce her participation in extended periods of lactation (substituting "modern" techniques of child nourishment); and it may reduce her acceptance of sexual taboos (extended abstinence during "hard times"). These impacts of education would increase the supply of children. Whether the net impact of education is positive or negative is therefore an empirical issue. It is more likely to be positive in situations where households are "supply constrained," i.e., where they desire more children than they are able to produce. It is more likely to be negative in situations where households have excess fertility.

These examples should be sufficient to demonstrate the exceptional complexity of the relationships between seemingly straight-

Figure 3.3 Intervening Variables and Fertility Determination

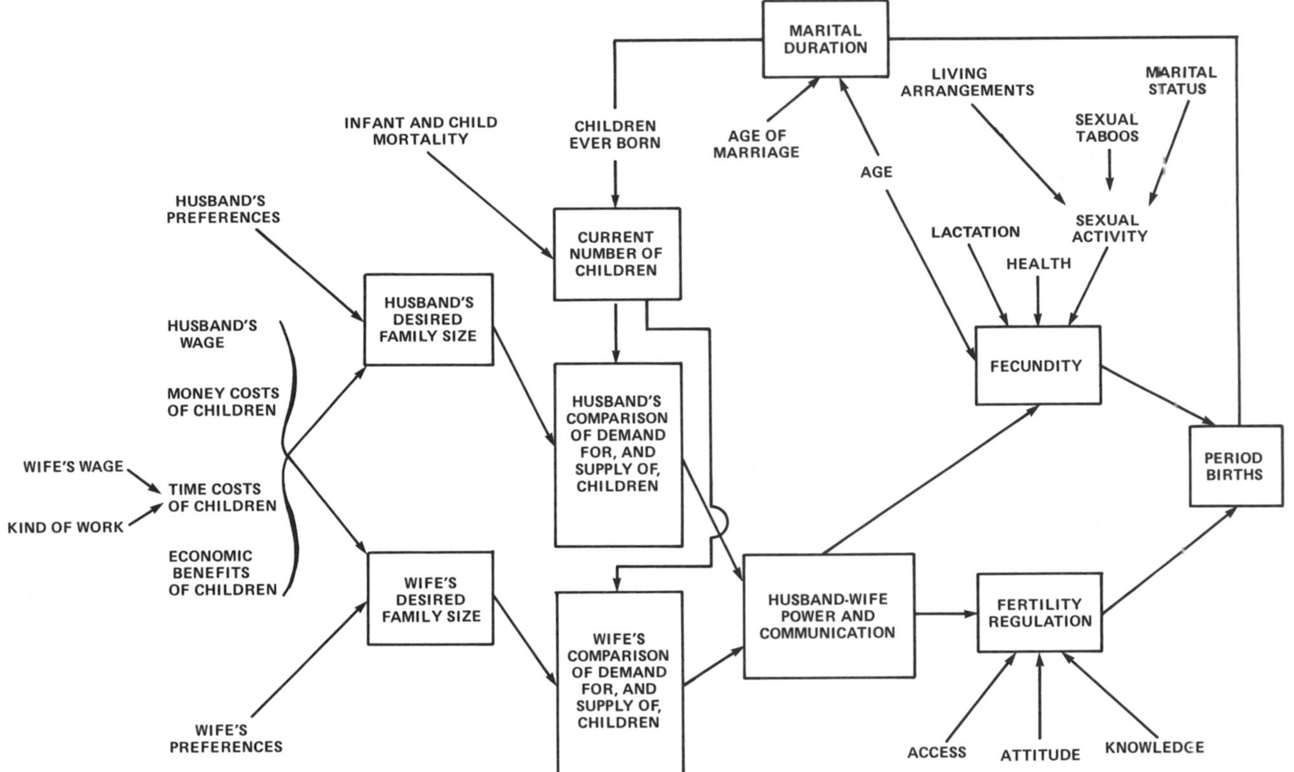

SOURCE: S. Cochrane [1979, p. 60].

forward variables, such as education and fertility, and to dispel some of the confidence in the widespread belief of a stable and negative relationship.

The key research question, then, is to identify the magnitude of the separate influences of education on fertility and/or completed family size. To answer this question we turn next to the statistical and methodological requirements for, and the pitfalls in, interrogating data to explore these relationships.

3.5.3 Pitfalls in Interpreting Multiple Causal Relationships[33]

As noted above, the household's observed family size is determined by factors which influence that household's demand for children, as well as its ability to supply that number of children. If there were no constraints on the supply of children, then in a perfectly contracepting world, observed family size would be determined totally by factors affecting the demand for children. If, on the other hand, some households desire more children than they are able to obtain, then factors influencing the supply of children determine completed family size. While there are many factors influencing the supply of and demand for children, for illustrative purposes we will continue to focus only on education. Figure 3.4 displays one possible relationship. The demand curve is downward sloping in part because increased education is associated with an increased value of the mother's time, which results in a higher cost of children. The supply curve is upward sloping in part because better educated women are healthier (they employ more appropriate health-care measures in food preparation and sanitation), and utilize knowledge that improves child survival.

Most data used to investigate the determinants of family size constitute cross-sections of women with widely varying levels of education. As shown in figure 3.4, an increase in education will increase surviving family size for some women in the sample (those to the left of point a) while decreasing it for others (those to the right of point a). Using a simple statistical technique which displays only the above variables (a single table displaying the education, surviving children relationship, or a single regression equation which shows the same variables), one could observe a nonlinear relationship. (Indeed, a simple regression technique that imposed a linear relationship might indicate *no* statistically significant relationship,

Figure 3.4 Impact of Education on Surviving Children

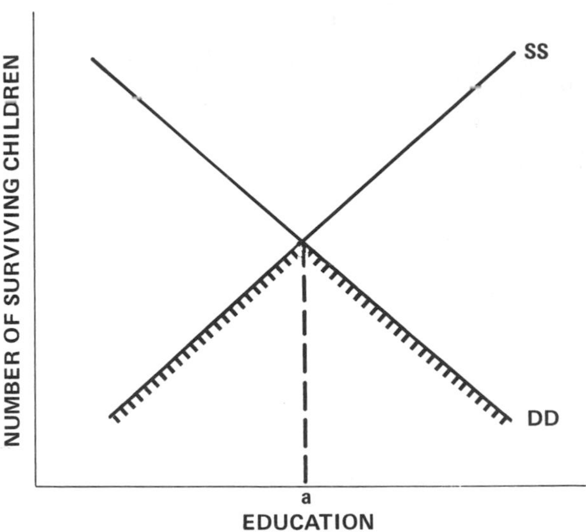

where in fact the underlying data incorporated one.)

The key point of this example is that in exploring a relationship between variables with multiple causation linkages, and especially between variables in the supply-demand framework of figure 3.4, simple tables and single-equation regressions present at most a "reduced form" relationship--the *net* result of supply *and* demand factors. The interpretation of the results must take this point into account. This discussion is neither a criticism of the underlying statistical methodology employed in our study, nor is it a caveat which may account for "unexpected" empirical results. Rather, we merely wish to reveal, through an important example, the extremely complex relationships between socioeconomic variables, fertility, and mortality.

Nevertheless, we conclude on an optimistic note. It is possible to resolve many of these statistical and methodological problems, but doing so requires additional theoretical specification, an expanded data base, and a more complex statistical methodology. In reference to the example in figure 3.4, it would be necessary to (1) specify separately the determinants of (and equations for) supply and demand and (2) insure that this specification is adequately identified (i.e., there are one or more measurable determinants of supply that are not common to demand, and vice versa).[34] If appropriate assumptions are satisfied with respect to the underlying statistical properties of each equation, then procedures are available to untangle the apparently nonlinear relationship described above.[35] In the present study, given time and especially data constraints, little use of these more sophisticated modeling techniques has been made. Our results therefore represent a first effort in ferreting out the broad relationships under investigation. On the other hand, we feel that with a careful interpretation of the results, some useful insights are obtained for policy analysis, as well as for identifying future directions of research into the determinants of demographic and economic change in rural Egypt.

4. RURAL EGYPTIAN SOCIETY: AN OVERVIEW

4.1 INTRODUCTION

Historically, Egypt has been a predominantly agricultural society. From the dawn of agriculture to the present time, the history of Egypt has recorded continuing efforts to control the river Nile. The Nile has brought fertility to a desert that knows almost no rain. The irrigated green tract of fertile land, which winds for 1500 kilometers from south to north, narrowly bordering the twisting course of the Nile, comprises less than four percent of the total land of Egypt. But the richness of the Nile valley has given agriculture a key position in the Egyptian economy. Even though about half of the Egyptian population presently dwells in urban or semiurban localities, the majority are descendants of peasants who for generations have tilled the soil.

About two-thirds of the rural population live in the Delta, the location of most fertile soil in Egypt, while the remainder reside in Upper Egypt. Within the rural agricultural environment, the village serves as an important social unit. Indeed, agriculture comprises the ecological and economic basis of the village, for it is the hard physical labor of plowing, sowing, weeding, harvesting, and threshing of the basic crops that is the central core of life in a traditional village.

As a physical unit, the village is constructed around a circular road. Initially houses are built within the circle along unpaved irregular streets, while new houses and service buildings are constructed outside. Each house is usually owned by its resident. Typically it is one story high and built most often of mud or red bricks or, less frequently, of stones.

For the peasant, land is the basic source of income and

production, although crafts and small local businesses provide other sources of income. Land ownership and wealth derived from livestock are the main factors contributing to position and status within the village. Consequently, villagers may be classified as upper class (rich landlords or the equivalent), middle class (tenant farmers and agricultural workers with 70 percent having less than one feddan of land), or lower class (laborers).

The division of labor within a village is governed by a number of factors, including social status, sex, and age. Well-to-do villagers plan and supervise, while hired laborers carry out the normal work of the land. Upper-class women are generally involved in household activities. In addition to housework, middle- and lower-class women work with men in the fields. Besides raising children, women have always played an important role economically. However, they usually remain unpaid family workers before and after marriage. When upper-class children are at school in a nearby city, it is commonplace to see young middle- and lower-class children leading water buffalo to the canal. Many children start to work in the fields at a young age, and they become an important economic resource.

The family occupies the most important position in the Egyptian village structure. It derives its significance from its economic functions and its role as an agent of socialization and social control. The rural family is patrilineal and patrilocal. The head of the extended family controls the family lands. As long as the father is the head of the family, the household management rests with the mother. Sons and daughters-in-law are expected to obey her. Islamic teaching provides that at the death of the father each son receives twice the amount of assets of each daughter. Typically there is no precise formal division, although the oldest son may assume the decision-making of the deceased father. Moreover, the land is usually kept intact and is not divided as part of the assets. As a result, the daughter's share of the assets often takes the form of produce, personal assets, and the like.

Culturally, Egypt is a male-dominant society. The status of a woman is determined largely by ownership of land or by possession of a house, gold, or jewelry. When women participate with their husbands in agriculture, they then enjoy a degree of equality.

Since marriage is regarded as natural and necessary, weddings usually occur at harvest time or during religious feasts to insure fertility and success. Early marriage for females is customary. In rural areas, many females marry before the age of 16, and many males before the age of 25. Most marriages are arranged and brides are normally selected by the couple's parents. The status of the young bride becomes settled once she bears children, for the larger the number of children, the greater her influence with her husband and the greater her security within the family. Childbirth is such an important event in the countryside that a childless woman, or one unable to produce a son, may be forced to allow a polygynous household or accept divorce, and her status in the community will be drastically reduced.

Prevailing social values and aspirations in the countryside are important for understanding rural behavior and attitudes. Islamic religious values encourage childbearing--children are a gift of God and are the result of God's will. As an economic value, children are a source of labor and income. Socially, they bring prestige to the family and recognition to the wife. Villagers aspire toward both the acquisition of land to provide a source of income as well as social status, and toward the development of the home as a social value and mark of achievement.

Because religious, economic, and social values encourage large families and the acquisition of land often demands labor, women in many age groups are usually pregnant or nursing. Since females marry young, two generations of women in the same extended family might be pregnant at the same time. Women normally give birth at home, assisted by older women or by the local midwife. It is only the upper class that has recently availed itself of some medical assistance.

In recent years, signs of social change have become evident. The traditional rural economic structure is changing. Although agriculture predominates, education and urban contact have introduced new ideas about the accumulation of wealth by nonagricultural means. Trade, small industries, and services coexist with agriculture. Mobility, once restricted, is now extensive. The foundation which has supported the extended family is changing, leading to individualism and a decline in rigid traditional principles. The altered conditions and attitudes of the people are reflected in their aspirations. The goals of parents for their sons have become directed toward education, thus transforming education into a socioeconomic value in its own right.

4.2 THE 1976 CENSUS

The conditions of rural Egyptian society can be more clearly understood by a comparison with urban areas. In 1947 the rural population included 12.6 million people, which represented 66.4 percent of the entire population. Since 1960 this proportion has decreased rapidly. Total population increased by 12 million between 1960 and 1976, which with a steady drift of migrants to cities, reduced the ratio of the rural population from 62.2 percent in 1960 to 56.1 percent (or about 20.5 million people) in 1976. Such a change is both a cause and result of large economic and social disparities between urban and rural areas. Of the 20.5 million Egyptians living in rural areas, about 95.5 percent are Moslem, compared to 91.6 percent in the urban areas. Population density is only 609 individuals per square kilometer in rural areas, compared to almost 10,000 in urban areas. It may reach 24,000 in metropolitan Cairo or be as low as 327 in the rural governorate of Kafr El-Sheikh. Rural-urban migration is predominantly male, thus increasing the sex ratio from 102 in rural areas to 105 in urban areas.

Table 4.1 reveals that about 42 percent of the rural population in 1976 is below age 15 and that about 54 percent is in the 15-64 age group. The resulting dependency ratio of .856 is one of the highest in the world--each 100 persons in the manpower ages support about 86 others in addition to themselves. However, since only 37 percent of the rural population above the age of 6 is classified as in the labor force, each person in the labor force supports about 3 other persons.[1] About 22 percent of the rural population are females in their reproductive ages, 15-49. Of these women, 79 percent are above the legal marriage age (16 years), and of this group 68 percent are currently married. The proportion of women single at ages 15-19 and 20-24 increased from 75 and 23 percent respectively in 1960 to 83 and 39 percent respectively in 1976.[2] Thus, the frequency of first marriages among younger women has decreased markedly after 1960. In addition, the singulate mean age at first marriage (the average age at first marriage that would be experienced by a hypothetical group of persons if, in moving from age 15 to 50, the group had the proportions single observed in a

Table 4.1 Rural Population by Age and Sex

Age Groups	Male	Female	Total
Less than 1	1.81	1.83	1.82
1-	12.90	13.03	12.96
5-	14.14	13.37	13.76
10-	14.46	12.83	13.65
15-	11.05	9.24	10.16
20-	7.32	7.43	7.38
25-	6.56	7.00	6.77
30-	4.99	5.86	5.42
35-	5.22	5.78	5.50
40-	4.75	5.30	5.02
45-	4.11	4.24	4.18
50-	3.82	4.37	4.09
55-	2.53	2.47	2.50
60-	2.71	3.02	2.86
65+	3.63	4.23	3.93
Total	10,419,502	10,170,299	20,589,801

Source: CAPMAS (1978b). *1976 Population and Housing Census: Detailed Results (Total Republic)*, Reference No. 1978-15111-93, Table 1, pp. 61-72. Cairo: Central Agency for Public Mobilization and Statistics. (Arabic).

census or survey), according to the National Academy of Sciences study, increased from 20.3 years in 1960 to 21.7 years in 1976 for all Egypt. No figures were available for Upper/Lower or urban/rural differentials. However, Loza and El-Khorazaty,[3] using a sample of 5,126 households conducted in 1978 covering 21 cities and villages in six governorates, found that the singulate mean age at marriage is 19.2 years for rural areas and 22.4 years for urban areas.

In spite of the growth of rural development, the rate of improvement of the peasant's condition has been meager. Lack of adequate educational, health, and social services, as well as employment opportunities, has contributed to unfavorable population characteristics in rural areas. This situation is further aggravated by illiteracy, which is widespread in villages, particularly among females (see table 4.2). About 70 percent of the rural population 10 years and over are illiterate; 17 percent have some education, but no certificate; and only 11 percent have at least a primary

Table 4.2 Characteristics of Rural and Urban Populations by Sex

Characteristics	Percentage Distribution								
	Rural			Urban			Total		
	Male	Female	Total	Male	Female	Total	Male	Female	Total
Population Distribution	50.6	49.4	100.0	51.3	48.8	100.0	50.9	49.1	100.0
Population by Age									
Less than 15	43.3	41.1	42.2	37.0	37.2	37.1	40.5	39.4	39.9
15-	53.1	54.7	53.9	59.9	59.7	59.8	56.1	56.9	56.5
65 and over	3.6	4.2	3.9	3.2	3.1	3.2	3.4	3.7	3.6
Total(000)=100	10,420	10,170	20,590	8,228	7,809	16,037	18,648	17,979	36,627
Marital Status[a]									
Single	26.1	16.6	21.1	35.6	27.1	31.1	30.6	21.3	25.6
Married	71.6	65.7	68.5	62.3	59.8	61.2	67.2	63.0	65.1
Divorced	.3	1.1	.8	.5	1.3	.9	.4	1.2	.8
Widowed	2.0	16.6	9.7	1.6	11.9	6.8	1.8	14.5	8.4
Total(000)=100	5,142	5,757	10,849	4,566	4,719	9,275	9,708	10,476	10,184
Educational Status[b]									
Illiterate	55.0	85.9	70.4	26.4	52.4	39.2	41.9	70.9	56.3
No Certificate	26.2	7.7	7.1	30.2	19.1	24.8	28.1	12.8	20.6
Primary Cert. +	17.1	4.1	10.6	41.9	26.6	34.3	28.5	14.2	21.3
Not Stated	1.7	2.3	2.0	1.5	1.9	1.6	1.6	2.1	1.8
Total(000)=100	7,414	7,299	4,713	6,263	5,926	12,189	13,677	13,225	26,902
Economic Activity[c]									
Economically Active	56.7	2.7	35.1	56.1	7.2	52.4	61.9	4.7	33.9
Not Econ. Active	33.3	97.3	64.9	43.9	92.8	67.6	38.1	95.3	66.1
Total(000)=100	8,461	8,263	16,724	6,970	6,598	13,568	15,431	14,861	30,292

Source: See Table 4.1.

a Total females 16 years and over and males 18 years and over. b Population 10 years and over.

c The data covers the main economic sector of the work place of individuals 6 years and over according to the international classification of economic activity.

certificate. Of those engaged in some form of economic activity, representing about 35 percent of the rural population aged 6 years and over, about 75 percent work in agriculture.

From table 4.2 we also see that a higher percentage distribution of married males and females is found in rural areas. Although the divorce rate for males and females is slightly higher in urban areas, the combined widow rate (males and females) in rural areas (9.7 percent) is higher than the combined rate for urban areas (6.8 percent). In rural areas, the illiteracy rate is higher for females, reaching about 86 percent, than for males (55 percent). The percentage of females economically active in rural areas is less than 3 percent, compared to about 67 percent for males. The picture in urban areas is not notably different from rural areas when comparing male and female characteristics. However, female economic and social characteristics in urban areas are somewhat more favorable than comparable female characteristics in rural areas.

Rural life in Egypt offers an expression of hospitality, solidarity, and mutual help. It is the socioeconomic and demographic aspects of life along the Nile which will receive attention in this study. While much of our analysis will be statistical and analytical in orientation, we must not lose sight of the richness of the Egyptian historical heritage, and we must be cautious in formulating policy prescriptions and conclusions that fail to relate to this culture. The present account of the statistical attributes of the rural area has therefore been couched with this broader perspective in mind.

4.3 THE RESEARCH DATA BASE

Two data sets, the Rural Fertility Survey and the Community Data Sheet, constitute the information base for the analysis in the present study. A description of these data completes our overview of the rural Egyptian society.

4.3.1 The Rural Fertility Survey

The Rural Fertility Survey (RFS) was executed in 1979 under the direct responsibility of the Statistics Office of the Population and Family Planning Board. The staff of the Statistics Office provided the major part of the personnel. The survey headquarters were based in the Board's premises in Cairo, with regional offices located in each of the governorates surveyed.

The sample represents a two-stage cluster stratified design. The seventeen rural governorates constitute the strata. Since the sample is aimed at providing information on the governorate level, it was decided to include an equal number of households from each governorate as opposed to a proportional allocation that would give rise to a small number of households in small governorates.

Using the results of the 1974/1975 National Fertility Survey in Egypt,[4] it was decided to include 250 households from each governorate to control for sampling error within 10 percent for the governorate's contraceptive prevalence rate, with a 95 percent confidence level.

In order to guarantee geographic representation within each governorate, and for field management considerations, the 250 households were selected in two stages: five villages were randomly selected in the first stage and 50 households were selected from each of the five villages in the second stage. The list of households was prepared two to four weeks before the actual field work.

The sample is not self-weighted. Hence, weights based on the population census of 1976 (which were not available at the time the sample was designed) were adopted. The planned sample size included 4,277 dwelling units; however, only 4,061 were actually reached in the field. Mainly because of cost considerations no further attempt was made to reach the missed dwellings. The nonresponse rate varied among governorates, ranging from .49 percent in Kalubia to 7.91 percent in Kafr El-Sheikh. The average overall nonresponse rate was about 3 percent.

Each dwelling unit may include more than one household. Indeed, 4,158 households were interviewed in the 4,061 dwellings, which results in an average of 1.02 households per dwelling unit. A total of 3,971 eligible women (ever-married women under 50 years of age) were found in these 4,158 households, giving rise to an average of .95 eligible women per household.[5]

Appendix table A.1 presents summary statistics on the main variables used from the Rural Fertility Survey. The first nine entries represent the dependent variables--those to be explained--while the remaining entries are independent variables. The statistics in the table are useful in obtaining some perspective on the magnitudes involved in interpreting the tabular and multiple regression results in chapters 5-10. Briefly, it is seen that for the entire RFS sample, (1) the average number of children ever born is 4.3, (2) child deaths average 1.0, (3) most women never participate in the formal workforce (89 percent), (4) women marry young (16.9 years), (5) the proportion of women who have ever used or are currently using modern contraceptives is fairly moderate (23.6 percent and 12.2 percent, respectively), and (6) education levels are quite low (62 percent of the men and 76 percent of the women are illiterate). For the subset of women who have largely completed their childbearing (women aged 35 years and over), (1) CEB are 6.6 and child deaths are 1.8, leaving 4.8 surviving children, and (2) education levels are somewhat lower than for the sample as a whole (71.7 percent of the husbands and 81.0 percent of the wives are illiterate).

4.3.2 The Community Data Sheet

The Population and Development Project (PDP) is a community-oriented program through which structural changes may be introduced on the community level to affect individuals' attitudes and behavior. Given this orientation, it was felt that a community data base was needed to assess, monitor, and evaluate the project's effects. To this end the Department of Population and Development of the Population and Family Planning Board developed a community data sheet with the technical assistance of experts in the fields of population, family planning, economics, agriculture, health, education, social affairs, and statistics. The Community Data Sheet (CDS) was to be completed prior to the initiation of the PDP. The observation unit is the village council, on the assumption that activities introduced in the "mother village" have their effect and impact on the neighboring satellite villages; thus, the village council unit is considered as one community from the standpoint of PDP programming.

Data are collected for each village council on the following items:

1. Population: population size (male, female), births, deaths, marriages, and divorces;
2. Family Planning: number of women in reproductive ages, number of contraceptive users, and distribution of different family planning

	methods;
3. Economics:	land tenure, number of tractors, irrigation units, agricultural development projects, and cottage industries;
4. Health:	number of health units, hospital beds, clinics, pharmacies, family planning centers, and family planning doctors;
5. Education:	number of schools, classes, and students in the primary, preparatory, and secondary levels;
6. Social Setting:	number of social units, society development associations, nurseries, youth centers, mosques, religious associations, cooperatives, police and fire departments, mayor's offices, water taps, and electricity units;
7. Recreation:	number of libraries, cinemas, theaters, and cultural centers;
8. Transportation & Communications:	number of post offices, bus stops, telegraph and telephone offices;
9. Mass Media:	number of radio and TV sets, newspapers and kiosks;
10. Projects:	number of socioeconomic projects by type of finance and type of activity.

The CDS information was collected by the headmen of the village councils and the local coordinators from different government offices. The CDS was updated in early 1980 for those village councils covered by the PDP before the end of 1979. By April 1980, the first CDS, collected at the initiation of the PDP program, was available for 311 of the 369 village councils in the project. The 58 unavailble CDS's are for those councils where PDP activities started after April 1980. The updated CDS is available for 271 of the 287 councils in the project by the end of 1979. Appendix table C.4 shows the availability of the CDS in different governorates by April 1980, and for the first and second rounds of the CDS.

4.3.3 Empirical Characteristics of PDP Village Councils

Of the 85 villages in the RFS, 32 were covered by the PDP at the time of the survey. However, 2 of these 32 villages were from the same village council. Since the CDS's are available only for the village council, community level variables are taken to be the same for these 2 villages. Thus, only 31 CDS's are investigated, and their data have been assigned to individuals and households in the 32 villages as their attributes.

Different indices were developed to reflect the socioeconomic situation in the village councils. These measures provide a useful picture of the environment in which individuals and households operate. The indices were developed as follows. First, per capita variables were created. Exceptions involve farm size and mechanization of agriculture (tractors and irrigation units) where per feddan variables were created. Second, per capita variables were grouped into three categories, namely, 0 = low, 1 = middle, and 2 = high. Third, per capita variables were classified into fifteen socioeconomic indicies. Fourth, for each index, categorized variables were summed.

Fifteen indices were developed.

1. MTENURE: mean size of tenure (feddans).
2. MECHAGR: mechanization of agriculture per feddan (tractors and irrigation units).
3. AGRDEV: agricultural development per capita (plows, nurseries, honeybee cultures, cooperatives, dairy products, animal breeding, etc.).
4. COTIND: cottage industries per capita (carpet, tile, and carpentery workshops, etc.).
5. HTHSER: health services per capita (health and rural units, clinics, pharmacies, hospital beds, family planning centers, etc.).
6. EDUCSER: educational services per capita (primary, preparatory, and secondary classes).
7. WEDUCL: women's education level per capita (female students in primary, preparatory, and secondary education).
8. SOCSER: social services per capita (children's nurseries, youth centers, society development associations, etc.).
9. RELACT: religious activities per capita (mosques, Koran teaching associations, etc.).
10. RECFAC: recreational facilities per capita (libraries,

cinemas, theaters, etc.).

11. TRCSER: transportation and communication services per capita (post, telegraph, and telephone offices, bus stops, etc.).
12. FOODSER: food supply per capita (consumer cooperatives).
13. WATSUP: water supply per capita (public water taps).
14. ELECSER: electricity services per capita (electric units).
15. MASMSER: mass media services per capita (radio and TV sets).

An index of development was then developed as the sum of the above fifteen indices (TINDEV: total index of development). In addition, three other indices pertaining to the PDP were constructed. These were:

1. DURATION: duration of the PDP in months.
2. PPRJPDP: intensity of the PDP socioeconomic projects per capita.
3. EXTWKS: extension workers (Raiyda Riyfia) per capita.

Table 4.3 shows the distribution of village councils and ever-married women by different socioeconomic indices, as well as the mean and standard deviation of each index.

The mean size of tenure per household in the PDP sample is about 2.6 feddan. The coefficient of variation is small, about 0.33. Indices with high coefficients of variation are mechanization of agriculture, electricity services, educational services, mass media services, and transportation and communication services. Of particular interest is the small coefficient of variation for the total index of development. About 95 percent of households achieve a low level of development of not more that 55 out of a possible score of 79. Other indices with a small coefficient of variation are health services, and agricultural development. However, it is the relative importance of each index either on the village level or on the individual level which will be highlighted in much of the following analysis.

The three indices pertaining to the PDP program are shown in table 4.4 along with their frequencies, means, and standard deviations. Of women surveyed in PDP villages, 41.2 percent live in areas where the project had a duration of 10 months or less. The maximum duration is 19 months with a mean value of about 10.5

Table 4.3 PDP Village Councils and RFS Women by Socioeconomic Indices

Indices and Possible Range	Village Councils		Ever-married Women	
	Frequency	Percentage	Frequency	Percentage
MTENURE: (feddan)		Mean = 2.605	S.D. = 0.866	
Less than 2	9	29.0	407	26.8
2-	15	48.4	699	45.9
3+	7	22.6	416	27.3
MECHAGR: (0-4)		Mean = 1.710	S.D. = 1.305	
Less than 2	15	48.4	712	46.8
2-	7	22.6	384	25.2
3+	9	29.0	426	28.0
AGRDEV: (0-14)		Mean = 6.173	S.D. = 2.957	
Less than 5	9	29.0	440	28.9
5-	13	42.0	6284	1.3
8+	9	29.0	454	29.8
COTIND: (0-6)		Mean = 2.538	S.D. = 1.571	
Less than 2	9	29.0	440	28.9
2-	16	51.6	758	49.8
4+	6	19.4	324	21.3
HTHSER: (0-10)		Mean = 4.785	S.D. = 1.578	
Less than 5	13	42.0	669	44.0
5-	13	42.0	637	41.9
7+	5	16.0	216	14.1
EDUCSER: (0-5)		Mean = 1.938	S.D. = 1.475	
Less than 2	12	38.7	596	39.2
2-	13	41.9	610	40.1
4+	6	19.4	316	20.7
WEDUCL: (0-4)		Mean = 2.371	S.D. = 1.298	
Less than 2	10	32.3	457	30.0
2-	15	48.3	722	47.4
4+	6	19.4	343	22.6
SOCSER: (0-5)		Mean = 2.327	S.D. = 1.494	
Less than 2	11	35.4	533	35.0
2-	14	45.2	651	42.8
4+	6	19.4	338	22.2

Table 4.3 (continued)

Indices and Possible Range	Village Councils		Ever-married Women	
	Frequency	Percentage	Frequency	Percentage
RELACT: (0-4)		Mean = 1.868	S.D. = 1.066	
Less than 2	10	32.3	534	35.1
2-	13	42.0	632	41.5
3+	8	25.7	356	23.4
RECFAC: (0-3)		Mean = 1.161	S.D. = 0.910	
0	9	29.0	472	31.0
1	8	25.8	384	25.2
2+	14	45.2	666	43.8
TRCSER: (0-8)		Mean = 3.617	S.D. = 1.967	
Less than 3	10	32.3	501	32.9
3-	11	35.4	530	34.8
5+	10	32.3	491	32.3
FOODSER: (0-4)		Mean = 1.923	S.D. = 1.255	
None	6	19.4	275	18.1
1-	16	51.6	761	50.0
3+	9	29.0	486	31.9
WATSUP: (0-3)		Mean = 1.646	S.D. = 1.057	
Less than 2	13	42.0	612	40.2
2-	11	35.5	538	35.4
3+	7	22.6	372	24.4
ELECSER: (0-3)		Mean = 1.558	S.D. = 1.203	
None	9	29.0	434	28.5
1-	13	42.0	608	40.0
3	9	29.0	480	31.5
MASMSER: (0-4)		Mean = 2.305	S.D. = 1.579	
Less than 2	10	32.3	457	30.0
2-	10	32.3	480	31.6
4	11	35.4	585	38.4
TINDEV: (0-79)		Mean = 36.927	S.D. = 9.699	
Less than 31	9	29.0	441	29.0
31-	14	45.2	672	44.2
41+	8	25.8	409	26.8
Total	31	100	1522	100

Table 4.4 PDP Village Councils and RFS Women by Selected PDP Indices

PDP Index	Village Councils		Ever-married Women	
	Frequency	Percentage	Frequency	Percentage
DURATION: (months)		Mean = 10.542	S.D. = 3.169	
Less than 11	13	42.0	627	41.2
11-	10	32.3	487	32.0
13-19	8	25.7	408	26.8
PROJECT INTENSITY/10,000		Mean = 0.257	S.D. = 0.355	
None	19	61.3	914	60.0
Less than 0.5	5	16.1	251	16.5
0.5+	7	22.6	357	23.5
RAIYDA RIYFIA/10,000		Mean = 1.993	S.D. = 0.789	
Less than 2	19	61.3	904	59.4
2	8	25.7	433	28.4
3+	4	13.0	185	12.2
TOTAL	31	100	1522	100

months. These figures suggest that it might be premature to expect noticeable changes in fertility behavior due to PDP programming. Of the 31 village councils, 19 did not have any projects supported by the PDP. The mean intensity is about .25 projects per 10 thousand inhabitants. The mean number of Raiyda Riyfia per 5 thousand inhabitants is about unity. Only 4 villages had more than one Raiyda Riyfia per 5 thousand inhabitants, and these villages included 12 percent of the total number of women in the PDP sample.

5. DETERMINANTS OF COMPLETED FAMILY SIZE IN RURAL EGYPT

5.1 CHILDREN EVER BORN: CUMULATIVE FERTILITY

This chapter presents an exploratory inquiry into the patterns and determinants of cumulative fertility, child deaths, and female workforce participation. Our objective is to examine some preliminary working hypotheses on the determinants of these three variables. For this purpose we rely on tabular analysis, and we present correlations between pairs of variables. (Many of the comparisons standardize for age of the wife.) On the other hand, the various relationships examined are in fact quite complex, and as a result, multivariate regression models will be required to identify more precisely the underlying empirical causation. This analysis is taken up in chapter 6.

The measurement of the number of children ever born (CEB), representing cumulative fertility, suffers from several limitations. First, women who died or emigrated before the survey date are excluded from the data. "To the extent that they differ from the remaining women with respect to the number of children ever born, the reported fertility for a given cohort of women will be biased. This bias is usually ignored in analysis."[1] Second, the figures on number of children ever born derived from survey data may be erroneous because of faulty memory of women, especially older women who bore their children many years ago.[2] Those live births who died shortly after birth are also more likely to be omitted.[3]

While underreporting is itself troublesome, the primary difficulty arises if this underreporting is related to individual attributes of interest in the analysis. The age and education of the woman represent examples of such attributes. Caution must therefore be exercised in the analysis of survey data as related to these particular attributes. Nevertheless, probing by interviewers should have minimized the extent of underreporting. Moreover, this particular survey included an extensive section on retrospective birth and pregnancy history, a feature that should not only raise the accuracy of recall, but also should provide checks on the cumulative figures for child deaths and children ever born.

Due to the cross-sectional nature of the survey, there is a systematic exclusion of women who had not married by the time of the survey. As a result, there is an underestimation in the mean age at marriage. This effect extends through the entire reproductive history of the respondents and results in a downward bias in the age at entry into each parity. Caution must therefore be observed when dealing with children ever born classified by birth cohorts of respondents.

Table 5.1 reveals that the overall average number of children ever born per ever-married woman is 4.3. This is a relatively high average, since the sample includes young women who anticipate long reproductive lives. (The mean age of ever-married women in the sample is 30.4 years.) The mean CEB for women in the age group 45-49 is 7.5, a high figure for completed fertility. The data show that by the time a woman is in the 35-39 age group, she has had more than 6 live births on average, therefore adding only 1.5 births in the remaining 10 to 15 years of her reproductive period.

It is further observed from table 5.1 that the mean number of children ever born increases steadily with years since first marriage. Control by marriage cohorts overcomes the bias inherent in birth cohorts due to the censoring effects.[4] However, while marriage cohorts overcome this inherent bias, they are themselves subject to bias in the opposite direction. This is due to the underrepresentation of earlier cohorts who first married late in life and were thus aged 50 or over at the time of the survey. However, marital duration is a very good indicator of the length of exposure to childbirth. The data show an average number of children ever born of 0.9 during the first five years of marital life. This is low, of course, because these five years include the newly married with a duration of less than one year. An average of 2.7 children ever born is observed in the second five years of marital life. The average increases notably since all women had an exposure to childbirth of 5-9 years. The average increases gradually until it reaches about

Table 5.1 Women by CEB, Age, and Years Since First Marriage

Characteristics	Children Ever Born											Mean	
	0	1	2	3	4	5	6	7	8	9	10+	CEB	N
Current Age													
15-	49.3	35.7	12.9	*	-	-	-	-	-	-	-	.68	337
20-	15.3	23.8	28.7	18.8	10.3	2.3	*	-	-	-	-	1.95	739
25-	7.5	8.6	15.6	20.5	20.5	14.1	9.3	2.3	*	*	*	3.40	782
30-	4.6	3.6	5.6	10.5	15.3	18.4	17.4	13.5	7.2	2.5	*	4.94	609
35-	3.4	2.9	4.0	6.7	9.1	15.0	14.5	15.6	10.5	9.4	8.9	6.02	552
40-	3.9	3.0	4.6	3.9	7.1	10.6	13.3	9.7	14.3	12.9	17.0	6.65	435
45-49	*	*	2.7	2.7	5.9	9.1	9.1	14.4	12.6	14.2	25.1	7.47	374
Years Since 1st Marriage													
<5	39.6	37.9	18.4	3.4	*	-	-	-	-	-	-	.88	760
5-	5.7	9.9	28.2	31.2	17.7	5.4	1.7	*	-	-	-	2.70	778
10-	3.4	3.2	7.1	12.2	23.5	23.5	17.0	6.8	2.0	*	*	4.44	648
15-	3.6	2.7	4.3	7.5	13.7	18.3	17.8	14.9	10.5	4.1	2.9	5.42	563
20-	2.5	1.7	2.7	4.6	7.2	11.8	16.1	16.3	13.2	13.0	10.9	6.60	484
25+	2.4	1.9	3.2	3.6	3.9	8.2	9.4	12.1	14.1	14.7	26.6	7.55	587

* Less than 10 cases.

7.6 for those with 25 or more years of marital duration.

The distribution of ever-married women by number of births by current age and by years since first marriage is also shown in table 5.1. It is to be expected that the number of children ever born increases as current age and/or marital duration increases. Women under 20 years of age who had one or more live births constitute 51 percent of the sample. The percentage increases to about 85 percent among women aged 20-24 and to over 92 percent for older age groups. The same trend is observed in marital duration. Figure 5.1 demonstrates the clear trend that as the length of years of exposure to childbirth increases, the shape of the percentage distribution of children ever born becomes wider, the mode tends to occur at higher numbers of children ever born, and the percentage having the modal value tends to decrease in magnitude. For example, the mode CEB for those with less than five years of marriage is zero with a percentage of 39.6; it increases to 3 for those of 5-9 years of marriage with a lower percentage of 31.2, and so on, until the mode for 25 or more is 9, and the corresponding percentage is 14.7.[5]

Table 5.2 presents the mean number of children ever born to all ever-married women, child deaths (CD), proportion child deaths (mean CD/mean CEB), and proportion working women by age at first marriage, current age, and selected attributes: wife's and husband's education, electricity in the home, women's employment, husband's occupation, and the levels of real and personal assets. Age at first marriage shows a clear trend: women who married early predictably tend to have a higher average number of children ever born. Those who first married before the age of 15 had an average of 5.4 live births (5.3 if adjusted by age).[6] This average decreases gradually until it reaches 2.6 for those who first married at the age of 24 or more (2.4 adjusted by age). These overall averages must be considered with caution due to the censoring effect and the variation of possible years of exposure to childbirth.[7] Women who married at an age of less than 15 had approximately 30 or more years of exposure; those who married at ages 25-29 had only about 20 years or so of exposure.

While the value of CEB decreases monotonically from 4.3 to 3.2 by level of wife's education, when adjusted by age there is a slight rise from the illiterate to no certificate education categories (from

Figure 5.1 Children Ever Born by Marriage Duration

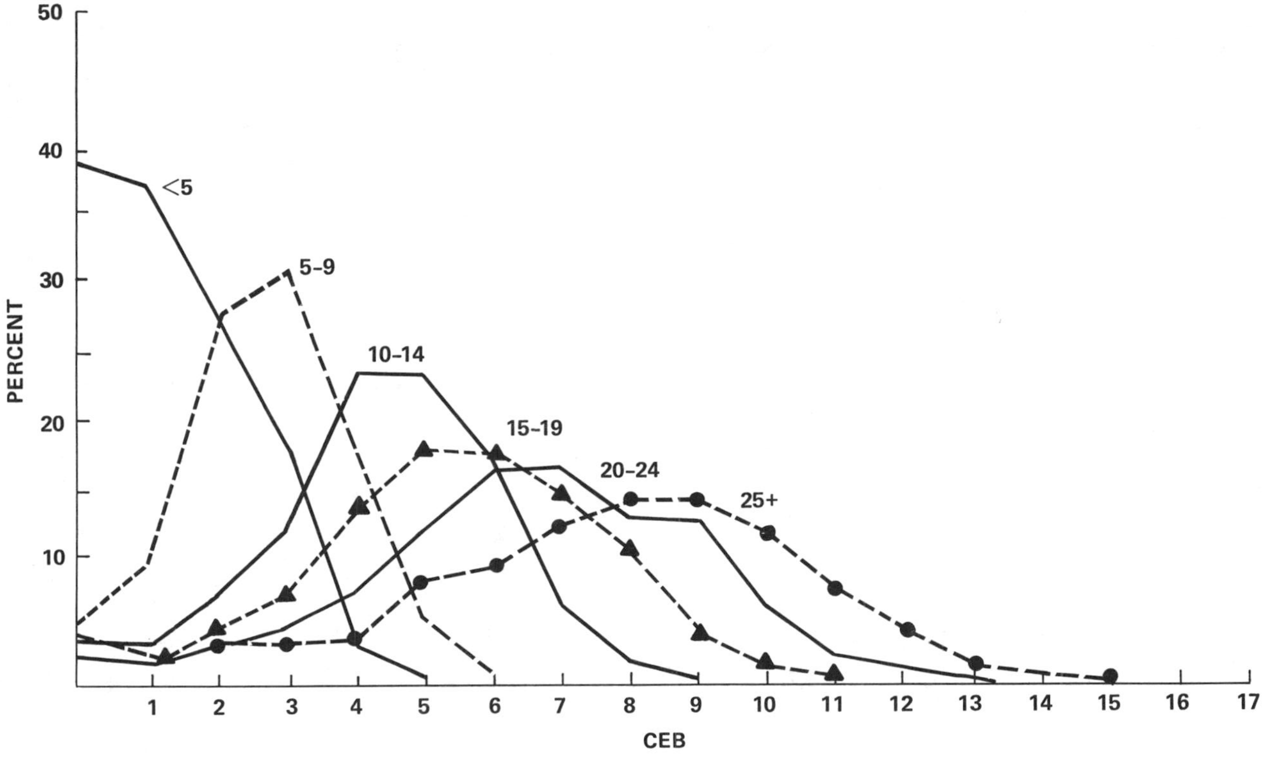

PERCENT
50
40
30
20
10
<5
5–9
10–14
15–19
20–24
25+
1 2 3 4 5 6 7 8 9 10 11 12 13 14 15 16 17
CEB

Table 5.2 Mean CEB, CD, Death Ratio, and Proportion Working Women by Selected Attributes

Characteristics	CEB		CD (Mean CD / Mean CEB)		% Working Women		N
	Unadj.	Adj.[a]	Unadj.	Adj.[a]	Unadj.	Adj.[a]	
Current Age							
15-	.68	-	.07 (.10)	-	12.38	-	337
20-	1.95	-	.35 (.18)	-	17.73	-	739
25-	3.40	-	.71 (.21)	-	18.69	-	782
30-	4.94	-	1.07 (.22)	-	19.74	-	607
35-	6.02	-	1.44 (.24)	-	16.49	-	552
40-	6.65	-	1.77 (.27)	-	16.13	-	435
45-49	7.47	-	2.27 (.30)	-	16.84	-	374
Age at 1st Marriage							
<15	5.35	5.26	1.34 (.25)	1.31	13.67	13.55	785
15-17	4.39	4.64	1.06 (.24)	1.13	18.50	18.71	1641
18-19	3.67	3.91	.81 (.22)	.88	17.14	16.88	672
20-21	3.91	3.83	.91 (.23)	.89	18.07	18.07	415
22-23	2.92	3.02	.70 (.24)	.74	16.90	18.65	142
24+	2.64	2.42	.54 (.21)	.49	21.21	21.83	165
Wife's Education							
Illiterate	4.34	4.24	1.05 (.24)	1.02	17.61	17.66	2930
No Certificate	4.21	4.48	.98 (.23)	1.04	14.75	14.77	739
Primary Cert.+	3.17	3.95	.59 (.19)	.77	24.68	28.74	154
Husband's Education							
Illiterate	4.45	4.39	1.11 (.25)	1.04	18.85	18.91	2386
No Certificate	4.25	4.50	.96 (.23)	1.03	15.67	15.71	889
Primary Cert.	4.00	4.28	.90 (.23)	.99	11.30	10.37	230
Prep. Cert. +	3.13	4.10	.54 (.17)	.78	14.52	14.36	311
Wife's Employment							
Not Working	4.27	4.27	1.02 (.24)	1.02	-	-	3160
Working	4.29	4.24	1.01 (.24)	1.00	-	-	664
Husband's Occupation							
Agriculture	4.33	4.25	1.05 (.24)	1.03	20.21	20.37	2236
Nonagriculture	4.19	4.30	.98 (.23)	1.01	13.18	13.22	1593
Electricity							
No	4.13	4.00	1.03 (.25)	1.02	19.41	19.44	2174
Yes	4.44	4.47	1.00 (.23)	1.01	14.61	14.53	1649

Table 5.2 (continued)

Characteristics	CEB Unadj.	CEB Adj.[a]	CD (Mean CD / Mean CEB) Unadj.	CD Adj.[a]	% Working Women Unadj.	% Working Women Adj.[a]	N
Real Assets							
0	3.95	3.99	.85 (.22)	.81	12.43	12.39	885
1	4.37	4.34	1.11 (.25)	1.10	18.24	18.17	1674
2	4.38	4.38	1.04 (.24)	1.04	20.35	20.45	1076
3+	4.22	4.44	.87 (.21)	.87	15.26	15.33	190
Personal Assets							
0	4.18	4.12	1.03 (.25)	1.01	19.17	19.22	1502
1	4.31	4.34	1.03 (.24)	1.03	17.02	17.01	1586
2	4.43	4.62	1.05 (.24)	1.09	14.48	14.38	449
3+	4.20	4.19	.91 (.22)	.91	14.04	13.85	285
Total							
Mean	4.27	-	1.02 (.24)	-	17.34	-	-
Number	-	-	-	-	-	-	3826

[a]Adjusted by age.

4.2 to 4.5), and the subsequent decline is much more dramatic (from 4.5 to 4.0). This nonlinear relationship is a puzzle that requires careful scrutiny. It may be based on data deficiencies; that is, as noted above, there may be a bias in the recall of deaths. However, as shown later in chapter 9, section 9.3, the increase in CEB from illiterate to no certificate education categories is observed at all age groups, not only for older women, which casts doubt on this speculation of memory lapse. Alternatively, the explanation of the nonlinear relationship should be qualified by the fact that age at marriage is itself increased by greater education, and the role of education may therefore be much more complex than that represented in table 5.2. Indeed, there are other interactions with education which, when adequately taken into account, may result in a different relationship with CEB than the one shown in table 5.2. These possibilities are considered in chapters 6 and 9.

Women living in houses with electricity had a higher mean CEB of 4.4 compared to 4.1 for women in houses with no electricity. Electricity may be interpreted as a proxy for higher income and wealth. Real assets also appear to be positively related to mean CEB. A gradual increase is observed from a mean CEB of 4.0 (adjusted for age) for women who own no real assets to a mean of 4.4 for women who own three items or more. As noted in chapter 3, children may be like many other items a household enjoys such that more will be demanded at higher income levels. Possible exceptions lie in the cases where the added income is due to higher wages of the wife, or where families elect to substitute child "quality" for child "quantity" at higher levels of prosperity. As an additional explanation of the positive electricity-CEB correlation, one might speculate that those households with electricity are able to supply more children, since they are households with higher incomes and can provide superior health and nutritional standards. And as an additional explanation of the real asset-CEB correlation, one might speculate that children are complements to production in households with extensive real assets (i.e., they are especially helpful on relatively well-equipped and prosperous farms), and thus the rate of return on children as productive agents increases with real-asset wealth.

Table 5.2 shows a curvilinear relationship between personal assets owned and mean CEB. Mean CEB is lower for those who own no personal assets (4.1) and for those who own at least three items (4.2) than for women who live in households with one (4.3) or two (4.6) items of personal assets. It thus seems that personal assets may exert a positive effect on CEB up to a certain level, and then the impact turns negative. On the other hand, these variations of CEB by personal asset level are small, and may be statistically insignificant, a hypothesis tested in chapter 6.

Whether the pairwise correlations observed in table 5.2 hold up to more detailed multivariate analysis must await the examination of chapter 6. These relationships do, however, suggest interesting working hypotheses that merit further inquiry.

5.2 CHILD DEATHS

The same set of variables--wife's current age, age at first marriage, wife's education, husband's education, electricity, women's employment, husband's occupation, real assets, and personal assets--are next examined in relation to child deaths. The proportion of children dead among all ever born, i.e., mean

CD/mean CEB, called the death (mortality) ratio, will also be examined along with mean CD. Since mean CD is strongly related to CEB and CD increases with age and marriage duration, it is misleading to make comparisons between subgroups without controlling for one or more of these variables. Our various comparisons control for age. More detailed control is provided in the multiple regression analysis in chapter 6.[8]

On average, of 4.3 live births, 3.3 are still living. As expected, the mean number of deceased children increases with age and parity. Women in the age group 20-24 lost 0.4 out of 2.0 live births; women 45 or more lost 2.3 of their live births. In general, the data reveal a very high mortality level. The survival rate, on the average, is 76 percent: one of every four children dies before the mother reaches the age of 50.

On the average, women who marry earlier lose more of their children. Table 5.2 shows that a woman who first married at an age below 15 loses an average of 1.3 children. This mean CD declines significantly with increasing age at marriage to reach 0.5 child for women who first married at the age of 24 or more. However, because CEB follows the same pattern, the death ratio represents a more reliable measure of differences in mortality among age-at-marriage subgroups. Table 5.2 shows that the proportion who died is slightly higher for the lowest age at marriage group compared to the highest age at marriage (25 percent compared to 21 percent), with fluctuating proportions in between.[9] This result is consistent with the hypothesis that early age at marriage is associated with higher child mortality, a result that is supported by the regression analysis in chapter 6. This conclusion holds generally true with each age group.

Wife's education reveals only a slight impact on both the proportion of children who died and on mean CD for the first two education categories. A decline in the proportion of children who died exists only for those women who hold at least a primary certificate. This same pattern is observed in the case of the husband's education. However, this relationship must be examined in relation to age at marriage, since better educated women tend to marry later and, as a result, the impact of education noted here may in fact be an age-at-first marriage effect.[10] The wife's employment and husband's occupation seem to exert no effect on child deaths.

The presence of electricity appears to exert a slight negative effect on child deaths. The percentage of children who died is 22.5 for women living in houses with electricity, and 24.9 for women in houses without electricity. Real assets owned, another indicator of household wealth, show a curvilinear relationship, where proportions who died are lowest for those who own nothing and those who own three or more items. An explanation of this result may require an inquiry into the type of real assets owned. For example, owning simply a small piece of agricultural land or a few head of cattle does not necessarily make the household better off than if the family were tenants on a large plot of agricultural land. Thus, while real assets, other things equal, raise the productivity of children (an interpretation provided above with respect to CEB), they may be a less than perfect index of household income. At any rate, child deaths for households with 0 and 3+ real assets is about the same, and the rise in the death rate in the intermediate asset-ownership levels is slight. For all practical purposes, we would conclude that real assets and child deaths are largely uncorrelated.

Personal assets in relation to the proportion of children who died show a slight negative impact, and only those households owning three or more personal assets begin to reveal a significant decline. As previously mentioned, this effect may follow if personal assets are accepted as a proxy for income and wealth.

We may conclude that these preliminary results reveal that deaths are relatively insensitive to several socioeconomic factors. For the most part, mortality is very high in rural Egypt, and within the fairly narrow ranges of the education and wealth variables considered in our analysis it is not likely that deaths will change dramatically during the slow evolution of socioeconomic development and modernization. Of course, in this chapter we have considered only the relationships between mortality and various *household* attributes. If *community-level* wealth is altered--health, and sanitation facilities--the mortality rate may well decline at a significantly greater pace.

5.3 FEMALE WORKFORCE PARTICIPATION

As noted in chapter 4, women in the upper class are generally confined to the house, while women in other classes work with men and remain unpaid family workers. Women who work outside the home as paid labor are still viewed negatively in rural Egyptian society. The analysis in this section deals with workforce participation differentials of all ever-married women. This overview is mainly provided to shed some light on the female workforce participation variable which is highlighted in many studies of fertility. However, a detailed study that would require an examination of many other aspects of women's work--such as employment status, occupation, timing, and duration--is beyond the scope of the present inquiry.

The survey questionnaire denotes "working women" as those performing activities other than "traditional housework," either inside or outside the home and even for a short period of time. The question on workforce status was designed to include as workforce those cottage industry activities done inside the home, and eliminate those housework activities done outside the home, such as food preparation in the fields and clothes washing in the canals. This definition of working women leaves much to be desired, especially in its treatment of the contributions of farm labor.

Table 5.2 presents the proportion of women currently working by selected background characteristics. Women work in smaller proportions in the younger and older age groups. The highest proportion is found among women in the 25-34 age group. Women who first married very early in life (less than 15) have the lowest proportion of labor market participation. The highest is found among women who married at age 24 or later (21.2 percent). This result may be because later marriage is associated with higher education, and women with a primary or higher certificate are more likely to participate in the labor market. (Adjusted by age, the percentage is 28.7 among women with at least a primary certificate, as compared to 17.7 and 14.8 for illiterate women and women with no certificate, respectively.)

Wives of illiterate husbands have the highest percentage of work (about 19 percent), while the lowest proportion is found among wives of husbands in the high-middle educational category. An explanation of the figures must await a detailed examination of wife's type of work. However, it might be speculated that if husband's education is positively related to income, then husbands in the lowest educational category must rely more on the income of their wives.

A similar income interpretation may be used to explain the higher proportion of women working among those living in homes with electricity (19.4 percent) versus those without (14.5 percent). Personal assets also to some extent reflect income levels and reveal a similar pattern. These various proportions do not change notably, however, and as a result little weight should be placed on these speculations at this stage of the analysis.

Wives of husbands working in agricultural occupations participate more in the workforce (20.4 percent) than wives of husbands in nonagricultural occupations (13.2 percent). This may indicate that wives work with their husbands on the farm, although the data are deficient for sorting out the length or form of work involved.

It is interesting to note that women's workforce participation increases, especially for women under the age of 35, with the number of real assets owned. As speculated above, this measure may be faulty as an index of income, yet it may reflect the productivity of workers on the farm--in this case, women as well as children. This complementarity of real assets to child and female labor, if true, may have important implications in assessing the impact of various development strategies on family size.

6. FURTHER DIMENSIONS OF EGYPTIAN FERTILITY AND MORTALITY

6.1 CONCLUSIONS AND POLICY SPECULATIONS

Children are highly valued in rural Egyptian society, due in part to the economic benefits they provide to their parents. Increases in the levels of wealth and income associated with socioeconomic development may well result in an increase in completed family size in the short to intermediate run. This is true whether the wealth is in the form of physical capital (land, implements, personal assets) or in the form of human capital (health and education).

The statistical analysis reveals that providing increased levels of education to women is unlikely to exert a direct, deterring impact on births in the near future. This may be due to the fact that employment opportunities for relatively educated women are limited in rural Egypt. In other words, the market value of a woman's education at the lower end of the education spectrum is virtually nil. Thus, if lowering population growth is an objective of public policy, government programs to increase female education might be coupled with employment programs that place a premium on that education.

These conclusions regarding the impact of education on children ever born (CEB) must be qualified to account for (1) the effect of education on the age at first marriage, and (2) the effect of education on the desired number of children.

Marriage is delayed for women who possess at least a primary education certificate, which in turn reduces CEB. However, only a small minority of rural Egyptian women receive a primary education certificate. Moreover, the impact of delayed marriage is not quantitatively large, and even after controlling for the age-at-first-marriage effect, there does not appear to be a discernible independent impact of education on children ever born.

Desired number of children is both strongly and negatively related to all levels of female and male education, as was reported in chapter 5. It is, therefore, necessary to reconcile these findings with the negligible impact of education on CEB. One possible explanation may be that some Egyptian women may desire more surviving children than they are able to obtain (or which they predict they can obtain). Thus, even though child mortality is very high in rural Egypt, statistical tests show that the "replacement effect" of child deaths on CEB is low for substantial numbers of Egyptians, particularly those in Upper Egypt. That is, the family size desired by women may be sufficiently large that the occurrence of a child death does not markedly change behavior. These findings suggest that, for some groups of Egyptian women, family size may be "supply constrained." Such families may desire more children than they can obtain. Even if family size desires were reduced by higher levels of education, the impact may not be sufficient to bring down actual family size. Note that while this interpretation reconciles the results of chapters 5 and 6, it does not diminish the potential role of education on children ever born. Rather, it suggests that the impact of education on desired family size may have to be large, and/or the child mortality impact on children ever born may have to be altered, before education reduces CEB with significant force. Moreover, it suggests that an education policy that is simultaneously designed to reduce CEB should focus on the subset of the Egyptian population where the antinatal impacts are greatest. Different policies (e.g., maternal and health care programs) may be more appropriate--at least initially--to that subset that is supply constrained. However, in the short run such a policy may, by reducing mortality, increase growth rates. A policy strategy that targets particular social services to subsets of the population is *not* one that discriminates in favor of one group versus another. Indeed, the investment in social services may well be the same among the various groups, but the *phasing* of the social welfare programs may be quite different.

Wealth effects exert a net positive impact on family size. Thus, policies that increase family economic status may, for a period of time, increase births. On the other hand, there may be some wealth-raising policies which work in the opposite direction. Policies that increase wealth but simultaneously reduce the value (or raise the costs) of children would have this effect. For example, the development of employment programs that place a premium on female labor outside the household would raise the costs of childrearing. Government promotion of farm practices that lower the premium on child labor but simultaneously increase output would also jointly accommodate population and economic goals. Labor-saving farm mechanization represents one such policy. In chapter 10 results will be presented to confirm the potential population impacts of this strategy.[1] It will be shown that agricultural mechanization reduces CEB. These findings are consistent with the above results, since the real assets measured in the RFS are not typically in the form of labor-saving equipment.

Age at first marriage has a potent effect on completed family size. Many Egyptian women in rural areas marry before the legal age of sixteen. Policies that raise the age of marriage will directly reduce births.

Mortality of offspring is high in rural Egypt. The statistical findings point to two factors that will significantly deter child deaths: an increase in the age at first marriage, and rural electrification programs. It should be noted that policies which directly reduce mortality may result in increased surviving children since (1) the replacement effect is fairly low for some groups of families, and (2) there is evidence that some families are supply-constrained in obtaining desired family size.

6.2 THE STATISTICAL MODELS

Modern theories of household behavior stress the interactions between the family's decisions relating to (1) children ever born, (2) the age at first marriage, (3) the wife's participation in formal workforce activities, and (4) child deaths. It thus seems appropriate to consider these four variables simultaneously and in a format that serves to draw out the interrelationships among them.[2]

6.2.1 Children Ever Born

Children ever born (CEB) is assumed to depend upon (1) the mother's current age, (2) the age at first marriage, (3) the number of child deaths, (4) the level of education of the mother and the father, and (5) the household's wealth. These variables have become standard in the literature on economic demography. Consequently, detailed comments justifying their selection and interpretation can be postponed until an examination of the specific empirical results is made.[4]

Equation 6.1 presents the main statistical model. (All of the variables are defined in appendix table A.1.)

$$[6.1] \quad CEB = \underset{(-12.45)}{-4.36^*} + \underset{(24.73)}{.55^*AGEW} - \underset{(-16.74)}{.0058^*AGEW2} - \underset{(-26.33)}{.21^*AFM}$$

$$+ \underset{(.71)}{.052WE2} + \underset{(.15)}{.02WE3} + \underset{(2.48)}{.16^*HE2} + \underset{(1.35)}{.15HE3} + \underset{(1.52)}{.17HE4}$$

$$- \underset{(-.06)}{.01ASSETP} + \underset{(3.31)}{.08^*ASSETR} + \underset{(4.80)}{.27^*ELEC} + \underset{(44.02)}{.89^*CD}$$

$r^2 = .73$
t values in parentheses
* significant at 90%

The age variables (AGEW, AGEW2) enter as expected and are very significant.[5] CEB increases with age, but the rate of childbearing diminishes at older ages. The functional form in age is plausible, with peak mean number of children ever born occurring at 47.5 years.[6] The turndown in the quadratic is for only 2.5 years, and a peak CEB in the late forties is acceptable.

Age at first marriage (AFM) has a large impact on CEB, a finding that is consistent with much of the demographic literature,[7] especially where a natural fertility regime is important and little birth control is practiced. For each year of marriage delayed, CEB decreases by .21 children. This is an average figure and holds only within the bounds of the age at first marriage variable, approximately from ages twelve through twenty-five.[8] A more detailed analysis of the impact of AFM on CEB (see appendix equations A.1 - A.3) permits an assessment of various government policies: the impact of enforcing the existing legal age of sixteen, and the impact of enforcing an alternative law that would set age at first marriage at eighteen. The estimates reveal that the first policy would reduce CEB by .95 and the second policy would reduce CEB by 1.16. While the second policy appears to have a smaller incremental impact *per family* (1.16 - .95 = .21), the *total* impact on population growth would be slightly larger than the first policy since many more women are involved. At any rate, enforcing the legal age at marriage would reduce CEB dramatically.

Some have argued that AFM does not represent a strong independent influence on CEB but primarily determines the *timing* of births and not completed family size. In an attempt to assess this hypothesis, the basic CEB equation was re-estimated for women whose ages exceeded forty. The regression coefficient on AFM in the basic CEB equation changed from -.21 in the full sample to -.14 in the sample of women with completed childbearing.[9] Thus, there is indeed some "catch-up" represented in this variable, although most (66 percent) of the impact of the variable constitutes a separate AFM effect. All of the main conclusions in the analysis with respect to education and assets are invariant to consideration of completed or age-specific fertility.

The education of the wife, when taken alone as an independent variable, does not exert a statistically significant impact on CEB.[10] Several factors may account for this. First, there may not be enough variation in the sample to reveal the underlying effects of education.[11] Moreover, the 740 women who are recorded as having attended some school, but not obtaining a primary certificate, may well overstate the amount of education received. The dropout rate is significantly higher for women than for men.[12] Within this broad education category (WE2), it is possible that the average level of education may be low, and also somewhat lower for women than for men. Second, the negative impact of education on CEB (women with higher levels of education may receive higher wages in market employment, thus raising the opportunity cost of childrearing) may not be large in rural Egypt since market job opportunities for educated women are scarce and/or low paying.[13] The positive income effect due to education may therefore offset the negative substitution (wage-price) effect. These results are plausible since studies showing a strong negative effect of education on CEB are generally based on urban samples where female opportunities in market jobs are relatively high.[14] Third, and perhaps most important, there may be an education/age-at-first-marriage interaction which is not controlled for in the above regression. That is, AFM may be delayed by women who take advantage of higher levels of schooling.[15] To test this hypothesis and to better untangle the AFM-WE-CEB relationships, two additional equations have been estimated. The first, presented in appendix equation A.5, estimates AFM as a function of WE. The second, presented as equation A.6, estimates the basic CEB model without AFM. In this model the WE parameter captures the impact on CEB of a delay in AFM due to higher levels of WE.

The findings are interesting. Women who participate in postprimary education delay their marriages by an average of 1.96 years. Thus, WE3 *does* exert a negative impact on CEB *when* the education variable incorporates the AFM effect.[16] (We interpret the equations as being recursive, especially since the age at first marriage is greater than age at completion of education for most rural Egyptian women. That is, AFM is a function of predetermined variables such as WE. AFM, in turn, influences the level of CEB.) An examination of the parameter estimates is also illuminating. Almost all of the education effect revealed in equation A.6 appears to be due to the impact of education on delaying marriage, and may not be the result of other pure education impacts (e.g., taste effects, changes in the opportunity costs of the woman's time, etc.).[17] In short, our original result showing education to have a negligible impact on CEB appears to hold. It *is* possible to reduce CEB by dramatically increasing WE, but this may occur primarily through lowering AFM--an effect that might take place directly.[18]

The education of the husband provides a positive impact on CEB.[19] In theory one would expect the income effect to dominate the substitution effect for the education of the husband. This is because husbands assume a small role (and thus bear small costs) in childrearing, and more children are presumably desired at higher income levels, *ceteris paribus.* It is a little surprising that higher education levels show no differential impact, although this may be a result of the fact that eduction levels within the ranges considered here have relatively minor impacts on income and wages in rural Egypt.[20] In contrast to women, there is more variation of education levels in the male sample: (1) illiterate, 2,387; (2) school, no certificate, 887; (3) primary school graduation, 230; and (4) preparatory school graduation, or above, 312.

The impact of family wealth on CEB can be distinguished separately for three types of assets: personal (mainly consumer durables), real (mainly house and land), and electricity. The latter may be interpreted as a measure of the quality of housing and other assets. On average, one would expect assets to exert a positive impact on CEB--a wealth-income effect.[21] This is confirmed by the results.[22] Assets are jointly significant; only personal assets are not individually significant.[23]

One would expect real assets to exert a stronger positive impact on CEB than personal assets since the value of children increases with their productive use in the household. An exception to this might occur if the assets were of a labor-saving type. Table 6.1 reveals that agricultural machinery constitutes a relatively small portion of the total asset stock, and thus the positive association noted above appears to be justified.

A digression on the interpretation of the electricity variable is appropriate at this point. Electricity may well represent a proxy for permanent income. For households that have electricity, hook-up charges may be significant. Only higher-income households can afford this expenditure and are likely to possess more expensive durables (refrigerators, televisions, etc.). Moreover, electricity represents a continuing expenditure and, thus, requires a fairly stable level of income.

Insight into the interpretation of the electricity variable can be obtained by examining its relation to the level and distribution of personal and real assets. This is shown in table 6.1, which illustrates that

1. the level of personal assets is higher for households with electricity than for those without (1.44 assets per household with electricity versus .55 assets per household without electricity);
2. stoves, refrigerators, and television sets are relatively more prevalent in households with electricity;
3. the level of real asset ownership is somewhat higher in households with electricity (1.71 assets per household with electricity versus 1.55 assets per household without electricity);
4. farmland, construction land and agricultural machinery are relatively more prevalent in households with electricity.

Child deaths (CD) is a highly significant determinant of CEB in equation 6.1. However, there is a spurious correlation in this

Table 6.1 Level and Composition of Household Assets

Asset Type	Percentage of Households with Each Asset		
	With Electricity	Without Electricity	Total
	Personal Assets		
No Assets	22.3	52.0	39.1
Refrigerator	3.4	.1	1.5
Stove	11.0	.8	5.2
Radio	70.9	46.3	56.9
Television	26.3	1.1	12.0
Sewing Machine	8.6	2.6	5.1
Clock	8.4	1.8	4.9
Tape Recorder	15.0	2.5	7.9
	Real Assets		
No Assets	16.8	19.4	18.2
Farmland	43.4	36.6	39.4
Construction Land	5.6	2.4	3.8
Agricultural Machinery	6.8	5.0	5.8
Buildings	68.7	65.0	66.4
Animals	46.1	46.3	46.1
Number of Households	1652	2160	3812

relationship. In particular, CD is part of CEB; having knowledge of CEB provides considerable information about CD. For example, if CEB were zero, CD would be zero as well. This spurious correlation will overstate the coefficient on CD. This is a particularly important parameter to estimate accurately since government policy may influence the level of child deaths. The magnitude of the "replacement effect" is, therefore, critical to determining the impact of government policy on total population growth. Moreover, some of the factors determining child deaths (e.g., education) enter the model with a sign opposite to their influence on CEB. Thus, the influence of these factors will be determined in part by the size of the CD parameter in the CEB equation.

While there have been several attempts in the literature to attenuate the spurious correlation problem, it is only recently that estimation models have been constructed which appear to be helpful in sorting out the replacement effect from the spurious correlation effect.[24] One procedure, proposed by B. Boulier, involves a simple adjustment of the CD variable which builds on the underlying assumption that households estimate an expected mortality equal to that of the average experience of the community, and that households then hoard children in expectation of child deaths (i.e., they replace expected, not actual deaths) on a one-for-one basis.[25] Another technique, developed and evaluated by J. A. Mauskopf, is based on a formulation of the decision-making process whereby households' replacement of children is based primarily on actual mortality experience.[26]

Mortality is high in rural Egypt. Table 6.2 presents the marginal distributions of child deaths for those women who have had at least one child and whose ages are greater than 35 and 40 years, respectively. For these two groups of women, the average number of deaths per family (and corresponding mortality ratio = (CD/CEB)) is 1.8 (.24) and 2.1 (.27), respectively.[27]

Appendix equations A.7 and A.8 present the basic CEB results for these two groups of women where the models are not corrected for spurious correlation. The parameters on the CD variable for the 35+ and 40+ samples are .86 and .83, respectively. When the Mauskopf framework is used these parameters drop to .41 (.07) and .36 (.01), respectively. (Standard errors are in parentheses.)[28] It is interesting to note that these all-Egypt results derive from quite different findings by region. In particular, for the 40+ sample the replacement parameters using the Mauskopf procedure for Upper and Lower Egypt are .21 (.19) and .47 (.19), respectively. Thus, for Egypt as a whole and for the individual regions, the replacement effect notably declines when account is taken of spurious correlation. Moreover, replacement is not significantly different from zero in Upper Egypt. The estimated parameter may approximate the biological replacement associated with the impact of breastfeeding. That is, in situations where mothers breastfeed, the occurrence of infant deaths reduces the interval of infertility, and as a result, some biological replacement occurs in the absence of any conscious attempt to replace lost children.

The CEB equations have also been estimated using the Boulier procedure, which effectively assumes that there is complete replacement of expected child deaths.[29] The resulting estimate thus represents primarily the replacement of unexpected deaths.[30] For the 35+ and 40+ samples statistically significant replacement

Table 6.2 Child Mortality in Rural Egypt

CD	Women Whose Ages Exceed 35[a]		Women Whose Ages Exceed 40[a]	
	Frequency	Percentage	Frequency	Percentage
0	286	28.9	129	23.6
1	220	21.5	104	19.0
2	186	18.2	97	17.7
3	144	14.1	91	16.6
4	95	9.3	61	11.2
5	39	3.8	29	5.3
6	29	2.8	20	3.7
7	9	.9	7	1.3
8	6	.6	5	.9
9+	8	.8	4	.7

[a] The sample is all women in the indicated age cohorts who have had at least one child.

rates are estimated as .39 and .33, respectively. These are less than, but still of approximately the same size, as those provided by Mauskopf's model. It is somewhat disconcerting, however, that similar results are obtained from two models which are based on very different interpretations of the parameters. This leads us to be somewhat cautious in drawing conclusions based on these particular results.

The findings from the Mauskopf and the Boulier frameworks permit us to conclude that the replacement effect is of plausible magnitude, but is on the low side for rural Egypt, and that for parts of this society (e.g., Upper Egypt), replacement may be unimportant as a motivating behavior. This latter finding is particularly noteworthy and raises two possible, related interpretations. First, some rural Egyptian families may not take replacement into account in planning their completed family size. This would be surprising, given the high prevalence of child mortality in Egypt and the importance and high value of children. On the other hand, because of the high mortality experience, one might argue that completed family size may be "supply constrained" by biological factors for some Egyptians, and as a result, those factors which influence the demand for, cost of, and (behavioral) supply of children are largely irrelevant in these cases. Second, if a substantial portion of the

Egyptian population were largely noncontracepting, then only biological replacement would be important, and the observed impact of CD on CEB could be expected to be small. On a constructed data set Mauskopf has shown this to be the case using simulation techniques, and her results are reinforced by the work and analysis of S. Preston.[31]

Additional insight into these results can be obtained by further statistical analysis. First, we have estimated our basic CEB equation without the CD term (appendix equation A.9) and have compared these results with the model that incorporates CD equation 6.1. The value of r^2 increased from .59 to .73. In largely noncontracepting populations, the sizes and significance of the other parameters should not be influenced by the inclusion or exclusion of the CD term. This was found to be the case. Second, we have estimated the CEB and CD equations simultaneously, hypothesizing that households explicitly take CD into account when they plan their desired family size. The results are found in appendix equations A.10 and A.11. Interestingly, in this model where there is *no* adjustment for spurious correlation in the CEB equation, the parameter on CD drops to insignificance. In this interactive model, the replacement effect is nil.

The finding that replacement effects are low or insignificant for portions of the rural Egyptian population has been obtained by three statistical procedures and three alternative behavioral models. Therefore, the result appears to be quite robust and has important implications for interpreting the results. First, as noted above, it elevates in importance the possible role of supply-oriented models for explaining Egyptian demographic behavior.[32] The Easterlin synthesis, which attempts to account for the switching point between biological supply constraints and models of micro-demographic behavior, becomes increasingly applicable. Second, it qualifies the impact of a government policy, which may be aimed at reducing child mortality. For example, if a substantial number of households were in fact attempting to have larger completed family sizes and if this desire were supply constrained (by mortality and/or by fecundity), then policies that reduce mortality would simultaneously increase completed family size (and population growth) with no corresponding reduction in CEB. Moreover, if the specific government policies that reduce mortality simultaneously increase fecundity (e.g., policies that improve the mother's health), then the supply constraint would be further relaxed. Therefore, a critical element in the appraisal of government population policies may depend on the turning point between the relative importance of supply constraints and behaviorally oriented factors in explaining micro-demographic behavior in rural Egypt. That is to say, particular attention must be paid to assessing when and how the "Easterlin turning point" will occur, since evaluation of government population policies may hinge on this judgment. For example, increased attention might be devoted to identifying which specific families are supply constrained. The choice of particular government programs that are designed to reduce population growth could then be varied according to whether the family is or is not supply constrained.

Analysts have surmised that the spurious correlation problem may be alleviated by using the family mortality ratio (CD/CEB) as the independent variable. This is in fact not the case.[33] Furthermore, Mauskopf has shown, using simulation techniques, that use of the mortality ratio biases the parameters of the remaining independent variables in the equation for the specific model of replacement behavior used to create the simulated data sets.[34] However, given the fairly widespread use of the mortality ratio variable in the literature on CEB, it would still be appropriate in concluding our analysis to include some results of the mortality ratio as well.

Two basic CEB models with alternative mortality ratio (CD/CEB) transformations substituted for CD are reported as appendix equations A.12 and A.13. Use of the mortality ratio does not alter our conclusions with respect to the remaining independent variables in the model, although in the CD model the education of the husband does appear to have a slightly larger and more significant impact. The comparisons between equation 6.1 and equations A.12 and A.13 are not ideal, however, since some 413 families with zero values for CEB are excluded from the latter equations. When the model in equation 6.1 is re-estimated on data excluding the 413 families (see equation A.14), the conclusions are the same as those derived from the model with all observations and the models with the two alternative death ratio transformations.[35]

While the analysis above has focused on rural Egypt as a whole, it is instructive to compare these aggregate results with those for Upper and Lower Egypt. Relevant regressions are presented as appendix equations A.30 - A.32. The results are basically the same for the two regions considered separately, and thus the all rural Egypt findings appear to be fairly representative.[36]

A final matter relating to the empirical specification concerns an issue raised by B. Boulier and M. Rosenzweig, who argue that the variables age, and age at first marriage, do not adequately capture the effects of marriage duration on CEB.[37] They use instead as the dependent variable a measure denoted as DRAT (duration ratio), represented as CEB divided by an estimate of natural fertility which takes into account both age and marriage duration. We have re-estimated our key regressions using DRAT and can report that the findings are generally invariant to the use of this revised specification.[38]

6.2.2 Female Workforce Participation

Most women have never participated in market workforce activity (2,996); a total of 800 have (21 percent).[39] To identify the determinants of workforce participation, equation 6.2 has been estimated for a dependent variable defined as whether or not (0,1) the wife has ever participated in market workforce activity.[40]

$$[6.2]\ WEW = \underset{(1.16)}{.10} + \underset{(1.56)}{.0088AGEW} - \underset{(-1.57)}{.0001AGEW2} - \underset{(-.86)}{.015WE2} + \underset{(2.97)}{.107^{*}WE3}$$

$$\underset{(-1.53)}{-.027HE2} - \underset{(-3.18)}{.091^{*}HE3} - \underset{(-3.34)}{.089^{*}HE4}$$

$r^2 = .0075$
t values in parentheses
* significant at 90% level

As found in chapter 5, younger and older women tend to participate less in the labor force than women in their middle ages. School attendance only for a short period of time (less than primary certificate) has no significant impact on female workforce participation, but school attendance for a somewhat longer period of time (primary certificate or above) exerts a positive impact. (156 women fall into this category.)

The education of the husband exerts a negative impact on the workforce participation rate of the wife. Two factors may explain this result. First, to the extent that the husband's education is positively associated with income, the marginal utility of income due to the wife's employment declines with increases in the husband's education. Second, average family size may increase with the husband's income; the value of the wife's time within the household may therefore be positively related to the husband's education level.

The results are somewhat different for Upper and Lower Egypt. (See appendix equations A.36 - A.38.)[41] The negative impact of husband's education on wife's workforce participation occurs in Lower Egypt only. In Upper Egypt, which is less prosperous, neither the education of the wife nor that of the husband has any effect on workforce participation.

6.2.3 Child Deaths

The number of child deaths[42] is assumed to depend upon (1) age of the mother, (2) the education of the mother, (3) the education of the father, (4) children ever born, (5) household wealth, and (6) age at first marriage.[43] Equation 6.3 presents the key results.[44]

$$[6.3] \quad CD = \underset{(7.12)}{1.20^*} - \underset{(-9.55)}{.081^*AGEW} + \underset{(8.72)}{.000021^*AGEW3} + \underset{(.09)}{.0040WE2}$$

$$+ \underset{(.20)}{.02WE3} - \underset{(-2.00)}{.09^*HE2} - \underset{(-.78)}{.06HE3} - \underset{(-1.54)}{.11HE4} + \underset{(45.32)}{.37^*CEB}$$

$$- \underset{(-.01)}{.0002ASSETP} - \underset{(-.16)}{.0025ASSETR} - \underset{(-3.39)}{.13^*ELEC}$$

$$+ \underset{(2.25)^*}{.08^*AFM{<}16}$$

$r^2 = .49$
t values in parentheses
* significant at 90% level

The age and age-cubed variables (AGEW, AGEW3) are each statistically significant. The child mortality rate is highest in infancy and is likely to be high for young mothers. This is not only because of biological factors, but also because young mothers are less able and/or less experienced in child care. Thus, for a *given* family size (recall the regression controls for CEB), the average number of child deaths declines with age since older mothers are more likely to have had their children at somewhat older ages, and to have spaced them more widely, than younger mothers. (Spacing is yet another possible determinant of child mortality rates.) At older ages, on the other hand, a countervailing influence emerges, which increases the child mortality rate; namely, after a certain point, the death rate rises with age, and, together with the accumulated exposure of children to the risk of death, there is a resulting increase in the average number of child deaths per woman. Our estimates reveal that for rural Egypt this aging impact dominates the infant mortality impact at around age thirty-six for the mother. The aging impact is considerably less powerful than the infant mortality impact; and hence, the resulting curve of deaths per woman as related to age is a "hook" with a decline over most of the ages and a mild upturn only at the older ages of the mother.

A detailed examination of the underlying data, for which plots have been made between average deaths per woman and age, and between average deaths per woman and alternative family sizes, reveals that the relationship summarized in equation 6.3 does not hold precisely for all family sizes. Indeed, it is explained in part as the composite of differing patterns by CEB. As can be seen in table 6.3 for women with one or two live births, the death rate fluctuates around .2, for 3-4 live births, it declines and then rises (as shown in equation 6.3); and for 5 or more live births, the rate increases over all ages. Similar results are obtained for the death ratio. Thus, an interaction term between age and CEB may be appropriate to capture the underlying relationships. At this stage the simpler model shown in equation 6.3 will be maintained. It is doubtful that the other variables in this model are sensitive to a fine tuning of the age-CEB relationship.

Age at first marriage (AFM<16), measured as those women who married before the age of sixteen (the sample includes 1,346 such women), has a positive impact on child deaths. Alternative binary specifications were tried, but the one selected here appears to best capture the effect of early marriage.

As a separate inquiry, we have examined the impact on child

Table 6.3 Means and Ratios of Child Deaths by CEB

	Mean CD Per Woman[a]			CD/CEB Ratio[a]		
Current Age	1-2	3-4	5+	1-2	3-4	5+
< 16	.167	-	-	.083	-	-
16-17	.138	-	-	.097	-	-
18-19	.092	-	-	.063	-	-
20-24	.160	.777	1.435	.099	.230	.271
25-29	.243	.559	1.528	.138	.158	.254
30-34	.196	.510	1.522	.108	.144	.223
35-39	.263	.425	1.838	.184	.122	.239
40-44	.333	.708	2.154	.227	.189	.261
45-49	.167	.718	2.608	.083	.185	.300

[a] For women with at least one CEB.

deaths of age at first marriage, controlling both for age and number of live births. The issue here is whether additional child deaths per woman are the result of early age at first marriage or whether they result from the fact that women who marry young have more children. The results, summarized in table 6.4 for the mean number of child deaths per woman and death ratio, confirm the findings in equation 6.3 that there is a fairly pervasive age-at-first marriage effect which is independent of the number of children ever born.

Education of the wife does not exert a statistically significant impact on CD. Apart from the point concerning the relatively low levels of formal education in rural Egypt, one might also speculate that to reduce CD, there must be a fairly sizeable income effect due to education; i.e., there must be a sufficient impact on income to permit the purchase of better and more food, refrigeration, stoves, health services, and the like. Given the findings on the impact of education on female workforce participation, the impact of women's education on income is likely to be slight. On the other hand, even without an income effect, more educated women should be able to allocate existing resources better and to identify illnesses and take appropriate action. The negligible impact of education on child deaths is somewhat surprising, possibly deriving in part from data deficiencies (e.g., deaths may be recalled less reliably by less-

Table 6.4 Means and Ratios of Child Deaths by Age, AFM, and CEB

Current Age	CEB	Age at First Marriage[a]					
		Less Than 16			16 Years and More		
		Mean	Ratio	N	Mean	Ratio	N
16-17	1-2	.161	.113	31	-	-	-
18-19	1-2	.085	.051	59	.098	.074	61
	3-4	.500	.167	6	-	-	-
20-24	1-2	.183	.092	71	.155	.101	317
	3-4	.685	.196	124	.901	.276	91
	5+	1.563	.296	16	1.143	.214	7
25-29	1-2	.320	.180	25	.231	.131	164
	3-4	.543	.145	81	.565	.162	239
	5+	1.574	.248	122	1.467	.262	92
30-34	1-2	.250	.125	16	.175	.100	40
	3-4	.561	.163	41	.491	.138	116
	5+	1.626	.220	155	1.446	.225	213
35-39	1-2	.333	.22	9	.241	.172	29
	3-4	.435	.134	23	.422	.117	64
	5+	2.087	.262	173	1.655	.222	235
40-44	1-2	.385	.231	13	.300	.225	20
	3-4	.643	.179	14	.735	.194	34
	5+	2.315	.260	130	2.053	.262	207
45-49	1-2	-	-	-	.200	.100	15
	3-4	.500	.132	12	.850	.217	20
	5+	2.860	.305	136	2.417	.296	180

[a] For women with at least one CEB.

educated women). Identification of the determinants of mortality for rural Egypt is certainly an area of demography requiring additional research, and our efforts using the RFS must be considered as but one exploratory foray into this important area of study.

It should be recalled that in identifying the impact of female education on CEB, we learned that most of the effect occurred through the impact of education on delaying marriage. This same finding appears to emerge with respect to the impact of education on CD. The basic CD equation, re-estimated without AFM<16, is presented as appendix equation A.15. The results indicate that the remaining parameter estimates (including those for education) are largely invariant in sign, size, and significance to the AFM<16 variable. Thus, female education, even in this reduced form expression, does not exert a statistically significant impact on child deaths. The husband's education exerts a negative impact on CD, although the effect is weak.[45]

One would expect child deaths to decline with family wealth.[46] This is confirmed in the regression results. The sign on each asset variable is negative, although two of the assets (real and personal) do not possess individually significant effects.[47] Interestingly, the presence of electricity notably deters child deaths. Those households with electricity experience an average of .12 less child deaths than those households without electricity. (For the sample, average deaths per household are 1.02.) Apart from the wealth effect noted above, the presence of electricity corresponds to households where stoves, refrigerators, and television sets are relatively prevalent. The first two assets exert a direct, positive impact on health: they increase the provision of boiled water and cooked food, as well as the safer storage of perishables.

Several studies in the literature use the death ratio (CD/CEB) as the dependent variable.[48] Such a model has been estimated for rural Egypt and is provided as appendix equation A.16. With only one exception (the impact of the primary education of the husband), the results for the death ratio are the same as those for the mean child deaths. It should be noted, however, that the samples are not strictly comparable; the death-ratio regression excludes households with zero CEB.

6.3 DISEQUILIBRIUM MODELS OF COMPLETED FAMILY SIZE

Most of the analysis of completed family size in the economics literature has assumed that families are able to obtain their desired number of children. On the one hand, the natural fertility of the family is assumed to be greater than the desired family size, and as a result, natural fertility does not constrain the attainment of family size goals. On the other hand, knowledge and methods of contraception are available and at a cost (broadly viewed) that permits families to limit their number of children to the number desired. Overshooting family size goals is of course possible, but this is a stochastic occurrence as distinct from a regularity due to behavioral and institutional conditions. However, such regularity in overshooting may be due to prohibitively high costs of contraception, or to ineffective use of contraceptive techniques that are available at a feasible cost. While the economist's model easily handles the situation where a high price results in zero consumption of a good or a service (e.g., contraception), empirical models showing the joint determination of contraception use and family size are rare in the economics literature.

In contrast, much of the literature in demography and sociology has focused on intermediate variables, and in particular, the determinants of natural fertility and contraception. The findings of this chapter, and those that follow, suggest that there are substantial numbers of rural Egyptian families that are not able to attain their desired number of children. For some of the families, supply constraints may be binding. As a result, the CEB variable itself cannot and should not be interpreted as a demand or equilibrium relationship, but rather as the net outcome of demand and various constraints on the household in attaining its desired family size. We have, therefore, attempted to be cautious in interpreting the findings relating to CEB.

This also argues for developing theoretical and econometric models that permit the identification of various "disequilibrium" aspects of household behavior. For example, presumably those households that are supply constrained will behave differently from those that are not. The statistical analysis of this situation could be handled by merely separating those households that are supply constrained from the rest, and estimating the behavioral relationships separately for the supply-constrained group, possibly with a modified model. However, the crux of the problem is one of identifying which households are in fact in the various categories: those with an excess demand for children, those with an excess supply of children, and those with an equilibrium number of children.

While the RFS data set provides observable information on children ever born, it does not offer observable data on family size desires. The only information available on "desires" is from statements by respondents on the "desired number of children (DNC)." But there is a wide literature that provides qualifications about, and notably questions the interpretation of, this DNC variable. Thus, the desired number of children variable is--to use the econometric terminology--an "unobservable." Having unobservable variables in econometric models does not pose an insurmountable barrier to the analysis, but it does require a model that uses additional information and/or assumptions so that the unobservable variable can be identified through a richer econometric structure. While such models are beginning to emerge in the economic-demographic literature,[49] these models typically require nonlinear estimation and are expensive to solve; they can also be somewhat difficult to interpret. Given the orientation of the present study, it is not appropriate nor is it feasible to mount such a modeling effort here. Our emphasis has been to provide an exploratory analysis of the Rural Fertility Survey data using relatively straightforward statistical procedures. On the other hand, one of the contributions of this study has been to reveal those data and modeling needs appropriate to a richer analysis of Egyptian demography. The construction of disequilibrium models of household behavior, and the development of econometric frameworks appropriate to testing these models, represents one such example.

Having said this, we should note that in chapter 8 an attempt is made to identify and analyze the experience of three groups of households that have largely completed childbearing (women aged thirty-five and above). These households are divided into subgroups according to a comparison of each family's desired number of children (DNC) with its number of surviving children (CS), as follows: excess supply of children (DNC < CS), excess demand for children (DNC > CS), and equilibrium number of children (DNC = CS). The difficulty of limiting the analysis to such a categorization can be illustrated by examining the resulting severe data reduction in several household attributes important to the analysis. For example, the number of women in the primary education certificate category declines from 156 in the total RFS to only twenty-four in the sample of women aged thirty-five or above. And when this latter group is further divided into the three excess demand states, the sample size in each subgroup is of course much smaller (16, 3, and 5 women), and is moreover constraining to reliable statistical analysis. As a result, a way must be devised to expand the number of observations if the excess-demand categorization is to be a focus of the empirical inquiry with this data set.

One way to accomplish this goal would be to use the entire data set. Note that families can be in "disequilibrium" *during* the period when they are having children. They may be having children too rapidly or too slowly with reference to their desires and expectations. The development of such disequilibrium models are rare in the economic-demographic literature, and this is not the place for their construction given the more limited objectives of the present study. Suffice it to say that future work on Egyptian demography could be productively directed to developing econometric models of disequilibrium behavior. This effort may not only yield results interesting in their own right, but should provide empirical findings useful for important areas of government policy, especially as this policy relates to health, family planning, and education.

7. FAMILY PLANNING: PROSPECTS AND PROBLEMS

7.1 INTRODUCTION

Two approaches are commonly used to investigate the determinants of completed family size. The first, employed in chapters 5 and 6, examines the direct impacts of socioeconomic variables such as education and wealth on fertility and mortality. The second, employed in this chapter and in chapter 8, examines the indirect impacts of socioeconomic change on fertility by focusing on proximate variables such as fecundity, contraception, abortion, age at marriage, and breastfeeding. Using data for many developing countries, J. Bongaarts has shown that these proximate variables account for most of the variation in fertility.[1]

Of the proximate variables that might be studied, contraceptive use and breastfeeding, when recognized as a contraceptive method, will be highlighted in this chapter, since together they constitute an important area of policy formulation.[2] Moreover, survey information is more readily available on these than on other variables in the Bongaarts' analysis. Preliminary studies for Egypt have further shown contraceptive use to be a relatively important intermediate variable and, as revealed in chapter 4, age at first marriage has relatively little variance in the rural setting. Using Bongaarts' framework, S. F. Loza and M. N. El-Khorazaty found that for rural Egypt contraceptive use is "the main intermediate fertility variable that is responsible for differences in fertility behavior...and for the decline [in fertility]."[3]

There are several distinct factors that need empirical investigation so that the relationships between socioeconomic change and contraception can be understood. These include the determinants of (1) knowledge, (2) approval, and (3) use of contraception. In addition, factors accounting for attitudes toward family size norms must be considered. In rural Egypt, as in many areas, knowledge of contraception is widespread, approval is considerably less prevalent, and use is disappointingly low. The reasons for this significant reduction in prevalence rates as one moves from knowledge to use are not well understood, nor will they be fully revealed in the present study. However, the empirical explorations in this chapter and in chapter 8 will permit us to advance some guarded speculations regarding the likely success of alternative family planning strategies and, in particular, how these strategies are related to various formats for socioeconomic change in rural Egypt.

7.2 KNOWLEDGE AND APPROVAL OF CONTRACEPTIVES

A necessary--though not wholly sufficient--condition for a successful family planning program is that the population for whom the program is designed be knowledgeable about contraceptive methods. This condition is met in rural Egypt where, as table 7.1 indicates, 89 percent of ever-married women have heard of at least one method. Knowledge of prolonged breastfeeding as a form of contraception comes in third place behind the pill and the IUD. Of particular interest, however, is the fact that only 37.7 percent of the women knew of prolonged breastfeeding, while 87.4 percent knew of at least one method of modern contraception.[4] This variation in the recognition of traditional versus modern contraceptive methods is not significantly affected by age or number of surviving children, although educated women are more likely to realize the contraceptive attribute of breastfeeding. Of the various explanations that might be offered to account for the low recognition of breastfeeding as a form of contraception, the most appealing concerns the lack of alternatives to child nourishment. As it has been for centuries, breastfeeding is still the safest and most economical form of infant nourishment. Seldom is any consideration given to alternatives, unless the mother is incapable of nursing the child, or else is wealthy enough for bottle-feeding to be economically feasible.

Two other interesting observations can be made with respect to the results presented in table 7.1. First, the impact of education on contraceptive knowledge occurs largely at the very low education levels, as women move from the illiterate category to having some education. Moreover, beyond the "no certificate" level, education is

Table 7.1 Knowledge of Family Planning by Selected Attributes

Characteristics[a]	At Least One Method	A Modern Method	Pill	IUD	Condom	Steril-ization	Prolonged Breastfeeding	N
Current Age								
< 25	88.1	86.4	86.3	50.5	4.5	13.0	34.5	1072
25-34	90.0	88.5	88.4	55.4	7.3	18.0	40.3	1391
35-44	89.2	86.8	86.5	54.5	6.9	15.0	39.0	987
45-49	88.2	87.7	87.7	56.0	5.6	10.2	34.2	374
Surviving Children								
< 3	85.1	83.6	83.3	49.4	4.8	16.0	35.[illegible]	1626
3-5	91.1	89.2	89.1	56.0	7.0	16.2	40.1	1533
6+	94.0	92.7	92.6	60.0	7.9	13.3	38.4	670
Wife's Education								
Illiterate	86.8	84.7	84.7	49.0	4.4	12.0	35.1	2933
No. Certificate	96.3	95.8	95.6	67.1	9.9	22.5	44.5	740
Primary Cert. +	98.1	98.1	98.1	80.8	23.9	29.0	54.5	156
Total								
Percentage	89.0	87.4	87.3	53.9	6.2	15.6	37.7	-
Number	3404	3344	3336	2062	238	597	1441	3824

[a] Ever-married women.

important only insofar as women become aware of the more esoteric methods of contraception: IUD, condom, sterilization. Only modest differentials exist as regards the impact of high levels of educational attainment on knowledge of basic methods such as the pill. Second, the modern contraceptive method of which rural Egyptian women are least aware is the condom. It will be shown below that men are less likely than women to approve of contraceptive methods. These two observations would appear to be related.

Table 7.2 presents data on the relationships between nine socioeconomic variables and the level of knowledge among women of a modern contraceptive method. Three observations useful to appraising family planning in rural Egypt can be offered. First, considerable variation in the percentage of women who have heard of a modern family planning method exists between illiterate women and women with some education ("no certificate" category). At higher levels of education little variation exists. This suggests a "threshold effect"--the impact of education on awareness of contraceptive methods, though positive at all levels, becomes less significant at higher education levels. Second, the level of contraceptive knowledge is higher for wives who participate in activities other than traditional housework or for wives of husbands working in nonagricultural occupations. Third, some variation in the percentage of women who have heard of a modern family planning method exists between households with no real assets and those with one real asset and, to a slightly lesser degree, between households with no personal assets and those with one personal asset. This again suggests a threshold effect: the impact of increases in household assets on the awareness of contraceptive methods, though positive at all levels, becomes less important at higher levels of household wealth. The same three threshold effects exist as regards the percentage of ever-married women who have heard of prolonged breastfeeding as a contraceptive method, by education levels, work status, and asset holdings. The impact of education on the awareness of the contraceptive effects of breastfeeding is greatest when moving from the "illiterate" level to the "some education" level, and it is less marked at higher levels. Moreover, the impact of asset holdings, especially real assets, is greatest when moving from the zero-asset level to the one-asset level and is less noticeable at higher levels.

Table 7.2 Knowledge and Approval of Contraception

Characteristics[a]	% Women Who Have Heard of Modern Family Planning Method[b]	% Women Who Have Heard of Prolonged Breastfeeding as Contraception	% Husbands & Wives Approving of Family Planning[b]		N
			Male	Female	
Current Age					
<25	86.6	34.3	47.1	59.6	1072
25-34	88.5	40.3	49.1	60.1	1391
35-44	86.8	38.8	46.4	54.9	987
45-49	87.7	34.2	39.8	47.3	374
Surviving Children					
<3	83.6	35.1	40.2	51.6	1626
3-5	89.2	40.1	50.3	59.7	1533
6+	92.7	38.5	55.4	66.0	670
Wife's Education					
Illiterate	84.7	35.0	42.7	52.6	2933
No Certificate	95.8	44.9	57.8	71.1	740
Prim. Cert. +	98.1	54.5	73.1	80.8	156
Husband's Education					
Illiterate	83.6	34.2	39.4	50.6	2387
No Certificate	92.5	40.6	53.3	66.2	887
Prim. Cert.	95.7	42.6	59.6	65.7	230
Prep. Cert. +	96.5	51.1	76.9	78.8	311
Wife's Employment					
Not Working	86.2	35.9	46.6	56.5	3160
Working	93.6	45.8	48.0	61.8	664
Husband's Occupation					
Agriculture	85.4	36.9	42.0	53.2	2237
Nonagriculture	90.2	38.8	53.7	63.2	1593
Electricity					
Yes	91.7	39.4	55.6	65.0	1652
No	84.2	36.4	40.4	51.6	2160
Real Assets					
0	73.3	23.9	37.7	46.0	700
1	88.7	40.4	49.1	61.0	1266
2	89.8	34.9	44.9	55.2	870
3+	93.7	46.3	52.2	62.7	994
Personal Assets					
0	81.3	32.4	34.5	47.0	1505
1	89.7	40.2	50.4	59.7	1588
2	94.2	42.4	62.1	70.7	451
3+	96.2	44.1	68.5	78.0	286
Total	87.5	37.7	47.0	57.4	3824

[a] Ever-married women.

[b] Unadjusted figures are presented for simplicity since percentages adjusted for age revealed no significant cohort effect.

To summarize the overall findings from tables 7.1 and 7.2, we conclude that knowledge of contraceptive methods does not appear to represent a constraint on family planning in rural Egypt. What appears to be true is that the extremely poor, illiterate, and nonworking (housewives) Egyptians are less aware not only of modern contraceptives, but also of the contraceptive effect of breastfeeding. Yet since this is the proportion of the population most likely to be "supply constrained" (that is, they desire more children than they are able to obtain), a program to increase contraceptive knowledge among it is likely to yield disappointing results. Indeed, it could well be that the lower knowledge of contraception relates to the need to know, and, as just argued, this need is low for the illiterate poor of rural Egypt.

Knowledge of contraceptive methods is only the first of the three steps necessary in the evaluation of family planning in rural Egypt; approval and use of contraceptive methods must be assessed as well. Table 7.2 also presents data on the degree to which husbands and wives approve of family planning. In assessing these results, it should be emphasized that the responses provided by wives may not reflect the views of their husbands. (Note also that the stated husband's views are those as provided by the wife.) Indeed, the RFS data evince that the approval of family planning methods among wives and their husbands is highly correlated--83.5 percent of the spouses share a similar view (43.9 percent approve and 39.6 percent disapprove). Only 13.5 percent of the wives approved of family planning while their husbands did not, and only 3 percent of husbands approved of family planning while their wives did not. Therefore, one should not overemphasize the significance of differences in the level of approval of males and females, in spite of the fact that the data show females to have a higher approval rate than males in all categories. Furthermore, it should be cautioned that "approval" is a somewhat nebulous term. It may indicate an actual "demand for" contraceptives, or it may simply translate into a "general acceptance" of contraceptives. After all, the approval rate is fairly high, but as shown below the actual usage rate is low. Whereas 47.0 percent of all males and 57.3 percent of all females approve of family planning methods, only 23.7 percent of women have ever used a modern contraceptive method, and only 12.3 percent were using one at the time of the survey.

The principal patterns in the data on approval reveal the same threshold effects that were found in the data on knowledge. In particular, considerable variation in the percentage of women and men who approve of family planning exists between illiterates and those with some education ("no certificate" category). But at higher levels the impact of education on approval tapers off. The same discontinuity exists between women from extremely poor households (zero-real-assets and/or zero-personal-assets) and women from households in the one-real-asset and/or the one-personal-asset categories. As asset holdings increase, their positive impact on approval diminishes. The results that pertain to approval of family planning measures--like those that assessed the impact of socio-economic change on knowledge of contraception--offer some insight into potential strategies which would focus on the extremely poor and illiterate segments of the rural Egyptian population. For this group, basic socioeconomic change might have to take place prior to the likelihood of any successful efforts to expand the approval and use of modern methods of contraception.

Besides overall approval, the reasons why women use modern contraceptives constitute another important part of the analysis of family planning. Of those currently married and living with their husbands, 60.1 percent approve of family planning. As for reasons justifying approval, 36.6 percent approve only when they have reached their desired number of children. In addition, 26.2 percent state that they want no more children, and/or that they are concerned for their child's health. Mother's health and economic reasons account for another 18.5 and 8.2 percent, respectively. The spacing of children (and a few related factors) account for the remaining 10.5 percent.

While most women approve of family planning only after reaching a desired family size, an examination of these family size targets is instructive: 21.7 percent of the women approving family planning use felt that birth control would be appropriate after having one or two children, 37.8 percent after having three children, and 40.5 percent after having at least four children.

Among those who did not approve of family planning, the most frequently cited reasons were religion (28.8 percent) and the importance of children to the family as a source of pride, assets, and security (27.3 percent). The remaining women cited discomfort caused by contraceptives, health, spouse disapproval, and sterility as reasons against contraceptive use.

7.3 USE OF CONTRACEPTIVE METHODS

Data on the patterns of use of various contraceptive methods are shown in table 7.3. Of the sample of ever-married women, only 27.9 percent have at some time ever used a family planning method, whether modern or traditional, and 15.0 percent are currently using a method. The percentage becomes less favorable as one moves closer to the actual practice of family planning. Indeed, almost all Egyptian women have knowledge of contraceptive methods; around one-half approve of family planning practices; approximately one-quarter have ever used modern contraception; and only around one-eighth are currently using family planning.

Of those who have used some method, the pill is by far the most frequently cited (22.6 percent). Prolonged breastfeeding recognized as a form of contraception is next (6.2 percent). A similar pattern is observed among women at risk of pregnancy (nonpregnant and currently married) where 18.4 percent were currently using a family planning method. Thus, over 80 percent of those at risk of childbearing at the time of the survey were not using any form of contraception. Among all women at risk of pregnancy, 15.0 percent were currently using modern contraception and 3.4 percent were using traditional contraception. Prolonged breastfeeding is the most frequently used method among the traditional forms, a pattern typical of developing countries where use of modern contraception is not widespread.

Surprisingly, family planning use for women twenty-five or above is largely unrelated to age (table 7.3). Instead, simple need (whether the family size is already large) and education (whether the mother has some, though not necessarily a great deal) are the most significant influences on contraceptive use. It is interesting to note, however, that the use of traditional methods is largely invariant to educational level.

Table 7.4 presents percentages of women ever and currently using modern contraception. Overall, 23.7 percent of the women have ever used a modern method, and only 12.3 percent are currently using a modern method. These percentages are consistent with those found in the 1974/75 National Fertility Survey (NFS) and

Table 7.3 Use of Family Planning by Selected Attributes

Characteristics[a]	Any Method	Pill	IUD	Condom	Sterilization	Prolonged Breast-feeding	N
Current Age							
<25	14.0	10.6	.6	.3	.0	3.6	1078
25-34	33.0	26.6	2.7	.9	.4	6.3	1391
35-44	35.5	28.3	3.9	1.1	.7	8.5	987
45-49	33.0	27.0	3.7	.5	.8	7.5	374
Surviving Children							
<3	11.5	8.9	.5	.3	.1	2.9	1626
3-5	37.1	29.0	4.0	1.2	.5	8.2	1533
6+	49.0	41.6	4.0	.9	.8	9.7	671
Wife's Education							
Illiterate	24.4	19.0	2.3	.3	.3	5.8	2933
No Cert.	39.8	32.8	3.1	1.8	.7	7.5	740
Prim. Cert. +	46.2	41.8	3.8	3.2	0.0	7.7	156
Total	27.9	22.6	2.5	.7	.4	6.2	3830

[a] Ever-married women.

the Egyptian Fertility Survey (EFS) conducted in collaboration with the World Fertility Survey in 1980. The proportions of ever-married women in rural Egypt who were using a family planning method at the time of the survey were found to be 12.9 percent and 11.7 percent for the two surveys, respectively.[5] The proportions for urban areas are 45.4 and 39.8 percent for the NFS and EFS, respectively. These rates reach 65.5 percent for Cairo and Alexandria governorates in the 1974/75 survey. Rural contraceptive use is, thus, very low, and factors accounting for this low prevalence rate constitute an important area for demographic research.

As noted above, age has a small effect on contraceptive use for women 25 and above. Predictably the very young women and the relatively older women use contraceptives less, but between the ages of 25 and 44, contraceptive use is largely invariant to age. However, the number of surviving children does reveal an impact on current family planning use, especially after three or more children have survived.

As was found in the data on knowledge of and attitudes toward

Table 7.4 Use of Contraception

Characteristics[a]	% Women Who Ever (Currently) Used (Using) a Modern Family Planning Method[b]		% Women Who Ever Used Prolonged Breastfeeding for Contraception[b]	Mean Breastfeeding Duration for Last Closed Birth Interval (mo.)
	Ever	Currently		
Current Age				
<25	11.1	5.9	3.6	15.9
25-34	27.8	13.7	6.2	18.0
35-44	29.8	16.9	8.5	20.2
45-49	28.1	12.3	7.5	20.2
Surviving Children				
<3	9.2	4.2	2.9	16.0
3-5	30.5	16.9	8.2	19.3
6+	43.0	20.8	9.7	19.9
Wife's Education				
Illiterate	19.8	10.0	5.8	19.1
No Cert.	34.7	19.1	7.4	17.1
Prim. Cert. +	42.3	19.9	7.7	16.0
Husb.'s Education				
Illiterate	17.8	8.8	5.9	19.6
No Cert.	29.0	14.5	6.7	17.5
Prim. Cert.	36.5	20.9	7.0	16.4
Prep. Cert. +	43.7	25.1	6.8	15.2
Wife's Employment				
Not Working	23.9	12.6	6.0	18.5
Working	22.7	10.1	7.1	18.8
Husb.'s Occupation				
Agriculture	19.0	9.7	5.9	19.1
Nonagriculture	30.1	15.7	6.7	17.8
Electricity				
Yes	33.2	17.4	6.4	17.8
No	16.4	8.3	6.1	19.3
Real Assets				
0	20.9	11.7	6.0	18.4
1	24.8	12.8	7.0	18.5
2	23.9	11.5	5.6	18.5
3+	23.9	12.3	5.8	18.8
Personal Assets				
0	14.5	6.3	6.1	19.4
1	24.1	12.2	6.7	18.4
2	36.8	20.8	4.4	17.3
3+	49.0	29.4	7.0	17.0
Total	23.7	12.2	6.2	18.6

[a] Ever-married women.

[b] Unadjusted figures are presented for simpliciy since percentages adjusted for age revealed no significant cohort effects.

contraception, a threshold effect appears evident in the data on education (especially that of the wife). If these correlations can be interpreted as causation, an increase in the use of contraceptive methods would be stimulated more by a policy of large numbers of illiterate women gaining some schooling rather than substantially increasing the number of women at higher education levels.

The association of occupational status and use of contraception is as expected for husband's employment, but contrary to that expected for women. Working in nonhousehold activities reveals no impact on family planning. The data are difficult to interpret since the nature of the wife's employment is not specified, but we would speculate that many of these activities (such as working in cottage industry jobs or helping husbands on the farm) are fully compatible with childrearing.

The most interesting correlation on contraceptive use pertains to the various measures of household wealth: electricity, personal assets, and real assets. While each of these measures represents an increase in wealth--and thus an increase in the demand for contraception would be expected--real assets may be, as noted in chapter 5, complements to children. This relationship is strikingly evident in the data, where contraceptive use is largely invariant to real asset ownership, but rises sharply with the use of electricity and the ownership of personal assets.

Studies have shown that the patterns between contraceptive use and various socioeconomic factors, found for all of rural Egypt, are broadly the same as those found in Upper and Lower Egypt when they are considered separately, although prevalence rates are significantly different between these areas.[6] While percentages of ever and current use of all methods, modern and traditional, among ever-married women are 38.2 and 21.1, respectively, for Lower Egypt, they are 17.3 and 8.1, respectively, for Upper Egypt. Ever and current use of only modern methods are 34.2 and 18.6 percent, respectively, for Lower Egypt and they are 11.9 and 5.1 percent, respectively, for Upper Egypt. The nature and significance of these differences are examined in more detail in chapter 8.

Another important dimension of family planning relates to the extent to which couples maintain their use of modern contraceptives over time, and is measured in terms of "continuation rates." Variations in continuation rates can result in misleading comparisons of contraceptive prevalence rates among different populations. For example, relatively low prevalence rates associated with low discontinuation rates might represent a more desireable situation than relatively higher prevalence rates associated with high discontinuation rates. The net outcome of prevalence rates and discontinuation rates is the woman/years protected by contraceptive use. It is an increase in this protection that is the objective of family planning programs, a goal that can be obtained by increasing prevalence rates, decreasing discontinuation rates, or both. Thus, the prevalence rates shown above for Lower and Upper Egypt reveal only part of the picture. It is necessary to compile information on continuation rates as well.

A rough measure of continuation rates is the ratio of current to ever users. The figures shown in table 7.4 for current and ever use of contraceptive methods indicate that this ratio for Lower and Upper Egypt is .55 and .47, respectively, for the use of modern methods. These ratios reveal that discontinuation rates are higher in Upper than in Lower Egypt. Thus, the gap between the percentages of woman/years protected in Lower and Upper Egypt is even wider than the gap of prevalence rates alone. The ratio for all rural Egypt is .54 for all methods and .52 for modern methods, showing slightly higher continuation rates for traditional methods than modern methods.

While the use of breastfeeding as a method of contraception is modest in rural Egypt, it is still second only to the pill as the most widely cited form of family planning. Table 7.4 shows the relationship between this traditional form of contraception and several socioeconomic factors. The most interesting result is the apparent *increase* in breastfeeding incidence with socioeconomic development indicators: wife's education, husband's education, wife's employment, husband's occupation, use of electricity, and personal asset ownership.[7] While many of these increases are slight, taken together they appear to provide some limited evidence that breastfeeding increases with development. This is contrary to expectations based on results found elsewhere in the literature. For instance, M. Nag has remarked that "sufficient evidence is available to demonstrate that the decline in the practices of breastfeeding and postpartum abstinence is generally linked with urbanization and the spread of education."[8] However, the increase observed here in the incidence of breastfeeding with socioeconomic development might be a result of more recognition of breastfeeding as a contraceptive method. More educated (as shown in table 7.3) women, and those with greater wealth, are more likely to know or cite prolonged breastfeeding as a contraceptive method.

The impact of breastfeeding as a contraceptive method relates not only to its incidence, but also its duration. "Breastfeeding cannot be regarded as a highly reliable contraceptive method for individual women, but its aggregate effect can be quite large in societies where women breastfeed for a prolonged period."[9] The average duration of breastfeeding reported in the RFS is 18.6 months among all ever-married women.

It may be fortuitous that in rural Egypt the incidence of prolonged breastfeeding as a contraceptive method may be increasing--however slightly--with socioeconomic development, and that this is occurring simultaneously with increases in the use of modern contraceptive methods. However, without more detailed longitudinal information regarding the duration of breastfeeding and its relationship to development, conclusions about the impact of these two forms of contraception must be guarded.

The RFS only provides data on the duration of breastfeeding of the last two children. The duration for the second to the last child is used in the analysis since it provides the last closed birth interval with no truncation. Table 7.4 shows the relationships between the mean duration of breastfeeding and various socioeconomic variables. Contrary to its incidence, breastfeeding duration decreases with modernization and development: small family size, wife's and husband's education, husband's occupation, electricity, and personal asset ownership. The decrease is more pronounced for younger wives, implying a cohort effect. (See appendix table A.7.) Thus, the increase observed in the incidence (cum recognition as a contraceptive) of breastfeeding is accompanied by a reduction in the duration, especially among younger women. J. Bongaarts has estimated that in a population with an infecundability interval of 24 months, fertility can rise by as much as 40 percent if the period is reduced to 12 months.[10] To prevent an increase in marital fertility in such a population, contraceptive use would have to rise from zero to nearly 30 percent.

These results provide some support to an important hypothesis, namely, a decline expected in the duration of breastfeeding with increased modernization in a society such as rural Egypt, where the use of modern contraceptive methods is modest and characterized by improper use and high discontinuation rates,[11] may lead in the short run to shorter birth intervals and a rise in fertility. (Chapter 8 examines this relationship between the use of modern contraceptives and fertility.) Indeed, as M. Nag has cautioned, "any theory of fertility should recognize the fertility-increasing effects of the process of modernization, at least in its early stages. In making predictions about fertility and in evaluating the fertility impact of any development or family planning program, the fertility-increasing effects of modernization are often not taken into consideration. The tendency of the fertility level to remain the same or even to rise should not necessarily be interpreted as a failure of a development program to generate demand for birth control or of a family planning program to provide effective service."[12]

7.4 ATTITUDES TOWARD FAMILY SIZE NORMS

Other things equal, the demand for family planning should vary inversely with family size norms. Two direct measures of these norms are available, desired family size and ideal family size, as well as two indirect measures, the desire for no additional children and ideal spacing between subsequent births. In order to obtain some insights into possible determinants of the demand for family planning methods, we will next provide an exploratory examination of the relationships between these various measures of family size norms and several socioeconomic variables. A more detailed inquiry into these relationships is made in chapter 8.

The RFS has two questions on family size aspirations. Women reported the "ideal" number of children in response to the question: What is the best number of children that *a* woman would have? Regarding *their* "desired" number, women were asked the following question: If *you* can decide about the number of children you would like to have all your reproductive life, what is this number?

For all ever-married women the mean desired and mean ideal number of children are 4.3 and 3.8, respectively. The mean desired number of children is equal to the mean number of CEB, while the mean ideal number is smaller than the mean CEB by about .5 child. The interpretations of the difference between desired and ideal family size are rather elusive, but it is thought that the ideal measure is closer to what is appropriate for an analysis of household behavior. The ideal family size question does not refer to what is ideal for the respondent, but for some other women in a similar situation. Hence, an attempt is made to abstract from peer pressures on accepted family size norms. This measure is not wholly reliable. In contrast to the responses women gave to the desired family size question, almost one thousand women responded that the ideal family size is "up to God."[13]

Table 7.5 presents the mean desired and mean ideal number of children by different background variables. Both measures increase by age, possibly reflecting a cohort effect (younger women have smaller norms) or, more likely, a rationalization response, since older women are more prone to state family size norms close to the actual number of surviving children they have *now*, which might be different from the norms they had at the start of their reproductive behavior.

It is interesting to note that family size norms decrease with age at marriage. While this may reflect an assessment by women about what is in fact possible (older marriages decrease possible family size due to the shorter marriage duration), it may also reflect a decision to marry later because smaller families are desired. If, in fact, it does reflect a decision to postpone marriage, then age at marriage cannot be considered as an exogenous determinant of fertility. Instead, it would have to be analyzed as an endogenous determinant responding to family size aspirations.

The remaining results are similar to those found for knowledge, attitudes, and use of contraceptives. Education reduces family size norms, but, as before, the largest discontinuity typically occurs as one moves from the illiterate to the "some education" categories. For example, some education of a woman (no certificate category) is associated with a reduction in the desired number of children by .66, whereas moving to a significant increase in educational attainment (at least primary certificate) is associated with a reduction of only an additional .38 children.

The highly consistent relationship found elsewhere in this study between household wealth and its form, and household behavior, is repeated with respect to family size desires. In particular, increased wealth is associated with a reduction in family size

Table 7.5 Attitudes Toward Family Size Norms

Characteristics[a]	Mean Desired Number of Children	N	Mean Ideal Number of Children	N	% Wanting No Additional Children	N	Mean Ideal Spacing (years)	N
Current Age								
<25	3.9	1028	3.6	777	16.2	1072	2.4	1000
25-34	4.4	1330	3.8	975	48.9	1391	2.5	1305
35-44	4.5	948	3.8	644	67.8	987	2.6	921
45-49	4.8	359	4.3	230	77.0	374	2.6	351
Age at First Marriage								
<15	4.6	753	4.0	536	56.9	785	2.4	737
15-17	4.4	1565	3.8	1102	46.0	1641	2.5	1536
18-19	4.2	648	3.7	486	42.3	672	2.5	635
20-21	4.1	397	3.6	285	48.0	415	2.5	386
22-23	3.9	134	3.6	97	38.7	142	2.5	130
24+	3.7	164	3.5	148	41.2	165	2.5	148
Surviving Children								
<3	3.9	1567	3.5	1110	14.9	1626	2.4	1493
3-5	4.4	1468	3.9	1056	65.8	1533	2.5	1454
6+	5.2	635	4.2	463	83.6	670	2.6	634
Wife's Education								
Illiterate	4.5	2798	3.9	1918	46.4	2933	2.4	2731
No Cert.	3.8	720	3.4	582	50.8	740	2.6	695
Prim. Cert. +	3.5	152	3.2	129	46.8	156	2.7	155
Husband's Education								
Iliterate	4.5	2287	4.0	1527	46.5	2387	2.4	2213
No Cert.	4.1	844	3.6	661	51.2	887	2.5	834
Prim. Cert.	4.1	221	3.6	177	47.0	230	2.6	217
Prep. Cert. +	3.5	306	3.2	257	42.8	311	2.6	305
Wife's Employment								
Not Working	4.4	3018	3.8	2173	47.3	3160	2.5	2959
Working	4.1	649	3.7	454	47.6	664	2.5	619
Husband's Occupation								
Agriculture	4.4	2136	3.9	1472	45.6	2237	2.4	2076
Nonagriculture	4.2	1535	3.7	1157	49.8	1593	2.5	1506
Electricity								
Yes	4.1	1589	3.5	1195	53.1	1652	2.5	1569
No	4.5	2065	4.0	1422	43.1	2160	2.4	2000

Table 7.5 (continued)

Characteristics[a]	Mean Desired Number of Children	N	Mean Ideal Number of Children	N	% Wanting No Additional Children	N	Mean Ideal Spacing (years)	N
Real Assets								
0	4.4	672	3.8	412	43.0	700	2.5	633
1	4.2	1219	3.6	923	48.4	1266	2.5	1189
2	4.5	832	4.1	587	47.1	870	2.4	810
3+	4.2	948	3.7	707	49.1	994	2.4	950
Personal Assets								
0	4.6	1437	4.0	942	42.3	1505	2.4	1371
1	4.2	1521	3.8	1124	48.6	1588	2.5	1504
2	4.0	436	3.5	341	54.6	451	2.5	431
3+	4.0	277	3.2	222	55.2	286	2.7	276
Total	4.3	3665	3.8	2626	47.4	3824	2.5	3577

[a] Ever-married women.

desires unless that wealth is in the form of real assets, which is a proxy for income as well as the ability to earn future income with the assistance of child labor.

Table 7.5 presents two additional measures relating to family size aspirations: desires for no additional children and ideal spacing of children. It is interesting to note that 47.4 percent of all ever-married women state that they want no additional children--a large percent considering the low contraceptive prevalence rates. This group of women is certainly a prime family planning target. Only two interesting unanticipated results are evident. The first is the absence of a monotonic association between education and the desire for additional children. The remaining findings are consistent with those found elsewhere in this section and in this chapter. The other finding of some importance is the relatively small variation in the ideal spacing measure in terms of its relationship to various indices of socioeconomic change. If this result can be believed, it would imply that the demand for contraceptives, which is associated with various components of socioeconomic change, relates more to completed family size than to the ideal spacing of children.

Overall, we can conclude that the various measures of socioeconomic change are fairly consistently related to family size aspirations. This association likely represents a major part of the explanation for contraceptive use in rural Egypt. While for all women who have largely completed their childbearing (ages 35-49) it is true that *on average* the desired number of children about equals the number of surviving children, such an equality does *not* imply that most Egyptians are successful in meeting their family size targets. In fact, there is considerable heterogeneity in rural Egyptian behavior. Many families are indeed successful in meeting their family size goals but many overshoot their goals and as a result have an "excess" number of children; still others are unable to meet their family size norms. The averages mask this wide variance in behavior. Understanding this variation, and how it relates to the demand for family planning services, is a theme that is considered in chapter 8.

8. CONTROL OF FAMILY SIZE: DETERMINANTS AND CONSTRAINTS

8.1 CONCLUSIONS AND POLICY SPECULATIONS

Attitudes among the rural Egyptian populace toward the desired number of children (DNC) and the use of contraceptives are in a state of transition. This transition can be examined by comparing the proportion of the population in which there is an "excess supply of children" (i.e., where the number of surviving children exceeds the desired number of children) to the proportion of the population in which there is an "excess demand for children" (i.e., where the number of surviving children is less than the desired number of children).

Though it is true that on average an excess supply of children exists for all of rural Egypt, almost one-third of the women who have largely completed their childbearing years have an excess demand for children. This indicates that many rural women are "supply constrained" since their desired family size exceeds their number of surviving children. As a result, socioeconomic development that lowers child mortality and improves living standards may cause an increase in completed family size for this segment of the population. Of equal significance, family planning programs may not be well received by this group until the situation of excess demand is alleviated. Such alleviation is unlikely without general socioeconomic change.

An increase in the level of education of the rural population is a key component of socioeconomic change. The evidence indicates that, as educational attainment rises, the desired number of children will diminish and modern contraceptive use will increase. For the poor and illiterate portion of the population, there is an excess demand for children, yet in families with some education, there is an excess supply of children. The level of education appears to represent a powerful influence on the desire for children.

Against this set of observations, it should be recalled from chapter 6 that educational attainment does not exert a statistically significant impact on CEB. Three explanations for this can be offered. First, rural Egyptians may use contraceptives inefficiently.[1] Consequently, even though relatively educated men and women have an excess supply of children and are more likely to use contraceptives, no reduction occurs in the number of children ever born. Second, a time lag may exist between the reduction of DNC and the subsequent use of contraceptives, eventually resulting in the realization of reduced family size. For the purposes of policy formulation, however, it makes little difference which interpretation is accepted. That the efficiency of contraceptive use improves with education--especially the education of the woman--has been documented in several studies. Further, DNC bears an inverse relation to educational attainment, in particular to the education of women. It is, therefore, reasonable to expect that increases in female educational attainment will, in time, lead to a lower number of children ever born, even if the current impacts of education are not yet apparent in the data.

Finally, the impact of education on the supply-constrained subset of the population may differ from the impact on the subset that has an excess supply of children. In the former group, increases in educational attainment may increase fecundity and CEB; in the latter group, higher educational attainment will likely decrease CEB and increase contraceptive use. At a transition stage of development, when the relative sizes of these two groups are approximately the same, the impact of education on CEB for the total population may be measured as being negligible, whereas its separate effects for the two population subgroups may be significant, but roughly offsetting. However, as the relative size of the population with an excess supply of children increases, the deterring impact of education on completed family size will become increasingly apparent. The lack of a measured impact of education on CEB for all of rural Egypt may well be due in part to these offsetting influences, and, if so, the deterring impact of education on CEB in the future can be predicted to increase as socioeconomic development takes place.

Nevertheless, the connections between education and socio-economic development, and between DNC and contraceptive use, are complex.[2] On the one hand, more highly educated families and families residing in communities with a relatively large supply of education facilities are more likely to use contraceptives. Yet on the other hand, contraceptive use occurs less in communities with relatively high levels of development, as measured by an aggregate index of community-level wealth.[3] To make the relationship even more paradoxical, it is found that if household wealth takes the form of *real* assets (land, buildings, and equipment), contraceptive use will decrease, but if community-level development emphasizes mechanized agriculture, contraceptive use will increase.

These various results are consistent with those for CEB. Namely, while increases in wealth in general may have a positive effect on the demand for children, the *form* of that wealth may be critical in determining the net impacts of wealth accumulation on child demand. If wealth accumulation takes the form of assets complementary to the enjoyment of children, then child demand will increase. This complementarity could be reflected by the level of the individual's real assets (which on average raise the benefits of child labor), or by the community's index of total development, since this particular index is heavily weighted toward items which increase the value of children in the production process in an agricultural-based setting. Indeed, the return on child labor is an important means by which such agricultural-based wealth accumulation takes place. But if wealth accumulation takes the form of investments in education (e.g., schools in the community, greater participation in schooling by individuals), then realizing the returns on such wealth may be competitive with rearing children. A similar consideration applies to the accumulation of wealth in the form of mechanized agriculture, which could result in a reduction of the return on investment in child labor.

Of the various possible government policies, one which provides increased primary education to the wife is likely to have the strongest positive impact on contraceptive use and the greatest negative impact on desired family size. These are interrelated relationships, both work toward reducing completed family size. If policies lowering the value of children to the household are implemented simultaneously (e.g., providing workforce opportunities for the wife that are *competitive* with childrearing), then the education policy noted above will in all probability exert an even stronger positive impact on contraceptive use. But it should be remembered that the possession of real assets *diminishes* contraceptive use. This might be interpreted as reflecting the increased value of children on the farm. In this case, children may be complementary to workforce opportunities, and consequently there is a decreased interest by the husband and wife to hedge against overshooting desired family size. In contrast, if economic development takes the form of mechanization of agriculture, DNC diminishes and contraceptive use increases. In sum, the *form* of economic development may be critical to determining the ultimate impact of government policies on completed family size.[4]

8.2 THE STATISTICAL MODELS

8.2.1 Use of Modern Contraceptive Methods

Two measures of contraceptive use are available: women who have ever used contraceptives and those who are currently using contraceptives.[5] Some researchers feel that the response reliability in survey data is greater for the current-use measure, although for some types of analysis (e.g., CEB, where *ever* born is the time frame), ever-used contraceptives may be the more appropriate variable. Regressions of both measures are provided for comparison.

The contraceptive use measure refers to "modern techniques," i.e., the pill (which is the most common method), IUD, and condoms. For the total sample, 900 women (23.6 percent) have ever used, and 466 women (12.2 percent) are currently using modern contraceptives. The estimated models are presented as equations 8.1 and 8.2.[6,7]

$$[8.1]\quad \mathrm{CUCM} = \underset{(-14.33)}{-.13} + \underset{(8.55)}{.08\mathrm{CS}} - \underset{(-5.04)}{.001\mathrm{AGE{\cdot}CS}} + \underset{(2.56)}{.003\mathrm{AGEW}} + \underset{(4.16)}{.06\mathrm{WE2}}$$

$$- \underset{(-.17)}{.005\mathrm{WE3}} + \underset{(2.12)}{.03\mathrm{HE2}} + \underset{(3.48)}{.07\mathrm{HE3}} + \underset{(4.85)}{.10\mathrm{HE4}}$$

$$+ \underset{(8.74)}{.05\mathrm{ASSETP}} - \underset{(-2.99)}{.01\mathrm{ASSETR}} + \underset{(1.85)}{.02\mathrm{ELEC}}$$

$r^2 = .12$

t values in parentheses

$$[8.2] \quad EUCM = \underset{(-4.84)}{-.18} + \underset{(10.83)}{.13CS} - \underset{(-5.48)}{.002AGEW \cdot CS} + \underset{(2.53)}{.003AGEW}$$

$$+ \underset{(5.40)}{.09WE2} + \underset{(2.60)}{.09WE3} + \underset{(3.88)}{.06HE2} + \underset{(4.09)}{.11HE3} + \underset{(5.92)}{.15HE4}$$

$$+ \underset{(9.24)}{.06ASSETP} - \underset{(-2.79)}{.02ASSETR} + \underset{(4.20)}{.06ELEC}$$

$r^2 = .20$

t values in parentheses

A comparison of the current- to the ever-used regressions reveals that the ever-used model (1) has a higher r^2, (2) shows a slightly greater statistical significance for the impacts of education and assets, and (3) reveals larger quantitative impacts. One of the reasons for the greater statistical significance of the ever-used model is the availability of more observations on this variable.

Several conclusions emerge from an examination of the ever-used model. First, the education of the wife and the husband both exert a positive impact on contraceptive use. Second, the impact of the husband's education is larger than that of the wife's for higher education levels, but slightly smaller for lower education levels.[8] This interpretation is reinforced by the qualification that for the first education category (no certificate), the wife's average years attended is usually less than the husband's. Thus, in terms of years of schooling attended, the impact on contraceptive use of the wife's education in the first six years is relatively understated.[9] (It is surprising, however, that WE3 is not significantly different than zero.) Third, asset ownership reveals mixed effects. On the one hand, electricity and personal assets exert positive impacts. Ostensibly this represents a wealth effect. Households at higher income levels are more likely to use modern contraceptives. On the other hand, real assets exert a negative impact. In this case there exists both a positive income effect (as with personal assets and electricity), and a negative effect--the greater the land and real asset holdings, the more valuable are children on the farm. Finally, the age and the surviving-children effects are as expected. Contraceptive use is more prevalent among older women.[10]

The results for contraceptive use for all of rural Egypt shown in equations 8.1 and 8.2 derive from quite different experience for Upper and Lower Egypt considered separately. For comparable region-specific regression models (see appendix equations A.39 - A.44),[11] contraceptive use is found to be considerably higher in Lower Egypt, and many of the impacts observed in the aggregate are absent in Upper Egypt. For example, husband's education, electricity, and real assets exert no statistically significant impact on contraceptive use in Upper Egypt. The people in this region hold more traditional values and more conservative religious beliefs, at least as regards their perception of Islamic precepts against birth control.[12] It is also interesting to note that the negative impact of real assets is larger in Lower Egypt for both ever and current contraceptive use.

8.2.2 Children Ever Born and Contraceptive Use

In an attempt to provide an exploratory description of the way in which contraceptive use is related to CEB, the ever-used and currently using modern contraceptives variables have been added to the basic CEB equation analyzed in chapter 6. In each instance, contraceptive use reveals a strong, highly significant, positive impact on CEB. However, the addition of the contraceptive use variables adds little to the total explained variance of the equations (r^2 increases by only .01 to .02 units); moreover, the remaining parameter estimates are largely unchanged. The results are presented as equations 8.3 and 8.4.[13]

$$[8.3]\quad CEB = \underset{(-11.48)}{-3.99} + \underset{(23.46)}{.52AGEW} - \underset{(-15.71)}{.005AGEW^2} - \underset{(-25.82)}{.21AFM} + \underset{(45.28)}{.90CD}$$

$$- \underset{(-.00)}{.0003WE2} + \underset{(.21)}{.03WE3} + \underset{(2.10)}{.14HE2} + \underset{(.76)}{.09HE3} + \underset{(.71)}{.08HE4}$$

$$- \underset{(-1.76)}{.05ASSETP} + \underset{(3.74)}{.08ASSETR} + \underset{(4.43)}{.25ELEC} + \underset{(10.34)}{.85CUCM}$$

$r^2 = .74$
t values in parentheses

$$[8.4]\quad CEB = \underset{(-10.62)}{-3.63} + \underset{(22.42)}{.49AGEW} - \underset{(-14.84)}{.005AGEW^2} - \underset{(-25.51)}{.20AFM} + \underset{(46.44)}{.91CD}$$

$$- .05WE2 - .06WE3 + .09HE2 + .03HE3 + .002HE4$$
$$(-.71) \quad (-.45) \quad (1.41) \quad (.26) \quad (.01)$$

$$- .07ASSETP + .09ASSETR + .20ELEC + 1.04EUCM$$
$$(-2.64) \quad (3.91) \quad (3.55) \quad (16.23)$$

$r^2 = .75$
t values in parentheses

These results apparently demonstrate reverse causation, since those women most likely to use modern contraceptives are those who already have relatively large families.[14] Many of these women have exceeded their desired family size. Indeed, in a more complete and complex model, the contraceptive-use variable would enter endogenously into the CEB equation. The reverse causation problem may be compounded by yet another factor. It is likely that extension workers and family planning personnel direct their efforts to those households in which the acceptance rate will be relatively high--those households predicted as having an excess supply of children.

A final factor, which may explain the positive "impact" of modern contraceptive use on CEB, relates to the relative efficiencies of alternative modes of contraception.[15] As noted in chapter 7, for some families modern contraceptives may represent a substitute for extended breastfeeding as a means of family size control. However, unless modern contraceptives are used regularly and properly, the overall impact on CEB could be positive when account is taken of the effect of reduced breastfeeding. (At a minimum, the negative impact of modern contraceptive use on CEB should be reduced.) We have no evidence to support or refute this possibility, but the issue looms as a critical area for future research in assessing the impact of Egyptian family planning programs.

Theoretically, the simplest model of CEB might be specified as follows: CEB = f(Desired Family Size, Error).[16] Desired family size may in turn be explained by several of the variables in the existing regression for CEB (education, assets, etc.), controlling for certain other variables (age, age at first marriage, etc.).[17] We have elected to estimate an equation for actual children ever born, in part because we have less confidence in the responses for desired or ideal family size. Household respondents may not be able to differentiate between the two measures: desired *now* and desired *ever*? Indeed, the fact that many of the responses cluster on actual surviving children (CS) lends some support to the hypothesis that many of the respondents are interpreting "desired ever" as "desired now."

Contraceptive use is also a function of "error," that is, the difference between desired and actual family size, as well as other variables (attitudes, cost, availability).[18] Errors in family planning can be of two types: a deficiency of children (due to infertility or other factors), or an excess number of children, due to overshooting desired family size. Use of contraceptives can thus be viewed as a means of reducing the variance in the error term. The precise way in which this occurs depends on the relative costs of the two alternative errors, and the efficiency and costs (socially and culturally) of contraceptive use.

Contraceptives are used for two related but different purposes: spacing of children as the family moves toward the desired family size, or reducing the stock of children due to overshooting the desired family size. The prevalence of contraceptive use by age will be better understood if these two factors are distinguished from each other.

More insight into the impact and use of contraceptives can be gained from further categorization. Table 8.1 shows the prevalence of contraceptive use for each of three age groups according to whether the woman (1) seeks more children, (2) has attained a number of children corresponding to her "desires" or "ideal," and (3) has more children than she desires. An entry in the table indicates the prevalence (percentage) of contraceptive users (current, ever) for each age cohort and for each fertility state (deficient, optimal, excess). For example, of the 661 women of ages less than 25 who have a deficient number of children, 3.8 percent are currently using contraceptives and 7.7 percent have ever used contraceptives.

The results from table 8.1 are consistent with the theoretical expectations outlined above. First, the prevalence of contraceptive use increases as women move from the state of deficient numbers of children to the state of excess numbers of children. Second, the prevalence for a given state may decrease with age, although this relationship is not particularly strong, especially for the excess-children state. Third, for women who describe their situation as optimal, the prevalence of contraceptive use does decrease with

Table 8.1 Prevalence of Modern Contraceptives by Age and Demand for Children

Contraceptive Use	Percentage Used or Using Contraceptives		
	Deficient Family Size	Optimal Family Size	Excess Family Size
		Ideal Family Size	
Women of Ages <25			
Current	3.8	23.8	33.3
Ever	7.7	38.6	44.4
Number	661	101	18
Women of Ages 25-34			
Current	4.9	25.7	28.5
Ever	15.2	42.2	54.6
Number	427	296	253
Women of Ages 35+			
Current	3.1	19.1	30.0
Ever	8.8	29.2	53.1
Number	194	209	473
		Desired Family Size	
Women of Ages <25			
Current	3.4	24.3	27.3
Ever	7.4	38.3	45.5
Number	904	107	22
Women of Ages 25-34			
Current	4.1	21.4	28.7
Ever	14.3	37.4	52.4
Number	684	393	254
Women of Ages 35+			
Current	3.0	13.4	27.7
Ever	7.9	24.9	49.7
Number	403	365	541

Notes: 1. "Modern" contraceptive methods include the pill, IUD, condoms, and sterilization.

2. "Ideal" family size refers to "...the best number of children required for a woman." 2,632 women responded numerically to this question. Women giving non-numeric answers including "up to God" were excluded.

3. "Desired" family size refers to "...the number of children you would like to have." 3,670 women responded to this question. Women giving non-numeric answers including "up to God" were excluded.

4. "Deficient," "optimal," and "excess" family size refers to conditions when surviving minus ideal or desired family size is <0, = 0, or >0, respectively.

age. Women at their optimal state may be more likely than others to use contraceptives efficiently, both with modern and with traditional techniques. As this group ages and fewer children are born (declining fecundity, intercourse, etc.), the need for contraceptives to maintain the optimal family size diminishes. In contrast, for women who have an excess number of children, even though the ability to conceive declines with age, the need and the ability to adjust to the target family size do not. Indeed, for these women the effective use of contraceptives increases with age if one adjusts for declining fecundity. The costs of overshooting also increase with age. Finally, the time remaining to reduce the stock of children to an equilibrium or optimal state declines with age, and this is yet another factor which accounts for the higher prevalence rate of contraceptive use with age.

The difference in the prevalence of contraceptive use between women with an excess number of children and those with an optimal number increases with age. (Comparisons of the less-than-25 age group are omitted because of the small sample size.) This may be explained by the fact that, as age increases, the time left to adjust to the target family size diminishes, and thus the relative prevalence of contraceptive use increases.

8.2.3 Desired Family Size

The Rural Fertility Survey furnished information on desired number of children (DNC) in an attempt to provide data on family size aspirations as distinct from family size outcomes. Such attitudinal measures are difficult to interpret. (The questions asked are given in chapter 7, section 7.4.) They are ambiguous as well as biased due to survey procedures and peer pressures.[19] As noted above, one possible ambiguity concerns the respondents' perception of the time frame in answering the question: does DNC refer to now or to ever? While the latter was the intended time frame of reference and was made explicit by the interviewer, some respondents undoubtedly incorporated elements of the former time frame when answering this question.

With respect to acceptable family size, peer influences likely entered the respondents' statements on DNC. This influence could well vary by age. For example, younger women may prefer smaller or larger families than older women. This does not represent a response error or bias in the DNC variable, but rather suggests that the age variable might be incorporated into the analysis to measure (and control for) a cohort effect in the responses.

There may be some bias toward women (especially older women) who state DNC close to their present number of surviving children, since any other response represents direct and observed evidence of a lack of success in achieving DNC. Thus, variables such as surviving children (CS) or children ever born (CEB) may enter significantly (and positively) as independent determinants of DNC, even though such measures are not attractive as explanatory variables *a priori*. Indeed, to the extent that CS or CEB do enter significantly in such statistical analyses, there is some evidence confirming the possible importance of response error and bias in explaining the DNC variable. One would expect that the importance of this bias would increase with age, and thus an interaction term between CS and AGEW might capture some of its influence. Whether such a variable adequately controls for response error, thereby permitting the true DNC influence to be revealed, is problematical.

The veracity of the DNC variable has been analyzed at length by M. S. A. Issa, who examines the consistency of the DNC responses to alternative hypotheses of behavior with respect to this measure. With specific reference to Egyptian data, he concludes "...the evaluation results are reassuring and they enhance the credibility of the information collected in the NFS (1974-1975) on desired family size in Egypt."[20] While we do not improve upon his research design to address this issue, we do expect the RFS to provide data at least as reliable as those found in the NFS.

The behavioral variables of interest in explaining DNC include measures of human capital (educational attainment of the wife and husband) and physical capital (personal and real assets). Education incorporates a positive income effect and a negative substitution effect. The negative substitution effect is likely to be larger for women (who bear the primary responsibility for childrearing) than for men. Education is also often taken as a measure of tastes and attitudes. It is commonly hypothesized that more educated parents possess tastes for smaller families.

Assets also possess both income and substitution effects. On the one hand, they permit larger families (an income effect); on the other hand, their consumption represents competition with the consumption of child services (a negative substitution effect). The *form* of the asset is significant. Personal assets are likely to be competitive with children. In contrast, real assets not only provide a flow of income to the household (and thereby permit the consumption of more children *and* other goods and services), but also this income flow may itself increase with the availability of child labor. Real assets and child services may therefore be complementary expenditures. We therefore hypothesize that personal assets will exert a smaller (possibly negative) influence on DNC than real assets, where the influcnce could even be positive.

Our basic model of DNC is presented as equation 8.5, which incorporates the primary behavioral variables of interest: education and assets.

$$[8.5]\quad \underset{}{DNC} = \underset{(55.36)}{4.61} - \underset{(-4.36)}{.49WE2} - \underset{(-2.38)}{.54WE3} - \underset{(-2.47)}{.27HE2} - \underset{(-1.31)}{.24HE3}$$

$$- \underset{(-4.03)}{.70HE4} - \underset{(-2.14)}{.10ASSETP} + \underset{(1.42)}{.05ASSETR} - \underset{(-.95)}{.09ELEC}$$

$r^2 = .025$
t values in parentheses

These variables enter as expected. The negative effect dominates for the education variable and this effect is larger for women than for men at comparable levels of education.[21] Interestingly, personal assets possess a negative sign, and real assets a positive sign (90 percent, one-tailed test). This result is consistent with the findings for CEB as well. In general, economic progress will reduce DNC, especially if the progress is tilted toward the provision of educational services and facilitates the purchase of personal assets. Programs of agricultural development that place a premium on child labor will work in the opposite direction.

As noted above, we expect some response error and bias to be incorporated in the DNC variable, as well as the possible existence of a cohort effect measured by age. It is therefore appropriate to determine if our basic findings presented in equation 8.5 are robust with respect to these hypothesized additional influences on DNC. Some evidence pertaining to this issue is provided in equation 8.6

which incorporates AGEW (age of wife) and CS (surviving children) as explanatory variables.

[8.6] DNC = 4.39 - .50WE2 - .45WE3 - .25HE2 - .20HE3
(25.03) (-4.48) (-1.99) (-2.47) (-1.10)

- .57HE4 - .11ASSETP + .03ASSETR - .18ELEC
(-3.25) (-2.37) (.86) (-2.01)

-.02AGEW + .25CS
(-2.75) (10.65)

r^2 = .061
t values in parentheses

Both AGEW and CS enter as statistically significant variables in the regression, although age enters with a negative sign. The most important result for the present analysis, however, is that the education and asset variables are at least as significant in the augmented model as in the basic model. Thus, our conclusions based on the results in equation 8.5 appear to be unaffected by the existence of possible response-error and cohort effects.

The results for desired number of children for rural Egypt as a whole are broadly the same in Upper and Lower Egypt considered separately. There are two notable differences. First, as seen in appendix equations A.45 - A.47, 1.16 more children are desired per household in Upper Egypt. Second, real assets exert a relatively larger positive impact on DNC in Lower Egypt. The desires for larger families in Upper Egypt are not derived simply from the role of children as productive agents in this area. These desires must be influenced considerably by cultural and religious values in specific regions.

As an exploratory inquiry, and with awareness of the ambiguities surrounding the measure of DNC, we may still compare this measure with the surviving children (CS) variable to ascertain whether there is an excess demand (DNC - CS > 0) or an excess supply (DNC - CS < 0) of children for each household. Furthermore, it would be interesting to determine whether this excess demand or supply is related to other key variables of interest. Table 8.2 provides some information on these relationships. Based only on the experience of those women who are toward the end of their childbearing span

Table 8.2 Excess Demand and Supply of Children

Characteristics[a]	Excess Demand[b] (Supply Constrained)			Equilibrium			Excess Supply[b]			Total	
	Mean No. Children	N	%	Mean No. Children	N	%	Mean No. Children	N	%	Mean No. Children	N
Total	3.12	402	100	0	363	100	-2.93	541	100	-.26	1307
Upper	3.28	263	65.3	0	179	49.3	-2.61	191	35.3	.58	633
Lower	2.79	140	34.7	0	184	50.7	-3.12	350	64.7	-1.04	674
Wife's Education[c]											
Illiterate											
Total	3.10	352	33.4	0	300	28.5	-2.91	402	38.1	-.07	1054
Upper	3.20	286	44.4	0	153	28.8	-2.58	143	26.9	.73	532
Lower	2.90	116	22.2	0	147	28.2	-3.09	259	49.6	-.89	522
Some Education											
Total	3.22	51	20.2	0	63	24.9	-3.01	139	54.9	-1.01	253
Upper	4.04	27	26.7	0	26	25.7	-2.71	48	47.5	-.21	101
Lower	2.29	24	15.8	0	37	24.3	-3.18	91	59.9	-1.54	152
Husband's Education[c]											
Illiterate											
Total	3.14	319	34.4	0	264	28.4	-2.90	345	37.2	0	928
Upper	3.28	213	44.7	0	134	28.1	-2.56	130	27.3	.77	477
Lower	2.85	106	23.5	0	130	28.8	-3.10	215	47.7	-.81	451
Some Education											
Total	3.04	84	22.2	0	99	26.1	-3.01	196	51.7	-.88	379
Upper	3.32	50	32.1	0	45	28.8	-2.72	61	39.1	0	156
Lower	2.62	34	15.2	0	54	24.2	-3.13	135	60.5	-1.50	223
Electricity											
No											
Total	3.25	272	36.0	0	229	30.3	-2.87	254	33.6	.21	755
Upper	3.52	201	44.2	0	127	27.9	-2.56	127	27.9	.84	455
Lower	2.51	71	23.7	0	102	34.0	-3.17	127	42.3	-.75	300

Table 8.2 (continued)

Characteristics[a]	Excess Demand[b] (Supply Constrained)			Equilibrium			Excess Supply[b]			Total	
	Mean No. Children	N	%	Mean No. Children	N	%	Mean No. Children	N	%	Mean No. Children	N
Yes											
Total	2.83	131	23.7	0	134	24.3	-3.00	287	52.0	-.89	552
Upper	2.54	62	34.8	0	52	29.2	-2.72	64	36.0	-.09	178
Lower	3.09	69	18.4	0	82	21.9	-3.08	223	59.6	-1.26	374
Personal Assets											
No Assets											
Total	3.15	192	36.3	0	156	29.5	-2.81	181	34.2	.18	529
Upper	3.23	143	43.5	0	93	28.3	-2.69	93	28.3	.64	329
Lower	2.90	49	24.5	0	63	31.5	-2.93	88	44.0	-.58	200
Some Assets[d]											
Total	3.09	211	27.1	0	207	26.6	-3.00	360	46.3	-.55	778
Upper	3.35	120	39.5	0	86	28.3	-2.54	98	32.2	.50	304
Lower	2.74	91	19.2	0	121	25.5	-3.17	262	55.3	-1.23	474
Real Assets											
No Assets											
Total	2.96	82	37.1	0	67	30.3	-3.03	72	32.6	.11	221
Upper	2.88	64	47.4	0	38	28.1	-2.73	33	24.4	.70	135
Lower	3.28	18	20.9	0	29	33.7	-3.28	39	45.3	-.80	86
Some Assets[d]											
Total	3.16	321	29.6	0	296	27.3	-2.92	469	43.2	-.33	1086
Upper	3.42	199	40.0	0	141	28.3	-2.59	158	31.7	.55	498
Lower	2.74	122	20.7	0	155	26.4	-3.09	311	52.9	-1.07	588

a The sample is ever-married women 35 years or over.
b Excess demand for children is the positive difference between the number "desired" and the number surviving (DNC - CS); excess supply is the negative of this difference.
c The no certificate and at least primary certificate education categories have been combined because of small numbers in the latter category.
d Ownership of "some" personal assets and "some" real assets pertains to the ownership of one or more items.

(those 35 or older), table 8.2 reveals some intriguing results.

For all of rural Egypt, roughly an equal proportion of the women 35 years or more are in the three childbearing states (excess demand, 31 percent; excess supply, 41 percent; equilibrium, 28 percent). Thus, quite surprisingly, almost one-third of the entire rural population is "supply constrained" by this measure; 31 percent of thc women desire more surviving children than they are able to obtain.[22] Of equal interest, the quantitative magnitude of this deficit in the number of children is large--3.12 children per family on average. While these results may be explained by large family size "desires," a significant portion of the explanation lies in the high child mortality in the rural area and the possibility that many families do not have the capacity to produce as many children as they desire.

This interpretation takes on greater force when considering the results for Upper and Lower Egypt separately. Again, considering only the aggregate results by region, Upper Egypt has an excess demand for children (0.58 child on average) while Lower Egypt has an excess supply (-1.04 children on average). It is not surprising, then, that contraceptive use is low in Upper Egypt, since a relatively large number of families have an excess demand for children. This excess demand is maintained on average for the region as a whole, while the opposite is the case for Lower Egypt.

What explains the likelihood that a family has an excess demand for children, i.e., that a family is in a situation of being supply constrained? Table 8.2 provides some relevant information by showing the numbers and proportions of the families in various child-demand states as related to different household attributes. Instead of examining these results variable by variable, we have elected to summarize the findings by compiling a set of regressions which reveal how each of the independent variables is related to the three child-demand states in the three geographic areas (total, Upper, and Lower rural Egypt). These results are presented in appendix table A.6.[23]

Interestingly, with one minor exception, the variables have little individual influence on whether or not a family has an "equilibrium" number of children. A somewhat similar result is found for the equations that explain excess demand and supply, with two notable exceptions. First, excess demand (i.e., a supply constraint) is less likely in those households in which women have some education and for households that own real assets, although these impacts are found only in Upper Egypt. The education impact was anticipated; the real-asset result was not. We expected households with real assets to desire more children and, as a result, reveal a greater excess demand. Evidently the households in Upper Egypt are able to fulfill their family size desires more successfully as their ownership of real assets increases (an income effect?). Second, those households most likely to have an excess supply of children are those in which family members are fairly well educated (especially in Lower Egypt), those in which there are real assets (Upper Egypt), and those with electricity. It is these households where family planning is most likely to be in demand. Indeed, these findings are generally consistent with those on contraceptive use.

Finally, in regressions that control for various asset and education variables by region and examine the regional impact on child-demand states, the strongest single individual influence explaining differential child-demand states is region. Consequently, while most of the independent variables are of small statistical significance, the regional variable is not. This may indicate that cultural and environmental factors are important in explaining demographic behavior in Egypt and suggests that government population programs should take the regional variations into account.[24]

In sum, Egypt appears to be at a threshold state with respect to the potential effectiveness of family planning programs. On the one hand, there are at present substantial numbers of Egyptians for whom family planning is likely to be ineffective. On the other hand, there is an even larger proportion of the population where modern family planning methods should be in considerable demand. As educational and socioeconomic development proceed, the desired number of children (DNC) will decrease and the capacity of families to produce surviving children (CEB - CD) may increase, thereby shifting ever larger numbers of families into the excess supply state where family planning has some appeal.[25]

In light of these results, what general assessment can be made about the prospects for family planning in rural Egypt? By most standards, the results to date of family planning in rural Egypt have been disappointing. Prevalence rates are low and discontinuation rates are high. Can we therefore conclude that an upper limit has been reached in terms of the use of family planning services? We think not. At least 40 percent of the rural women in Egypt have more children than they would ideally seek. This group, a prime target for family planning, is more than three times the size of the group currently using contraceptives. In addition, many of the Egyptians who are among the 28 percent of families that ostensibly have the number of children they desire will, and do, practice some form of contraception (and as a result have a demand for family planning services).

Although there is at present a sizeable fraction of the rural populace that is supply constrained, there still exists a much larger number of families who could now or in the near future demand family planning services. Of course, whether this demand is operationally translated into actual use of modern contraceptives is quite another matter, and this depends in part on the "cost" of family planning as well as the efficiency and effectiveness of the service delivery system. This cost must be broadly viewed to include not only monetary and time outlays, but religious, psychological, and social factors as well. At any rate, over time the demand for family planning services will increase and the rate of this increase will depend significantly on the impact of education on family size attitudes, child mortality, and child supply, as well as the impact of socioeconomic development in general. These two issues will be addressed in chapters 9 and 10, respectively.

Without anticipating the detailed results of those chapters, we conclude that while family planning represents an important component of population policy in general, without socioeconomic development conducive to changing family size aspirations and rural mortality rates, major efforts to increase family planning in rural Egypt may be disappointing. However, an integrated population and development strategy which has an active family planning component could well be appropriate.[26] Fortunately, it is this integrated family planning and development strategy that presently commands substantial support among Egyptian policymakers.

9. THE EFFECTS OF EDUCATION ON FERTILITY

9.1 OVERVIEW AND SUMMARY

The present chapter examines the relationships between the education of the wife and fertility and family planning. The wife's educational attainment is taken as the independent variable, which works through various interrelated intermediate variables to influence fertility. Several of these relationships have already been examined in various parts of this study using regression and tabular analysis, but education per se was not highlighted. This chapter will focus on the education variable, using tabular presentations of the data, extending the analysis, and, simultaneously, relating these results to those discussed in other chapters of this study.

As we indicated in chapter 3, the education-fertility relationships are highly complex because of the nature of "education" as a variable itself. The complexity has been reviewed exhaustively by T. W. Schultz, and his assessment merits repeating:

> The education of parents, notably that of the mother, appears to be an omnibus. It affects the choice of mates in marriage. It may affect the parent's preferences for children. It assuredly affects the earnings of women who enter the labor force. It evidently affects the productivity of mothers in the work they perform in the household, including the rearing of their children. It probably affects the incidence of child mortality, and it undoubtedly affects the ability of parents to control the number of births. The task of specifying and identifying each of these attributes of the parents' education in the family context is beset with analytical difficulties....[1]

Although the relationship between education and fertility has been frequently studied, the precise pattern is still uncertain. In an extensive review of the available empirical evidence, S. H. Cochrane concludes "that the relation between education and fertility is not always inverse. The earlier generalization about such a relation probably resulted from scarcity of data in the poorest, least literate societies and in rural areas where the inverse relation is less likely to occur."[2] She further shows that education in urban areas is more likely to be inversely related to fertility than in rural areas. However, her literature review reveals that relatively fewer studies exist for rural than for urban areas, particularly in less literate societies.

J. M. Stycos has suggested that the relation between education and fertility tends to be more uniformly inverse in countries with higher levels of education.[3] Cochrane concurs by presenting evidence indicating that countries with an illiteracy rate over 60 percent [the case of rural Egypt] "show lower proportion of inverse results, but there are relatively few studies available for those countries."[4]

S. Timur has reviewed several empirical studies for countries in stage I of demographic transition, i.e., countries with high fertility and high mortality. She concludes that "the scattered evidence reviewed in relation to stage I countries reveals no cut and dried fertility-education pattern. Although for a few countries there is the semblance of a hump-backed curve with fertility highest for the intermediate educational categories, in others the relationship is negative, notably for the higher educational categories."[5]

Timur's conclusion conforms to the empirical results of the present study, which has found that those rural Egyptians with limited amounts of education appear to have higher levels of fertility than illiterate Egyptians, although those with more substantial educational levels have the lowest fertility rates. Previous studies on the fertility-education relationship in rural Egypt have also revealed this "hump-backed curve."[6] However, due to the "omnibus" nature of the education variable, these results need to be reexamined. Some researchers have failed to control for possible avenues through which education may have an affect on fertility. One important way, as indicated in chapter 5, is the deferral of marriage through increased age at marriage. Another avenue is through supply factors influencing fertility.[7] In this case, as noted in chapter 3, less educated women are more likely to be supply constrained than highly educated women. At low educational levels, one impact of education is to release these supply constraints through improved nutrition, health, and related factors. At a certain educational level, women are able to achieve their family size desires, and the impact of further education is more likely to deter completed family size. Other factors explaining this nonlinear relationship between education and fertility will also be explored.

The present chapter attempts to examine the education-fertility relationship within a more comprehensive framework by examining the influence of education on several intermediate variables. The education of the wife has been classified into three categories. The low category includes all illiterate women. Women with some formal education, but not with a primary school certificate, are classified in the middle category. Women with at least a primary certificate are classified in the high category. The majority of women (76.6 percent) are in the illiterate category; approximately 19.4 percent are in the no certificate category, and only 4.0 percent are in the at least primary certificate category.

Husbands are relatively better educated than their wives: 62.6 percent of the husbands are illiterate, 23.3 percent are in the no certificate category, and 6.0 and 8.1 percent hold a primary or at least a preparatory certificate, respectively. The interaction between the education of the wife and that of the husband is significant where 64.5 percent of the spouses have the same educational level, 27.7 percent of the husbands have an educational level higher than their wives, and 7.8 percent of the wives have an educational level higher than their husbands.

To summarize the main findings of the present chapter, we have learned that education:

1. increases age at first marriage for women who possess at least a primary education certificate;
2. has a slightly positive impact on children ever born at low educational levels of the wife (when adjusted for her current age);
3. has an insignificant direct impact on children ever born at higher educational levels, although it indirectly reduces children ever born at the educational levels through a delay in age at first marriage;

4. slightly reduces child deaths, but is invariant to pregnancy loss;
5. diminishes desired and ideal family size;
6. increases knowledge, acceptability, and use of modern contraceptive methods, and;
7. reduces incidence and duration of breastfeeding; however, education increases the incidence of prolonged breastfeeding among those who recognize it as a contraceptive method.

This set of findings presents a puzzle, the dimensions of which we have discussed earlier, and about which we can reach no firm conclusions. If education reduces the desire for children, increases contraceptive use, and reduces child deaths, why then do children ever born remain unaffected by, or even increase with education over ranges of the education continuum (from illiteracy to the primary certificate level)? There are several possible answers, and these have been discussed in chapters 5 and 6, but two are particularly interesting and merit pursuing in future research on Egypt. (We are inclined to downplay, but not reject, the hypothesis that the results are explained by differential recall rates by education, i.e., the hypothesis that the relative understatement of deaths diminishes with education. This is discussed in detail below.)

First, at low education levels the use of "modern" contraceptives may not be effective. This explanation of inefficient contraception, however, would only explain a lack of association between contraception and children ever born, not a positive relationship. On the other hand, a positive relationship could materialize if women were substituting a less efficient form of contraception (e.g., a "modern" technique) for a relatively efficient one (e.g., breastfeeding) as education rises. Modern contraceptives are usually considered to be more efficient than traditional techniques. This may well be the case at high educational levels. At low educational levels, however, women may not, for example, use the pill with great regularity and as a result breastfeeding could well constitute a more effective deterrent to pregnancy. It might be hypothesized, then, that the relative efficacy of contraception, as between the alternative techniques, varies systematically with educational levels. As shown in section 9.6, breastfeeding incidence among all ever-married women declines with the increase in educational levels. Whether this trend in rural Egypt represents an intended substitution in contraceptive forms (it may in part be biologically explained), and/or whether one form is relatively more effective than the other, has not been revealed by our study. Thus, the above speculation must be considered only as a testable hypothesis at this stage of demographic research in rural Egypt.

Second, another possible explanation for a positive fertility-education relationship may lie in the fact that at low educational levels some women desire more children than they are able to obtain--they are "supply constrained." These supply constraints may be eased with the provision of education. Moreover, age at first marriage may not be delayed at low levels of education, so the negative impact of AFM on CEB is nonexistent. (Chapter 8 has provided some tabulations on "excess supply" and "excess demand" for children, classified by mother's education level, which are generally consistent with this hypothesis.) At the same time, education diminishes the desire for children. When the difference between desired and actual family size becomes negative (i.e., when the supply constraint is relaxed), then attributes of education that work against large families take on an increasingly powerful role.

Neither of the above hypotheses is conclusively evaluated in this study. Our findings are useful in pointing out the possible existence of a "humped" fertility-education relationship, and in suggesting two hypotheses--also consistent with various findings in the present study--why education may over certain ranges stimulate births. We have, we think, provided substantial evidence to cast doubt on the hypothesis that the relationship between education and fertility is uniformly negative in rural Egypt. Identifying the reasons why a nonlinear relationship may exist must constitute one of the more important areas of future research in Egyptian demography.

9.2 WIFE'S EDUCATION AND AGE AT FIRST MARRIAGE

There is substantial evidence that educational attainment and female age at first marriage are negatively related. Most studies show a fairly strong direct relationship, "but the nature of this relationship is highly complex and the causal mechanisms as yet little understood."[8]

Table 9.1 presents the percentage distribution of ever-married women married before age 20 and now 20 or more by age at first marriage and educational level.[9]

Table 9.1 Women by AFM and Education

Wife's Education	Age at First Marriage			Total	Mean
	Less than 15	15-17	18+		
Illiterate	25.3	52.4	22.3	2139	16.2
No Certificate	24.9	51.9	23.2	538	16.2
Primary Cert. +	13.3	45.8	41.0	83	18.8
Total					
Number	686	1438	636	2760	16.3
Percentage	24.9	52.1	23.0	100	-

χ^2 is statistically significant at .001 level. The sample are those women who first married before the age of 20, and are now 20 or more.

It is seen that age at first marriage increases only for those women in the high educational category. (The mean age at marriage is 18.8 years for those with at least primary education as compared to 16.2 for the illiterate and no certificate categories.) An explanation of this nonlinear education-marriage age relationship cannot be obtained directly from our data. Withdrawing from school is related only partially to academic achievement, and is largely determined by parental decisions relating to their daughter's marriage. At any rate, having just "some" education (less than a primary certificate) has little impact on marriage rates in rural Egypt.

9.3 WIFE'S EDUCATION AND CHILDREN EVER BORN

Based on unadjusted data, the results in table 9.2 show that education has a negative impact on fertility. Those women with primary education or more reveal the lowest level of fertility. The same pattern is maintained after adjusting for age at first marriage. However, after standardization for current age, a different pattern emerges where the adjusted mean CEB for women with some education (4.48) is slightly higher than for the mean CEB for illiterate women (4.24). Only women with at least a primary education certificate reveal a lower fertility level (3.95). These results obtain some support from the 1972 study, the 1974/75 National Fertility Survey analyzed by Sayed and El-Khorazaty, and Issa, and from the Menoufia Governorate survey analyzed by

Table 9.2 CEB by Age and Education of Wife

Current Age	Wife's Education						N
	Illiterate		No Certificate		Primary Cert. +		
	Mean	N	Mean	N	Mean	N	
1979 RFS							
15-19	.66	248	.78	75	.14	14	337
20-24	1.94	526	2.09	172	1.51	41	739
25-29	3.39	583	3.52	153	3.04	46	782
30-34	4.93	474	5.15	103	4.43	30	607
35-39	5.95	435	6.32	105	5.92	12	552
40-44	6.59	368	7.29	59	6.75	8	435
45-49	7.43	299	7.53	70		5	374
Total Unadjusted	4.34	2933	4.21	737	3.17	156	3826
Adjusted (Age)	4.24		4.48		3.95		
Adjusted (AFM)	4.33		4.20		3.79		
Adjusted (Age & AFM)[a]	4.23		4.43		4.53		
1972 Survey[b]							
Unadjusted	5.73	966	5.73	78	3.86	56	1100
Adjusted (Age)	5.67		5.84		4.71		
1970 Gadalla Survey[c]							
Unadjusted	5.63	3774	4.42	346	3.57	208	4328
Adjusted (Age)	5.42		5.79		5.42		

[a] Due to the sensitivity of direct standardization to cells with small number of observations, indirect standardization was used when adjustment is made for two variables (age and AFM). See note 5, chapter 5.

[b] The 1972 surveys were conducted in three Lower Egyptian Governorates (rural areas only). A. M. Khalifa and M. Abdel-Kader (1981a).

[c] Gadalla's survey was conducted only in rural areas of Menoufia Governorate. S. M. Gadalla (1978).

Gadalla.[10] Our RFS results, and those of the other three studies, reveal a nonlinear relationship between education and children ever born when controlling for only current age. This nonlinear relationship may be due to the small number of women (4 percent of all ever-married women) with at least a primary education certificate. Alternatively, recall lapse in accounting for child deaths may be cited as another reason. However, table 9.2 shows that the nonlinear relationship holds for *all* seven age groups, not just for older women. Moreover, the relationship holds for Upper and Lower Egypt, and for almost all age groups in these two regions.

When standardization is made for both current age and age at first marriage, a third pattern emerges where the adjusted mean CEB increases with education from 4.23 to 4.43 to 4.53 for illiterate, no certificate, and at least a primary certificate education categories, respectively. These results may appear to be inconsistent with those in chapter 6 where multiple regression analysis showed that education at all levels exerted no statistically significant impact on CEB. There are two reasons for the discrepancy in the findings between chapters 6 and 9. First, it can be shown that the positive impact of education on CEB in table 9.2 is not statistically significant. (This was done by replicating the model in table 9.2 with multiple regression analysis and employing standard tests of significance.) Thus, the basic findings of the two chapters are indeed consistent--education has little or no impact on CEB. Moreover, this experiment highlights the notable caution one must exercise in interpreting tabular results. Second, and equally important, when more variables are added to the analysis, as was done in chapter 6, the findings change. In particular, the education of the wife is correlated with the education of her husband and with the ownership of personal assets. When "control" is additionally made for these intervening influences on CEB, the residual CEB-education relationship is altered. It should be further noted that the methods of controlling for intervening impacts of education are important, and in some instances more endogeneity might be added to the framework. This line of inquiry could be productively explored in future studies in Egyptian demography.

The effect of little education on fertility may also be measured by an index *U*, defined as the ratio of cumulative marital fertility of women with less than 6 years of education (no certificate category) to that of illiterate women[11] for different marriage duration categories. (This index is useful since marriage duration differs among women in different education levels.) Table 9.3 shows the fertility effect of little education by duration since first marriage. The value of *U* will be greater than 1 if little education has a positive effect on fertility. For all ever-married women and for all marriage duration categories, the values of *U* exceed unity, although as with the findings in table 9.2, it is not clear whether these results are statistically significant. Thus, using this measure,

Table 9.3 Fertility Effect of Little Education on CEB

Duration Since First Marriage	Wife's Education			Total		*U* Values[a]
	Illiterate	No Cert.	Prim. Cert. +	Mean	N	
<5	0.83	1.00	0.93	0.88	760	1.20
5-9	2.66	2.77	2.87	2.70	778	1.04
10-14	4.42	4.45	4.66	4.44	648	1.01
15-19	5.37	5.61	5.39	5.42	563	1.04
20-24	6.53	6.94	7.62	6.60	484	1.06
25+	7.48	7.80		7.55	587	1.04
Total						
Unadjusted	4.34	4.21	3.17			
Adjusted (Marriage Duration)	4.22	4.42	4.27			1.05

[a] See text for a discussion of this index.

little education appears to have a positive effect on fertility. At any rate, as suggested by Jain, the fertility effect of little education might be a function of the illiteracy level and the fertility of illiterate women.[12] Our data show that the illiteracy level is higher among women with higher marriage duration. Changes in marital fertility also depend, as shown later, on shifts in the use and effectiveness of breastfeeding and contraceptive methods.

The interaction between wife's and husband's education and its impact on fertility also sheds some light on the education-fertility relationships. Table 9.4 shows the mean CEB for all ever-married women by wife's and husband's education. For illiterate wives or illiterate husbands, the mean CEB declines systematically with the increase in the educational level of the spouse. However, for wives or husbands with no certificate, the mean CEB increases with the increase in the educational level of the spouse until the primary certificate level and then decreases. For wives and husbands holding at least a primary certificate, the nonlinear relationship between education and fertility is maintained. These results suggest that the increase in educational levels of the spouses to a medium level (no certificate) is associated with an increase in fertility. However, achieving at least a primary certificate level of education of both parents results in a depressing effect on fertility.

Education may have an indirect effect on fertility through its relationships to the ownership of personal and real assets. As noted

Table 9.4 CEB by Education of Wife and Husband

Wife's Education	Husband's Education				Total
	Illiterate	No Cert.	Prim. Cert.	Prep. Cert. +	
Illiterate	4.47	4.17	3.88	3.38	4.34
No Certificate	4.31	4.34	4.41	3.42	4.21
Prim. Certificate +	3.79	4.74	3.50	2.35	3.17
Total	4.45	4.24	4.00	3.13	4.27

in chapters 5 and 7, there is a fairly consistent inverse (direct) relationship between personal asset ownership and fertility (use of modern contraceptives); the opposite is the case with the ownership of real assets. Could it be that these asset-fertility and asset-contraceptive use relationships are in part related to education? In particular, possibly the "taste" for personal assets increases with education, and that part of the personal asset-fertility and contraceptive use relationships is the result of increasing educational levels. Or, as we have speculated above, possibly the ownership of personal assets is "competitive" with having large famililies. Table 9.5 presents information on asset ownership by educational levels of the husband and wife. It is seen that personal assets increase systematically with education and that there is no apparent relationship of real asset ownership and education levels. Thus, the personal asset relationship to CEB and contraceptive use could well be due in part to a "taste" effect associated with education. Moreover, our interpretation of real assets as a proxy for an "income" effect, where real asset ownership is complementary with large families, is also clarified by the results in table 9.5.

In sum, the results of this section reveal that education does not appear to have a statistically significant impact on CEB, although the direction of the relationships, even if insignificant, is quite sensitive to the type of control that is made for intervening influences of education. These findings suggest that it would be productive to move to models where the intervening influences of education are explicitly and endogenously taken into account. (The theoretical basis of this suggestion is summarized in chapter 3, section 3.5.) Unfortunately, the RFS data show little variation in the education variable, and moreover, the categorization of this

Table 9.5 Asset Ownership by Education of Wife and Husband

Education	Personal Assets	Real Assets
Wife's Education		
Illiterate	0.81	1.56
No Certificate	1.15	1.83
Primary Certificate +	2.24	1.71
Husband's Education		
Illiterate	0.07	1.55
No Certificate	1.02	1.72
Primary Certifcate	1.46	1.63
Preparatory Certificate +	2.12	1.78
Total	0.94	1.62

variable is quite rough (only three discrete categories are available). Thus, at the present time more sophisticated modeling does not appear appropriate to the data.

9.4 WIFE'S EDUCATION, PREGNANCY LOSS, AND CHILD MORTALITY

It is plausible that more educated women have lower rates of pregnancy loss and higher rates of survival of their live born children. Table 9.6 presents means and ratios of pregnancy loss and children deceased (both unadjusted and adjusted by age and age at first marriage) for the three educational levels. Dividing pregnancy loss and child loss by CEB provides two meaningful ratios to measure these attributes since both phenomena are strongly related to CEB. Adjustments by age and/or age at marriage are also conducted since they are highly correlated with both losses.

The results for both measures are the same. In particular, with reference to the loss ratios, and especially those where control has been made for age and age at first marriage, it is seen that the impact of education is quantitatively small and likely insignificant. For pregnancy loss, moving from illiterate to some education and then to primary certificate education yields ratios of .13, .12, and .12, respectively; comparable figures for child loss are .20, .19, and .17. The latter results accord with those in chapter 6, where it was also found that child deaths are largely invariant to household

Table 9.6 Pregnancy and Child Loss by Education of Wife

Items	Education			Total
	Illiterate	No Cert.	Prim. Cert. +	
		A. MEANS		
Pregnancy Loss[a]				
Unadjusted	.45	.51	.29	.46
Adjusted (Age)	.45	.55	.38	
Adjusted (AFM)	.45	.51	.31	
Adjusted (Age & AFM)	.47	.44	.32	
Child Loss[b]				
Unadjusted	1.05	.98	.59	1.02
Adjusted (Age)	1.02	1.04	.77	
Adjusted (AFM)	1.30	1.19	1.07	
Adjusted (Age & AFM)	1.05	.96	.66	
Number of Cases	2930	740	155	3825
		B. RATIOS		
Pregnancy Loss[c]				
Unadjusted	.13	.12	.13	.13
Adjusted (Age)	.13	.12	.14	
Adjusted (AFM)	.13	.12	.10	
Adjusted (AGE & AFM)	.13	.12	.12	
Child Loss[c]				
Unadjusted	.20	.20	.15	.20
Adjusted (Age)	.20	.20	.13	
Adjusted (AFM)	.20	.20	.17	
Adjusted (Age & AFM)	.20	.19	.17	
Number of Cases[d]	2614	670	129	3413

[a] Includes all pregnancies that did not end in a live birth.
[b] Includes only deaths of live born children.
[c] Pregnancy and child loss ratios are defined by dividing each loss respectively by CEB.
[d] Defined only for women with CEB>0.

attributes, including the education of the wife.

A convincing explanation is not readily available for the negligible impact of education on pregnancy loss and child deaths, unless we accept the above speculation about the possible effect of environmental factors and conclude that education has a relatively small negative impact in the low ranges of this variable. Indeed, it is interesting to note that there is almost no variation in child deaths as one moves from the illiterate to the no certificate educational level, but that the CEB relationship displayed in table 9.2 changes in this range. We are, therefore, inclined to downplay the data-bias explanation of the CEB results, although clearly some bias is possible and may explain a portion of the findings in the CEB-education relationship. Another possible explanation would rest on the finding below that the prevalence and length of breastfeeding diminishes with education. In rural Egypt other forms of feeding may be more hazardous to infant health. However, whether or not increased education brings improvements in nutrition and health practices which are sufficient to offset the increased hazards of alternative forms of infant feeding is an open empirical issue.[13]

One of the possible impacts of child mortality on fertility as cited in the literature is through the "insurance effect," which is a response to a change in child mortality in the community. Other results of the present survey have revealed a statistically significant relationship between wife's educational level and her perception about child mortality trends in the community. The proportion of women who perceive a decline in infant mortality over time increases with education (43 to 51 to 60 percent, respectively, for the three levels of education). Furthermore, the survey data reveal a direct relationship to education in responses to a question that women should now have fewer children because child mortality is declining. However, previous results in the present study also suggest that for some women fertility may be supply constrained, and the actual "insurance effect" may be small in magnitude. Several independent tests in chapters 6 and 8 have been provided to support this interpretation. In other words, it seems that although more educated women have stronger perceptions about the declining level of infant mortality, this recognition may not be translated, as yet, into declining fertility behavior.

9.5 WIFE'S EDUCATION AND ATTITUDES TOWARD FERTILITY AND FAMILY PLANNING

This section presents information on the relationships between the education of rural Egyptian women and their attitudes towards several aspects of childbearing: desired and ideal family size, desire to cease childbearing, child spacing, and contraceptive approval. As has been seen from the results above, and as will be seen from some that follow, the expressed attitudes of women may not be fully translated into revealed behavior. On the other hand, we believe that a guarded interpretation of these data on attitudes provides additional insights into revealed behavior, which is the primary focus of the present study.

Table 9.7 shows that the education of women, even the smallest amount, alters their attitudes toward a smaller family size. This relationship is inverse for both ideal and desired number of children. For example, the mean ideal number of children (adjusted by age) decreases from 3.92 to 3.41 to 3.32 for illiterate to the at least primary educational level. The same pattern is found when means are adjusted by number of living children instead of age.

The desired number of children is based on a question phrased in terms of the respondent's own position on the total number of children she would like to have. Thus, it is likely that women who have large families will state that they want more to the extent that desired fertility is the reflection of their fertility performance, i.e., women who have a large number of children are more likely to state a desired number equal to that. The differences may therefore be exaggerated. The mean number of children desired shows a clear inverse pattern with education. The mean is 4.41 for illiterate women, and decreases to 3.85 and 3.61 for women in the two higher levels of education (adjusted means).

Measures on desired and ideal family size are broad in scope, but are useful as summary indices of women's aspirations. There are two additional and more specific measures available in the data, which serve to clarify the family size plans of the wife: desires to cease childbirth, and preferences (and reasons) for the spacing of children. We consider each of these measures in turn.

As regards the desire to cease childbearing, the trend by educational level is positive, although the differences are small. Data from the RFS reveal that while 48.8 percent of illiterate

Table 9.7 Ideal and Desired Children by Education of Wife

Items	Educational Level			Total
	Illiterate	No Cert.	Prim. Cert. +	
Ideal No. of Children				
Unadjusted	3.93	3.41	3.24	3.78
Adjusted (Age)	3.92	3.41	3.32	(2629)
Desired No. of Children				
Unadjusted	4.49	3.83	3.45	4.32
Adjusted (Age)	4.41	3.85	3.61	(3670)

( ) = total number of women who provided a numerical answer and not, for example, "up to God."

women wish to cease childbearing, this prevalence rises only to 56.6 and 59.5 percent among women with no certificate and at least primary educational levels, respectively (percentages adjusted by current age). These small differences may be surprising given the wide variances in desired and ideal family size by educational level. On the other hand, 59.5 percent of the women with at least primary education desire to cease childbearing with an average of less than three living children, while 48.8 percent of illiterate women wish to cease childbearing with an average of about four living children. Thus the wider variance in family size desires can be partially reconciled with the narrower variance in the wishes to cease childbearing by taking into account the range of numbers of children desired when childbearing is to cease.

Another influence on completed family size is child spacing. Data from the RFS reveal that as education increases, the attitudes of wives shift toward larger spacing intervals. Illiterate women expressed a desire for an average of 2.3 years as an ideal spacing period between each two live births; the mean intervals increase to 2.4 and 2.7 for the two higher educational levels, respectively.

The reasons for these spacing preferences are interesting and important. Higher educated women responded in higher proportion that the longer the interval between live births, the better the health of the mother and the child. Furthermore, when women were asked about their opinions on the effect of the number of children born on the health of the mother and on the care and health of the child, education revealed a clear impact. In all three areas the relationship is significant (χ^2 is statistically significant at the .01 level). As shown in table 9.8, more educated women indicated in higher proportions that more children born makes all three--mother's health, children's care, and children's health--worse.

These results help to explain rural Egyptian family size behavior. In particular, it is seen that one of the impacts of education is to create an awareness of the relationships between family size and health. Yet, as shown above, actual family size does not diminish at low levels of education--or at least until a threshold educational level is reached. If, in fact, there are supply constraints on family size at low educational levels, the results of the present section suggest that these constraints will be relaxed by education through the lowering of desired family size *and* the increasing awareness of the health costs of larger families. Thus, while observed children ever born does not decline at low education levels, the effective supply-constraint gap (which is not revealed in the data presented here but which is presented in chapter 8) may be closing through the application of ever increasing amounts of education.

9.6 WIFE'S EDUCATION AND CONTRACEPTIVE USE

Contraceptive use, yet another intermediate influence affecting fertility, depends on several factors, such as the knowledge of methods, approval of use, and availability of methods. This section examines attitudes on contraceptive use, and then takes up revealed behavior of actual contraceptive use.

Table 9.9 presents the percentage of ever-married women who disapprove of using any contraceptive method, whether modern or traditional, by number of surviving children and educational level. The relationship between education and the percentage who disapprove of the use of contraception is inverse. However, overall disapproval is not high (25 percent). Among illiterate women, the percentage of disapproval is 28.6 percent; this proportion decreases to only 16.8 and 12.2 percent among women in the no certificate and at least primary education categories. Further, table 9.9 shows that resistance to approval of contraceptive use decreases as the number of living children increases, and this is true for all educational levels. We may conclude, then, that low levels of education do not pose as a notable constraint on attitudes toward

Table 9.8 Attitudes Toward Health and Care Issues by Family Size and Education

% Responded "Gets Worse" in Relationship to:	Education			Total
	Illiterate	No. Cert.	Prim. Cert. +	
Mother's Health	76.5	83.4	92.3	76.6
Children's Care	74.8	83.1	90.3	76.6
Children's Health	73.7	82.8	90.3	76.6
Number of Cases	2932	740	155	3827

Table 9.9 Disapproval of Contraceptive Use by Surviving Children and Education

Surviving Children	Education			Total	
	Illiterate	No Cert.	Prim. Cert. +	Percentage	N
<3	32.2	20.1	13.4	28.8	1626
3-5	27.3	16.8	9.8	24.7	1533
6+	23.2	7.9	*	20.2	670
Total					
Percentage	28.6	16.8	12.2	25.7	-
Number	2933	740	156	-	3829

* Less than 10 cases.

contraceptive use. Indeed, 72 percent of the illiterates do not disapprove of contraceptive use, and even with small amounts of education, this disapproval rate diminishes dramatically. It is particularly interesting that the nonlinearity in the disapproval rate is visible at low, as distinct from high, educational levels--a pattern different from that observed in various measures of revealed outcomes (e.g., children ever born). Why is it that attitudinal changes are more sensitive to education than actual behavioral changes? Again, the supply-constraint gap thesis offers an intriguing hypothesis to explain these results. While education, even at low levels, changes attitudes rather dramatically, the disequilibrium supply-constraint gap can still persist until a threshold level of education is reached.

Another variable that reveals differences by education of women relates to attitudes toward abortion and sterilization. Better educated women are more likely to approve of both. Among illiterate women, the percentages approving of abortion and sterilization are 5.4 and 9.5, respectively; these percentages rise to 8.8 and 19.6 for women with primary certificates. However, for the total rural area, approval of abortion and sterilization is generally low: 5.8 and 11.1 percent, respectively. These two techniques do not appear to offer much promise as means of birth control in rural Egypt.

Knowledge of contraceptive methods, especially the more effective techniques, is as essential as approval as a determinant of contraceptive use. Data from the RFS, as shown in chapter 7, section 7.2 and chapter 8, section 8.2.1, indicate a direct relation between education and knowledge of contraception. In general, knowledge of at least one modern method of contraception is high (87.4 percent). Among illiterate women, that percentage is 84.7; the rate increases to 95.8 and 98.1 percent among women with no certificate or at least a primary certificate. While the pill and IUD are the two modern methods known best (87.3 and 53.9 percent, respectively), prolonged breastfeeding comes in third place with 37.7 percent. Knowledge of prolonged breastfeeding as a contraceptive method increases from 35.1 percent among illiterate women to 44.9 and 54.5 percent for women with no certificate and with at least a primary certificate, respectively. In rural Egypt education does not appear to pose a notable constraint on knowledge of contraception. Interestingly, as was the case of attitudes toward contraception, the impact of education is comparatively strong at low levels. Indeed, the provision of relatively more advanced education appears to represent an unproductive strategy for changing family planning knowledge.

Most research into the relationships between education and contraceptive use indicates that better educated women use contraceptives more frequently and more effectively. Both ever use and current use can be examined in relation to education in the present study. Table 9.10 shows for each educational level the percentage of past and current users of modern and traditional methods of contraception. The percentage of ever users increases from 20.3 to 35.7 and to 40.7 as women rise from illiterate to no

Table 9.10 Use of Modern and Traditional Methods of Contraception by Education

Education	% Past Use		% Current Use		% Ever Use		N[c]
	Modern[a]	Traditional[b]	Modern	Traditional	Modern	Traditional	
Illiterate	9.6	2.4	10.7	2.8	20.3	5.2	2710
No Cert.	15.4	2.0	20.3	3.8	35.7	5.8	694
Prim. Cert. +	20.3	2.0	20.5	3.4	40.7	5.4	148
Total	11.2	2.3	13.0	3.0	24.2	5.3	3552

[a] Modern methods include pills, IUD, condoms, and sterilization.
[b] Traditional methods include creams, foam tablets, jelly, rhythm, breast-feeding, and others.
[c] Only currently married women.

certificate to at least primary educational levels, respectively. The same pattern is found for both current and ever users.

Two results from table 9.10 are particularly relevant to the analysis of rural Egyptian family planning. First, the contraceptive use rates among currently married women are low. A 25 percent rate of ever use of modern contraceptives and a 13 percent rate for current use are lower than would be expected from a family planning program of the historical length of Egypt's. Second, the nonlinear relationship of contraceptive use by education level appears at low levels of education. This finding is particularly notable since it represents the only revealed behavior in our study where the impact of small amounts of education appears to have changed attitudes at low education levels. Note that the proportion of ever-users rises by 15 percent in moving from illiterate to no certificate educational levels; it rises only an additional 5 percent when advancing to the at least primary educational level.

It may seem puzzling that although women at the no certificate educational level have more favorable attitudes towards lower fertility and family planning and tend to use contraceptives in higher proportions than illiterate women, the mean number of children ever born to these two groups of women is not significantly different. (There may be a slight increase in CEB.) Any interpretation of this result would represent only speculation. It may be hypothesized, however, that women in the no certificate educational level do not use contraceptives efficiently nor do they use them for prolonged periods.

An alternative interpretation would focus on the prevalence and length of breastfeeding for women at different levels of education. Prolonged breastfeeding does indeed play a major role in keeping fertility in check. Results from the RFS show that both the incidence and the duration of breastfeeding decline with increased education. The proportion of women who have never breastfed is slightly lower among illiterates, and this group engages in breastfeeding for a longer duration on average. For example, the rate of breastfeeding is 97.8, 97.1, and 97.4 for illiterate, no certificate, and at least primary educational levels, respectively. However, only 6.2 percent of ever-married women have ever used prolonged breastfeeding as a contraceptive method while recognizing its fertility depressing impact. The percentage increase is from 5.8 to 7.5 to 7.7 for the three educational levels, respectively (see section 7.3).

It is expected that the mean duration of breastfeeding will decline with increased modernization, including increased levels of education.[14] The RFS provides data on breastfeeding duration for the next to last and the last child for pregnant women, i.e., for the last closed birth interval. Mean breastfeeding duration was calculated for three groups of women: (1) all ever-married women with closed birth intervals (2,929 women representing about 76 percent of all ever-married women in the sample), (2) women who have heard of prolonged breastfeeding as a contraceptive method, and (3) women who have ever used prolonged breastfeeding as a contraceptive method. Table 9.11 shows the results for these three groups of women. The mean breastfeeding duration increases for those women who recognize it or used it as a contraceptive method. The mean increases from 18.6 months for all ever-married women to 18.9 to 20.2 months for women who knew or used prolonged breastfeeding as a contraceptive method. However, in all three groups of women the duration decreases as women move from illiterate to no certificate to at least primary certificate educational categories. Thus, the increase in the use of prolonged breastfeeding (as a means of contraception) with education is compensated, to some extent, by a decrease in the duration of three

Table 9.11 Breastfeeding Duration for Last Closed Birth Interval

Wife's Education	All Ever-married Women		Women Who Knew of Prolonged Breastfeeding as a Contraceptive		Used Prolonged Breastfeeding as a Contraceptive	
	Months	N	Months	N	Months	N
Illiterate	19.1	2247	19.6	827	20.6	169
No Certificate	17.1	577	17.2	278	19.4	53
Primary Cert. +	16.0	105	16.1	57	18.0	11
Total	18.6	2929	18.9	1162	20.2	233

months, on average, between the two extreme educational categories.

The above discussion leads to a hypothesis that could help explain either a lack of association between children ever born and low educational levels, or even a positive relationship. As education advances, women are effectively substituting one form of contraception for another. Whether this substitution is behaviorally or biologically determined cannot be ascertained from our data. However, the relative efficacy of the two methods of contraception may well play a role in determining observed children ever born. If the switch from "traditional" to "modern" methods resulted in lowered contraceptive efficacy on average, due to improper use or high discontinuation rates of modern techniques, then in certain ranges of the educational continuum, a positive relationship between CEB and contraceptive use could be observed. This result has been found not only for rural Egypt, but for other countries as well.[15] Clearly other explanations are possible for the nonlinear relationship between education and CEB, but this hypothesis concerning the relative efficacy of contraceptive methods certainly merits additional research and analysis. In a recent paper, A. K. Jain states that "whether or not the average marital fertility of women in a country would rise with advancements in female education would depend upon the relative shifts in levels and effectiveness of these two [breastfeeding and contraception] intermediate factors."[16] Thus, he concluded that this positive relationship does not imply an increase in demand for children and may be a temporary phenomenon.

9.7 POLICY SPECULATIONS

Women who want no more children are likely to practice contraception and possibly use modern contraceptive methods. This might be considered as "consistent behavior." On the other hand, the behavior of many women in the RFS may appear to be inconsistent. The causes of this apparent inconsistency may be quite rational, stemming from social and cultural sources. A relevant issue arises, however, as to the extent to which rural Egyptian women on average use modern contraceptives and in what way this use is related to education.

Table 9.12 shows that the proportion of currently married women, who are consistent insofar as they employ modern contraceptives to implement their desire to cease childbearing, rapidly increases with the educational level. While only 19.4 percent of illiterate currently married women who do not want more children use modern contraceptives, the percentage increases to 34.1 and 39.7 for women with no certificate and at least a primary certificate, respectively.

Part of the inconsistency may be temporary if nonusers have intentions to use contraceptives in the future. The proportions of women who have never used modern contraceptives but who intend future use are largely invariant to educational level (23.3, 20.2, and 23.3 percent for the three educational categories, respectively). However, there are clear differences in the proportions who do not intend future use. The proportion of women who do not want more children and who have no intention for future use of modern contraceptives decreases with education. The percentages are 35.5, 17.2, and 5.5 for illiterate, no certificate, and at least primary educational categories, respectively.

Overall, then, we observe that only a relatively small proportion of women who want no more children are using modern contraceptives (23.4 percent). Many who want no more children have used modern contraceptives in the past (16.9 percent) and, for some reason, are not presently using contraceptives. The percentages for traditional methods are 3.7 and 3.0, respectively. The majority of rural Egyptian women who desire no more children have never used

Table 9.12 Contraceptive Use by Desire for More Children and Education

<table>
<tr><th rowspan="2">Desire for More Children</th><th colspan="2">Never Users</th><th colspan="2">Past Users</th><th colspan="2">Current Users</th><th rowspan="2">N[a]</th></tr>
<tr><th>Intend</th><th>Do not</th><th>Modern</th><th>Traditional</th><th>Modern</th><th>Traditional</th></tr>
<tr><td>Want More</td><td></td><td></td><td></td><td></td><td></td><td></td><td></td></tr>
<tr><td>Illiterate</td><td>35.7</td><td>55.3</td><td>3.7</td><td>1.8</td><td>2.0</td><td>2.1</td><td>1232</td></tr>
<tr><td>No Cert.</td><td>47.2</td><td>36.4</td><td colspan="2">9.8</td><td colspan="2">6.7</td><td>286</td></tr>
<tr><td>Prim. Cert. +</td><td>57.4</td><td>20.6</td><td colspan="2">6.9</td><td colspan="2">4.4</td><td>68</td></tr>
<tr><td>All Who Want More</td><td>38.7</td><td>50.4</td><td>4.7</td><td>1.7</td><td>2.4</td><td>2.1</td><td>1586</td></tr>
<tr><td>Do Not Want More</td><td></td><td></td><td></td><td></td><td></td><td></td><td></td></tr>
<tr><td>Illiterate</td><td>23.3</td><td>35.5</td><td>15.4</td><td>3.1</td><td>19.4</td><td>3.3</td><td>1354</td></tr>
<tr><td>No Cert.</td><td>20.2</td><td>17.2</td><td>21.0</td><td>2.7</td><td>34.1</td><td>4.8</td><td>372</td></tr>
<tr><td>Prim. Cert. +</td><td>23.7</td><td>5.5</td><td colspan="2">26.0</td><td colspan="2">45.2</td><td>73</td></tr>
<tr><td>All Who Want No More</td><td>22.7</td><td>30.5</td><td>16.9</td><td>3.0</td><td>23.4</td><td>3.7</td><td>1799</td></tr>
<tr><td>Total</td><td></td><td></td><td></td><td></td><td></td><td></td><td></td></tr>
<tr><td>Percentage</td><td>29.8</td><td>40.7</td><td>11.2</td><td>2.3</td><td>12.0</td><td>3.0</td><td>100.0</td></tr>
<tr><td>Number</td><td>1059</td><td>1445</td><td>397</td><td>81</td><td>463</td><td>107</td><td>3552</td></tr>
</table>

[a] Currently married women.

modern contraceptives (53.2 percent), and of these, almost one-half do not intend to use contraceptives in the future. While increased education reduces opposition to contraceptive use and increases use prevalence, even at high educational levels, only 39.7 percent of women who want no more children are currently using modern contraceptives. It appears that education itself, while conducive to the use of modern contraceptive techniques, has not been sufficient to insure high prevalence rates in rural Egypt. This is particularly the case since the data presently considered pertain only to those desiring no more children.

For two reasons, a major government program to augment female education in rural Egypt as an avenue for population control is not likely to influence notably the number of children ever born in the foreseeable future. First, while our results indicate that family size desires decline and contraceptive use increases with increasing educational levels, CEB is little influenced except through marriage delay. And even here this influence is for a small group of relatively well-educated rural Egyptian women. In chapter 6 we also learned that the education of husbands may exert a positive influence on CEB. This may represent an "income effect" where children are desired in larger numbers in prosperous households. It may also represent the result of a supply constraint whereby some households with more-educated parents are able to have more children and, thus, are more effective in meeting their family size goals. The low rates of contraceptive use observed in the RFS are, thus, consistent with these interpretations which stress rational economic and social behavior.

A second reason for the relatively low effect of educational policy on children ever born relates to the timing of the impact. While, as noted above, education of parents appears to have a small impact on CEB, current educational policy applies not to parents, but to their children. The impact of education on CEB will therefore be long delayed.

These are rather pessimistic conclusions on the role of educational policy for population control. On the other hand, if in fact a number of rural Egyptian families are supply constrained, then one of the ways by which this constraint may be relaxed is through education, by (1) lowering family size desires, and (2) enabling families to produce more children. Other things being equal, there may be a "phase" of modernization with increasing educational levels where the impact of education on population is counter to national policy goals.[17]

To move toward an educational policy that is relatively consistent with population goals, it is critically important to obtain more detailed information on the underlying determinants of a possible supply-constraint gap, as well as information on the relative efficacy of alternative contraceptive technologies.[18] Unfortunately, our findings do not provide answers to these important issues. However, one of the contributions of the present study is to document clearly that simple policies such as universal education will not, by themselves, necessarily result in desired population outcomes.

Moreover, and most important, our study has now pinpointed a set of research questions which, if answered, are likely to have important repercussions for public policy. In technical terms, research must be increasingly oriented toward the determinants of natural fertility, using disequilibrium rather than equilibrium models of family size determination. Referring to the Easterlin model described in chapter 3, we must identify the determinants of the "switching point" between supply and demand phases of family size determination. Recently economists and demographers have begun to identify specific methodologies for confronting these issues. We hope that the findings of the present study encourage this empirical and theoretical development.

10. THE POPULATION AND DEVELOPMENT PROJECT: PROSPECTS FOR SUCCESS

10.1 PDP: OBJECTIVES AND SCOPE

Population policy in Egypt has evolved from its early exclusive emphasis on family planning to the present state where policymakers stress the importance of integrating population and development planning. As mentioned in chapter 2, this "comprehensive approach" to population policy is exemplified by the Population and Development Project (PDP), initiated by the Population and Family Planning Board (PFPB) in 1977. The PDP is a community-based program to reduce population growth through the manipulation of socioeconomic activities at the local level.[1] While the PDP provides improved family planning delivery systems, it also stimulates socioeconomic development in general, and those activities in particular that are believed to deter population growth and to improve population characteristics (e.g., health, education, women's employment).

The philosophy of the program is "clear and unassailable: (a) to involve all groups within the local community in self-help efforts for their own development; (b) to integrate population and development objectives at the level closest to the people concerned; (c) to utilize and strengthen existing local government institutions to achieve these objectives, by improving their representative character, by coordinating the executive committees and elected representatives, and by strengthening their capacity for planning, management, and evaluation of the results of their efforts; and (d) to support the process of decentralization of governmental authority to the governorate level and to the village councils."[2] Given this comprehensive approach to population-development programming, the PDP explicitly formulates activites to augment local management capabilities which are needed to develop and administer PDP activities. The aims of the PDP are threefold:

1. to promote family planning services,
2. to mobilize local resources and human participation to increase the pace of socioeconomic development, and
3. to upgrade management capabilities at the local level.

The PDP is more than a program of rural socioeconomic development. It introduces the population issue and family planning into all developmental activities with which it is involved. These activities include, for example, expanded education facilities, transportation and communication systems, health clinics, village cottage industries, and agricultural mechanization. Before PDP funding is provided to any of these areas, local government leaders and volunteers, who are organized to provide substantial local resources of money and time, set targets and programs for population growth reduction.

The development programs are themselves associated with elements of population reduction and characteristics in varying degrees. Cottage industries in villages, for example, are designed to offer rural women productive opportunities in villages as an alternative to childrearing and farm labor. Clinics provide not only traditional elements of health care, but also special services for maternal and child care. Communication services are designed to increase the opportunities of rural residents to participate in "urban" (village-level) life, such as the educational, health, family planning, and employment opportunities available there. Agricultural mechanization is offered in a format that increases the productivity of land while lowering the value of child labor on the farm. At every stage, these traditional developmental activities, through the administrative network organized by the PDP, are related to targets for reducing population growth and improving population characteristics.

10.2 PDP COVERAGE TO DATE

The PDP was initiated in Sharkia governorate in Lower Egypt in July 1977 and in Giza, Fayoum, and Beni Suef governorates in Upper Egypt on an experimental basis the following October. Twenty village councils (VCs) comprising 107 villages were covered. A village council typically constitutes a "mother village" and, on the average, four satellite villages. By September 1978, eleven governorates were partially covered, six in Lower Egypt and five in Upper Egypt. The VCs numbered 171 and represented 809 villages. By September 1979, the total number of VCs reached 287, including 1,491 villages with a population of around 7.5 million and representing 37 percent of the total rural population of Egypt. While the number of governorates remained at twelve, the PDP increased its coverage to 369 VCs by the end of April 1980, including 1,912 villages and a population of 9.7 million.

In October 1980, the project covered all the VCs and villages in eight out of the twelve governorates. The number of village councils reached 525, including 2,848 villages representing 57 percent of the total number of VCs and 72 percent of the total number of villages in Egypt. The number of persons covered by the project reached about 14 million, representing 70 percent of the total rural population in Egypt.[3] It is expected that the PDP will eventually cover not only all of the rural area, but also the country as a whole. However, the emphasis in the early eighties will be on strengthening and intensifying the PDP activities in the already existing village councils.

Since 1971, the UNFPA has assisted different types of population related activities in Egypt. Beginning in 1977, the "UNFPA has provided more assistance specifically directed towards the population and development project, which was considerably expanded in 1980."[4] The UNFPA support through 1980 amounted to about 3.2 million U.S. dollars, covering all local costs of 325 VCs, including incentive income payments[5] to the PDP central administration, coordinators, and extension workers, loans and grants, and socioeconomic projects. The USAID support, begun in 1980, covered the local costs of an additional 200 VCs and amounted to about 0.6 million dollars, incentive income payments to the PDP coordinators and extension workers, loans and grants, and socioeconomic projects. Starting in 1981 the Egyptian government allocated about 4.3 million dollars to the PDP for the fiscal year 1981/82.

10.3 PDP ORGANIZATION AND ACTIVITIES

The institutionalization of the PDP exists at three levels: (1) village (local), (2) governorate (regional), and (3) national (central). The PDP provides for coordinators at each of these levels, who act through various committees to plan and implement family planning and development efforts. These coordinators are critical to the success of the PDP and are provided training in population policy, fertility-socioeconomic interrelationships, and techniques of management.

Responsibilities vary according to level. Local coordinators, usually village headmen, typically possess a university degree, have been raised in a rural area, and are conversant with a wide range of rural activities and needs. Their responsibilities include planning, coordinating, and monitoring specific PDP activities on a day-to-day basis, insuring contraceptive supply, and supervising extension workers in the dissemination of family planning methods. Regional coordinators, responsible for about five village councils, make biweekly visits to identify problems, offer technical advice, and assist in project formulation and evaluation. Central coordinators deal largely with administrative aspects of project development and implementation and offer expertise and advice on a persuasive rather than a supervisory or authoritarian basis. The PDP is decentralized to a great degree, one of the keys to its potential success.

On the local level, a PDP Advisory Committee (PDPAC) is established for each village council. The PDPAC consists ot government-appointed officials who are heads of various government offices in the VC, elected officials from the village councils including representatives from all satellite villages, and recognized opinion leaders from among women, youth, and elders. The PDPAC coordinates the activities of all officials, seeks to avoid contlicts through integration, and sets a common goal to be achieved. More specifically, the committee is responsible for insuring a sufficient stock of contraceptives, promoting family planning, collaborating with health officials in villages, supervising and monitoring community developmental efforts, solving program problems, and collecting data for evaluation. The PDPAC meets once a month on an informal basis where collective discussions take place to encourage wide participation of all concerned individuals. Regularly scheduled meetings and progress reports within and between all levels bind the entire network together.

Volunteer female (extension) workers, known as Raiyda Riyfia (which in Arabic means "rural pioneer"), are recruited by the PDPAC from the village where they will be employed. The Raiyda

Riyfia (RR) makes visits to the homes of eligible women (those of reproductive age) to encourage contraceptive practice. She offers information, answers questions, corrects misunderstandings, supplies contraceptives, and collects data. There is at least one RR in each village. The plan is to assign not more than 250 eligible women to each RR so that she can visit them once a month to follow up cases of discontinuation of contraceptive use.

Administratively, the PDP is headed by the Director of the Department of Population and Development at the PFPB. He has four assistants. On the governorate level, there is a regional council for population and family planning headed by the governor. Members of the council are all regional leaders from the governorate. In mid 1979, at the time of the RFS, 287 VCs were covered by the project. Manpower serving at different levels included 5,015 PDPAC members, 1,471 RRs, and 574, 56 and 12 local, regional, and central coordinators, respectively. By the end of 1980, when 525 VCs were covered, the five numbers, respectively, were 9,330, 2,428, 1,050, 77, and 12.

The PDP promotes small-scale socioeconomic projects appropriate to the village, with the objective of offering new ways of life that may influence values and attitudes. This, in turn, may eventually reduce family size norms and increase family planning acceptance and use. Examples of projects and objectives include: increasing the socioeconomic status of women, improving health, sanitation, nutrition, electricity, education, transportation and communication, agricultural mechanization, and cottage industries. These projects are meant also to upgrade the socioeconomic status of the population, to "urbanize" the Egyptian village and, hence, to discourage migration to the major urban centers.

The socioeconomic projects are to be PDPAC initiated to ensure community commitment and participation. Local communities are to participate in proposing, developing, financing, and managing the projects. Local financial participation must be at least 25 percent of the total budget, and local management must be at least 50 percent of the total project board. The PDP supplies technical advice when needed and an interest-free loan when communities cannot raise the required capital.

By mid-1979, about 176 project proposals had been submitted to the Department of Population and Development, where they were first screened to insure that an adequate population dimension and commitment had been established. Those projects passing the test were then screened from an economic perspective by the Organization for Development of Egyptian Villages (ORDEV). Finally, a joint committee with representatives from the PFPB and the ORDEV made final approval or rejection, taking into consideration social goals as well as population and economic objectives.

Out of the 176 proposals, forty projects were approved and classified as follows: twenty-two for transportation, eight for mechanization of agriculture, three for women's employment (sewing machines), four for cottage industries, and three for food preparation. The estimated value of these projects is about 360 thousand U.S. dollars. Total interest-free loans to the projects amounted to 260 thousand dollars. If a project is not funded by the Board and the PDPAC still holds it to be viable, funds can be sought elsewhere. The criteria developed for PDP projects are presently being adopted by other government agencies as well.

By the end of 1980, about 878 projects were proposed, out of which 518 were financed. A new dimension was also introduced in 1980: the projects approved covered social and service (nonincome-generating) as well as economic (income-generating) activities. Thus, 369 service and 149 economic projects were financed with a 1.6 million dollar estimated value. The PFPB's contribution amounted to about one million dollars. About 200 thousand dollars were supplied for service projects in the form of grants. These grants represented about one-half of the project's cost. The social service projects included infrastructure projects, nurseries, schools, women's clubs, health services, and youth centers. About 800 thousand dollars were provided for 149 economic projects: 59 for the employment of women (sewing machines and dairy equipment), 43 for transportation, 14 for cottage industries, 9 for mechanization of agriculture, 18 for food preparation, and 6 for community health (sewerage, cleaning, etc.).

10.4 THE IMPACT OF THE PDP: SOME RESEARCH QUESTIONS

The PDP started initially on an experimental basis, representing a prototype program. It is consistent not only with current Egyptian population policy, but also with the strategies emphasized in the international community. As pointed out by the UNFPA:

> . . . there has been increasing interest on the part of policymakers and administrators in the integration of family planning services with other socieconomic development activites, especially those designed for rural development. This is partly due to a realization of the limitations of unifunctional family planning programs in dealing with the multifaceted nature of fertility regulation. It is also due to a growing awareness, as exemplified in the World Population Plan of Action, that effective fertility regulation must be accompanied by the improvement of socioeconomic conditions of the rural population.[6]

It is far from clear what the impact of the PDP will be in the short run. It represents a complex package of integrated activities designed to meet several objectives, one of which is the reduction in population growth rates. In some instances, these activities may increase population growth rates--at least in the short run. Yet, this increase may also constitute a necessary prerequisite to establishing the conditions for fertility reduction in the intermediate to long run. In this sense, the PDP may be viewed as an attempt to shorten the period of rising population growth rates, which have been pervasively observed as a part of the demographic transition, and to facilitate the rate of reduction from these high levels once a trend in declining birth rates has been established.

The difficulty in evaluating the impact of the PDP can be illustrated. The PDP will predictably raise the level of economic prosperity and reduce the child mortality rate. These outcomes could increase the rate of population growth, especially if there exists in rural Egypt substantial numbers of families who desire more children than they are able to obtain. Thus, more children will be demanded as income increases, and the *ability* to obtain more children will simultaneously be augmented by the reduction in the child mortality rate.

Whether these population-increasing influences of the PDP are translated into actual increases in average family size depends on the magnitude and the timing of offsetting PDP impacts. Increased education, for example, will likely act to reduce desired family size, a result that has been found in numerous research studies. However, this impact will occur only with a substantial lag, and thus education is not likely to exert a notable short-run influence sufficient to offset the effects of increased income and reduced child mortality.

In terms of timing, other PDP activities may be more opportune, in particular, the development of cottage industries and the mechanization of agriculture. Cottage industries will provide employment opportunities to women in villages as an alternative to farm labor and childrearing. This in turn will increase the cost of children while economic development is taking place and will constitute a short- to intermediate-run deterring effect to offset the increased demand for children. (Note, however, that the "income effect" of female workforce participation may still act as a stimulating effect on average family size.) Similarly, the impact of agricultural mechanization will diminish the benefits of child labor in the short to intermediate run. Finally, there are also some PDP programs which may be fairly immediate in offsetting the positive impacts on population growth. The provision of improved transportation services represents one such example. Greater access to urban locations afforded by upgraded transportation services will, on the one hand, augment income and reduce child mortality, and, on the other hand, increase the access to family planning services, female employment opportunities, and education. Which of these sets of influences on birth rates will be more important, even in the short or intermediate runs, is an empirical issue.

The discussion of the complexity of the likely impacts of the PDP on population growth rates itself justifies the launching of a substantial research effort to ferret out the *net* impacts of such an integrated program. This need and the complexity outlined above have also been pointed out in the UNFPA 1980 report, which urges that "evaluation systems are to be developed to assess its [PDP] progress."[7] The results of this chapter represent a step in that direction. The research agenda for evaluating the PDP has been divided into three broad questions.

1. What has been the *net* impact of the PDP on children ever born, child deaths, contraceptive knowledge, approval or use, and attitudes toward desired family size?
2. What have been the impacts of specific aspects of PDP projects on children ever born, child deaths, contraceptive knowledge, approval or use, and attitudes toward desired family size?
3. What types of data and what research methodologies appear to be most appropriate to evaluating programs such as the

PDP?

Through the PDP, Egypt is one of the first countries to develop a focused program which puts forth a coherent "population-development strategy" for the rural area.[8] Aspects of this project may constitute a paradigm for other countries. Therefore, the PDP merits careful evaluation to identify areas of strength and possible avenues for improvement. In this chapter we provide a preliminary evaluation, which primarily draws upon information available in the Rural Fertility Survey (RFS), as well as a specially compiled data set of community-level variables collected by the Population and Family Planning Board. We also incorporate, where relevant, some recent results compiled from the 1980 Contraceptive Prevalence Survey.

To be realistic, it is premature to provide a detailed assessment of the impact of the PDP since this program had only been in operation for an average of ten months in the villages sampled by the RFS.[9] Moreover, the magnitude of the programming on a per capita basis is low. However, many of the impacts of the PDP will, in the long run, occur through community-level effects; some will occur through household behavioral responses to PDP programs. Our statistical analysis of the RFS should be useful in identifying the impacts on key demographic variables of some of these community-level and household variables that will be influenced by the PDP. At the very least, the analysis below can be considered as a documentation of prevailing economic-demographic relationships and the socioeconomic environment, which will produce a baseline picture to be used in the future assessment and evaluation of the PDP. At the most, the empirical results can be considered as highly tentative findings, which follow from a prototype evaluation and statistical methodology which itself may represent a useful contribution to the long-run assessment of the PDP.

10.5 A COMPARISON OF THE PDP, NON-PDP, AND TOTAL RFS SAMPLES

Heretofore, the statistical analysis in our study has pertained to the total RFS sample. But the eighty-five villages in this sample can be divided into those which participated in the PDP (thirty-two villages) and those which did not (fifty-three villages). If the original selection of the PDP villages had been made on a random basis, then the RFS sample of PDP and non-PDP villages might form the basis of a control and experimental research design from which insight could be obtained with respect to the impact of the "PDP treatment." In fact, such an explicit research design was not part of the original PDP programming. As a result, the PDP villages in the RFS data set may or may not be representative of the RFS in the aggregate. Some insight into whether there is bias in the selection of PDP villages can be obtained by ascertaining whether the PDP and non-PDP villages in the RFS are similar in key attributes. Accordingly, this section attempts to answer the following question: considering only the variables used in this study, in which ways do the PDP and the non-PDP villages differ?

Table 10.1 is designed to answer this question. A probability level, based on a chi-square statistic, is presented to indicate whether or not one can reject the hypothesis that the two sets of villages are the same for the attribute under consideration. Summarizing the tabular results, it is found that the PDP and non-PDP villages are broadly the same in the following attributes: (1) age of wife, (2) age at first marriage, (3) child deaths, (4) children ever born, and (5) use of electricity. Thus, in terms of the key demographic attributes and the use of electricity, the samples are the same.

In contrast, some of the economic and social variables between the samples differ. PDP villages:

1. are currently using contraceptives with greater prevalence,
2. have used contraceptives in the past with greater prevalence (however, the ratio of current to ever users does not differ significantly between PDP and non-PDP villages),
3. have more men and women who attended school but less men with at least a preparatory certificate and less women with at least a primary certificate,
4. have fewer personal assets, and
5. have more real assets.[10]

Thus, strictly speaking, PDP households do not appear to represent a random sample of the rural Egyptian population. On the other hand, in terms of a composite index of development, it is not at all clear whether the PDP villages are either more or less prosperous than the non-PDP villages. A close examination of the data reveals mixed results: (1) school participation is higher in PDP

Table 10.1 Comparison of PDP and Non-PDP Samples for Selected Variables

Variable	PDP		Non-PDP		Total	
	No.	%	No.	%	No.	%
			Children Ever Born			
0	160	10.5	253	11.0	413	10.8
1 - 2	348	22.9	539	23.4	887	23.2
3 - 4	354	23.2	512	22.1	866	22.7
5 - 6	299	19.6	460	20.0	759	19.6
7+	362	23.8	544	23.5	906	23.7
		[χ^2 = .8	DOF = 4	Prob. = .94]		
			Child Deaths			
0	823	54.0	1189	51.5	2012	52.5
1	336	22.1	481	20.8	817	21.3
2	172	11.3	286	12.4	458	12.0
3	91	6.0	177	7.7	268	7.0
4	59	3.9	89	3.8	148	3.8
5+	42	2.7	87	3.8	129	3.4
		[χ^2 = 9.2	DOF = 5	Prob. = .10]		
			Ever Used Modern Contraceptive Methods			
No	1117	73.3	1809	78.4	2926	76.4
Yes	406	26.7	500	21.6	906	23.6
		[χ^2 = 12.7	DOF = 1	Prob. = <.001]		
			Currently Using Modern Contraceptive Methods			
No	1317	86.5	2049	88.8	3366	87.8
Yes	206	13.5	260	11.2	466	12.2
		[χ^2 = 4.4	DOF = 1	Prob. = .04]		
			Age at First Marriage			
Ls 16	518	34.0	837	36.2	1355	35.4
16+	1005	66.0	1472	63.8	2477	64.6
		[χ^2 = 2.0	DOF = 1	Prob. = .16]		
			Current Age			
Ls 20	250	16.4	354	15.3	604	15.8
20 - 24	335	22.0	494	21.4	829	21.6
25 - 29	295	19.4	445	19.3	740	19.3
30 - 34	227	14.9	374	16.2	601	15.7
35 - 45	416	27.3	641	27.8	1057	27.6
		[χ^2 = 1.9	DOF = 4	Prob. = .76]		

Table 10.1 (continued)

Variable	PDP		Non-PDP		Total	
	No.	%	No.	%	No.	%
			Wife's Education			
Illiterate	1111	72.9	1822	78.9	2933	76.5
No Cert.	360	23.6	382	16.5	742	19.4
Primary Cert.+	52	3.5	105	4.6	157	4.1
		[χ^2 = 31.0	DOF = 2	Prob. = <.001]		
			Husband's Education			
Illiterate	918	60.3	1469	63.6	2387	62.3
No Cert.	418	27.4	471	20.4	889	23.2
Primary Cert.	93	6.1	138	6.0	231	6.0
Prep. & Above	94	6.2	231	10.0	326	8.5
		[χ^2 = 37.2	DOF = 3	Prob. = <.001]		
			Availability of Electricity in the Home			
Not Available	866	56.9	1313	56.9	2179	56.9
Available	657	43.1	996	43.1	1653	43.1
		[χ^2 = 0	DOF = 1	Prob. = .99]		
			Personal Assets			
None	528	34.7	973	42.2	1501	39.2
Refrigerator	8	.5	53	2.3	61	1.5
Stove	76	5.0	125	5.4	201	5.2
Radio	943	62.0	1237	53.6	1280	56.9
Television	183	12.0	277	12.0	460	12.0
Sewing Machine	62	4.1	133	5.8	195	5.1
Clock	41	2.7	145	6.3	186	4.9
Tape Recorder	102	6.7	198	8.6	300	7.9
			Real Assets			
None	330	13.1	302	21.7	933	24.4
Farm Land	674	44.3	835	36.2	1502	39.3
Construct. Land	64	4.2	80	3.5	144	3.8
Agri. Mach.	99	6.5	122	5.3	221	5.8
Building	1095	72.0	1447	62.7	2542	66.4
Animals	741	48.7	1024	44.4	1765	46.1

villages, but the availability of relatively educated families is greater in non-PDP villages; and (2) personal (real) assets are less (more) prevalent in PDP villages. While one might speculate that real assets are on average more valuable than personal assets (and thus PDP villages might be more prosperous), what can one conclude about the impact of the relatively more educated households in non-PDP villages? In sum, the differences between PDP and non-PDP villages are quantitatively slight; in terms of general levels of prosperity, the two sets of villages are remarkably similar. While in a precise statistical sense we cannot conclude that the PDP villages are absolutely representative of the RFS sample, the differences observed are sufficiently small and in offsetting directions so as to allow for guarded comparisons of PDP and non-PDP villages.

10.6 THE IMPACT OF THE PDP: A FIRST EXPLORATION

Table 10.2 presents the results of six basic regression models for children ever born (CEB), child deaths (CD), female workforce participation (WEW), ever-used modern contraceptive methods (EUCM), currently using modern contraceptive methods (CUCM), and desired number of children (DNC). The last term in each equation is a dummy variable for the "PDP effect." Such a regression specification constrains the coefficient of the variables in the model to be the same across all villages and represents the PDP effect as a shift factor.[11] The results show that the PDP effect is:

1. positive, and statistically significant for CEB,
2. negative, and statistically significant for CD,
3. positive, and statistically significant for ever used modern contraceptives,
4. positive, and statistically significant for currently using modern contraceptives,
5. positive, and statistically significant for workforce participation of wives,
6. negative, and statistically significant for desired number of children.

For all of these models, the signs, sizes, and significance levels of the remaining parameters, with reference to the model without the PDP effect, are maintained. This provides some basis for concluding that the PDP effect is *not* capturing differential mea-

Table 10.2 Regressions for CEB, CD, DNC, WEW, EUCM, and CUCM With Impact of PDP

Eq. No.	Dep. Var.	Intercept	Independent Variables									
			AGEW	AGEW2	AGEW3	AFM	AFM<16	CD	CEB	WE2	WE3	HE2
10.1	CEB	-4.40 (-12.55)	.55 (24.71)	-.0058 (-16.71)		-.21 (-26.35)		.89 (44.13)		.04 (.53)	.02 (.16)	.16 (2.37)
10.2	CD	1.23 (7.33)	-.08 (-9.56)		.000021 (8.69)		.08 (2.34)		.37 (45.42)	.02 (.33)	.02 (.19)	-.08 (-1.85)
10.3	DNC	4.68 (53.46)								-.47 (-4.16)	-.54 (-2.37)	-.25 (-2.34)
10.4	WEW	.09 (1.00)	.009 (1.53)	-.0001 (-1.54)						-.02 (-1.08)	.11 (2.99)	-.03 (-1.68)
10.5	ECUM	-.20 (-5.20)	.003 (2.60)							.09 (5.16)	.09 (2.60)	.06 (3.73)
10.6	CUCM	-.14 (-4.52)	.003 (2.60)							.05 (4.02)	-.005 (-.17)	.03 (2.04)

Eq. No.	Dep. Var.	HE3	HE4	CS	AGEW·CS	ASSETP	ASSETR	ELEC	PDP	r^2
10.1	CEB	.15 (1.35)	.18 (1.66)			-.01 (-.35)	.07 (3.05)	.28 (4.82)	.14 (2.57)	.73
10.2	CD	-.06 (-.79)	-.13 (-1.73)			-.0005 (-.03)	.002 (.15)	-.13 (-3.42)	-.12 (-3.44)	.49
10.3	DNC	-.24 (-1.30)	-.72 (-4.15)			-.10 (-2.15)	.06 (1.65)	-.09 (-.97)	-.22 (-2.53)	.03
10.4	WEW	-.09 (-3.18)	-.08 (-3.18)						.04 (3.01)	.01
10.5	ECUM	.11 (4.10)	.16 (6.10)	.12 (10.75)	-.002 (-5.43)	.06 (9.27)	-.02 (-3.09)	.06 (4.24)	.04 (3.35)	.21
10.6	CUCM	.07 (3.41)	.10 (4.94)	.08 (8.50)	-.001 (-5.01)	.05 (8.75)	-.01 (-3.15)	.02 (1.87)	.02 (1.87)	.12

t values in parentheses.

surement effects on the variables included in the study. (For example, it is possible that the average years of schooling attended *within* the fairly broad education categories included in this study are different between PDP and non-PDP villages. The PDP term would then capture some of this effect.)

It is implausible that the PDP has already exerted a notable direct impact on CEB.[12] When such an impact is revealed, it is possible that it will be positive, at least for a period of time. On the one hand, increased prosperity may increase the supply of children through improvements of nutrition and health. On the other hand, since the basic microeconomic regressions reveal that "wealth" (human and physical) exerts a mildly positive impact on children demanded in the rural Egyptian setting, many of the PDP activities that increase the economic prosperity of villages may exert a positive impact on CEB as well. Indeed, the existing positive parameter on the PDP variable may measure such a wealth effect at the community level. Since this prosperity relies largely on the agricultural productivity of an area, and since children are in many instances productive agents on the farm and in the village, then an increased demand for children may be associated with an increase in general prosperity. This situation is likely to change over time as alternative forms of economic activity develop in which children are more competitive with the possibilities for taking advantage of the new forms of economic activities.

The PDP also appears to exert a negative impact on child deaths, although it is problematical whether this reduction is largely the result of PDP programming. Since some PDP activities relate directly to maternal and infant health, it is still possible that one of the early effects of the PDP will be to reduce child mortality.

Current and ever use of contraceptive methods are more prevalent in the PDP villages. This result may be due to PDP programming. The evidence that supports this hypothesis shows that even within the set of PDP villages, when control is made for indices of socioeconomic development, contraceptive use responds positively to PDP programs--in particular, to the availability of extension workers.[13] However, PDP programming in the area of family planning has two goals: (1) to increase the use and effectiveness of contraceptive methods, and (2) to decrease discontinuation rates. That is, the existence of high discontinuation rates is held by some observers to be responsible for the positive relationship between contraceptive prevalence and birth rates in recent years. One measure which may reveal the impact of the PDP on discontinuation rates is the ratio of current to ever users of modern contraceptive methods. The RFS data show that the two ratios for the PDP and non-PDP villages are .51 and .52, respectively. Thus, at the time of the RFS, PDP villages appeared to show a slightly higher rate of discontinuation. This relationship, however, was reversed over time. Using data from the 1980 Contraceptive Prevalence Survey, conducted almost twenty months after the RFS, the two ratios are .55 and .52 for the PDP and non-PDP villages, respectively.[14] These sets of results, taken together with those above, suggest that while the PDP may encourage higher contraceptive prevalence rates in the short run, it takes a period of time (one or two years) for its impact on continuation rates to emerge and augment the influence of the PDP on the control of family size.

Female workforce participation is higher in PDP villages, an expected outcome, given the greater intensity of development programming at all levels in these villages. It is possible that one of the stronger deterring impacts of PDP on births will occur through the development by the PDP of increased employment opportunities for women. This will be especially true if the jobs created are of the type that are competitive with childbearing. (Such jobs may be away from the home and demand regular hours competitive with housework.)

Desired number of children, a variable more likely to change in the short run, is lower in PDP villages. Since a decline in the desired family size will likely precede a reduction in CEB, we might speculate that, if the effect measured here is reflective of the program's impact, then CEB will in time be lowered by the PDP.

The present study had concentrated almost exclusively on the analysis of rural Egypt as a unit. However, it might be of some interest at this point to compare the results showing the impact of the PDP in Upper and Lower Egypt. The relevant regressions, provided in appendix table A.5, permit the estimated parameters of all of the independent variables to vary by region. Here it is seen that the impacts of the PDP have been largely in Lower Egypt where deaths are deterred, contraceptive use increased, and family size desires reduced; there is no impact on CEB. In contrast, in Upper Egypt deaths, contraceptive use, and family size desires are largely uninfluenced by the PDP, but CEB is increased. These results are consistent with the possibility that supply constraints may be relatively more important in Upper Egypt. That is, the immediate impacts of the PDP may be to release some of these constraints. While we place little confidence in the result showing a positive impact of PDP on CEB, it is worth noting that the impact on contraceptive use and on child deaths is statistically insignificant.[15] These measures will be more immediately affected by the PDP in the short run.

There have been three studies, in addition to the present one, which have analyzed the impact of the PDP. The first, representing a report commissioned by the UNFPA (J. M. Stycos and R. Avery), uses the RFS data, considers households with intact marriages, and analyzes the experience of Upper and Lower Egypt separately. The second (A. M. Khalifa, H. A. Sayed, and M. N. El-Khorazaty) also uses the RFS data and analyzes PDP impacts on family planning knowledge, contraceptive attitudes and behavior, pregnancy incidence rates, and the employment of women. The third study (A. M. Khalifa and A. Way) uses data from the 1980 Egyptian Contraceptive Prevalence Survey, collected under the direction of the Population and Family Planning Board with the assistance of the Westinghouse Health Systems.[16] A comparison of our results with those of Stycos and Avery (S/A), and with Khalifa, Sayed, and El-Khorazaty, shows not surprisingly that the findings are identical. To make this comparison with S/A, however, we have run our models using our data coverage of all rural households--though for Upper and Lower Egypt separately--and have examined only the impact of the PDP. While our specific regression models differ from the S/A specifications and while our statistical techniques are different, it is encouraging that the findings appear to be consistent. The Khalifa and Way (K/W) findings using the 1980 Contraceptive Prevalence Survey data are somewhat different from those using the RFS. K/W found CEB and CD to be unaffected by the PDP. We and S/A find CEB to be positively affected and CD to be negatively affected by the PDP. Overall, the impact of the PDP on contraceptive use (prevalence and continuation rates) is slightly stronger in the K/W study, although the effect of PDP on desired (or ideal) number of children is the same in the three studies. These results suggest that while attitudes towards family norms are affected by PDP activities in the short run, the impact of the PDP on contraceptive use emerges with only a lag. Thus, as time elapses, contraceptive prevalence rates increase in PDP villages, and discontinuation rates decrease, as shown above.

10.7 INTERACTION BETWEEN COMMUNITY-LEVEL INDICES AND CEB, CD, DNC, AND CONTRACEPTIVE USE: A SECOND EXPLORATION

In this section an attempt is made to analyze the relationships between community-level indices (including the intensity and duration of the PDP) and CEB, CD, DNC, and contraceptive use. Since community-level indices are available only for the thirty-two PDP villages, the empirical results presented here relate only to the PDP portion of the total rural sample. The results are especially preliminary for several reasons.

1. The community-level indices apply to a village council administrative area covering on average four villages from which one village is drawn in the RFS sample. Furthermore, different activities are concentrated and implemented in the "mother" village where governmental bodies usually exist. As a result, many of the community-level indices will exert a relatively small direct impact on the sampled households selected from one village which is usually not the mother village.
2. Some of the village-level variables are inappropriate for use in the present study. "Physicans per capita," for example, measures only that subset of doctors assigned to provide family planning services. While this measure may be relevant to explaining contraceptive use, it cannot be employed as an index of village-level health services, a potentially important influence on CD.
3. The community-level indices are arbitrarily constructed, many of which require modification (or sensitivity analysis) to provide meaningful results. For example, in early regressions "PDP Duration" was coded in three binary categories and in this form showed little or no impact on the dependent variables. In contrast, when PDP Duration was

recoded as a continuous variable (months), its impact was significant and in the expected direction.

The data file contains many community-level variables. We have elected to focus on seven indices because they are judged *a priori* to be potentially important and also illustrate some of the methodological possibilities and difficulties of using this set of data. The indices are:

1. total index of development (TINDEV)
2. intensity of PDP projects (PPRJPDP)
3. duration of PDP (DURATION)
4. mechanization of agriculture (MECHAGR)
5. transportation and communications services (TRCSER)
6. health services (HTHSER)
7. education services (EDUCSER).

Table 10.3 provides the mean, standard deviation, and range for each index. All variables included in the constructed indices, except DURATION, are in per capita terms.[17]

Total index of development (TINDEV) represents a composite of many development attributes, including such diverse features as land tenure, agricultural mechanization, cottage industries, agricultural development projects, education, health and social services, communications, mass media, recreational facilities, electricity, water, food, transportation, and religious activities. TINDEV has a fairly wide variance and likely represents a reasonable index of the "developmental" attributes of the villages.

PDP projects' intensity (PPRJPDP) represents the number of PDP-sponsored projects (mainly transport and communications, cottage industries that emphasize female employment, agricultural mechanization, health, etc.) in the village council area. Project size is not taken into account, nor is there any weighting for *a priori* impacts (e.g., whether the project represents a marginal addition to an already established activity, or whether it represents a new area of development programming). DURATION measures the number of months between the start of the PDP program activities and the date of the survey. PPRJPDP and DURATION each have a low mean and a small variance. This underscores the relatively small quantitative impact PDP is likely to exert on the dependent variables considered in the present study.

In contrast to PPRJPDP which represents the flow of services

Table 10.3 Means, Standard Deviations, and Ranges of Community-Level Indices

Index	Mnemonic	Mean	S.D.	Range
Total Development	TINDEV	36.927	9.699	14 - 55
PDP Intensity/10,000	PPRJPDP	0.257	0.355	0 - 1.119
PDP Duration	DURATION	10.542	3.169	5 - 19
Agricultural Mechanization	MECHAGR	1.710	1.305	0 - 4
Transportation Services	TRCSER	3.617	1.967	0 - 8
Health Services	HTHSER	4.785	1.578	1 - 8
Education Services	EDUSER	1.938	1.475	0 - 5

from *new* development programming attributed to the PDP, the remaining four indices--MECHAGR, TRCSER, HTHSER, and EDUCSER--represent services flowing from *existing* stocks of activities. Agricultural mechanization (MECHAGR) is a composite index of per capita tractors and per capita irrigation units. Transportation services (TRCSER) is a composite index of per capita bus stops, post offices, telegraph and telephone offices. Health services (HTHSER) is an index which aggregates per capita health units, family planning centers, hospital beds, clinics, and pharmacies. The education services index (EDUCSER) combines per capita primary, preparatory, and secondary classes.

To assist in interpreting the impact of the community-level indices in the basic CEB, CD, DNC, and contraceptive-use regression equations presented below, it is useful first to examine the correlations between the various community-level variables and then to analyze the nature of some of the more important relationships. These correlations are presented in table 10.4.

The key observation to emerge from an examination of the correlations is that the intensity of PDP projects is positively and strongly related to the level of socioeconomic development. A building-on-strength strategy represents an inherent feature of the PDP administrative structure, since many PDP projects "attach"

Table 10.4 Correlations Between Community-Level Indices

	TIN-DEV	PPRJ-PDP	DURA-TION	MECH-AGR	TRC-SER	HTH-SER	EDUC-SER
TINDEV	1.000	.523	.037	.478	.569	.324	.672
PPRJPDP	.523	1.000	.100	.240	.212	.284	.502
DURATION	.037	.100	1.000	-.165	-.129	-.067	-.113
MECHAGR	.478	.240	-.165	1.000	-.004	.181	.426
TRCSER	.569	.212	-.129	-.004	1.000	.210	.250
HTHSER	.324	.284	-.067	.181	.210	1.000	.257
EDUCSER	.672	.502	-.113	.426	.250	.257	1.000

themselves to existing programs. In short, PDP projects tend to be located in already relatively developed areas (the correlation between PDPINT and TOTDVT is .52), and these very areas are the ones with existing high intensities of development programming.[18]

The organization of the regressions with community-level indices is as follows. Each regression includes TINDEV, which controls for the overall level of development in the village. Two PDP variables are then added to each regression: projects intensity (PPRJPDP) and DURATION. These variables are designed to measure the impact of PDP for a *given* level of socioeconomic development, with the realization, of course, that there is interaction between TINDEV, PPRJPDP, and DURATION.

For each regression one or more additional indices have been appended. Additional indices were selected on the basis of *a priori* judgments relating to their predicted impacts. Some of these indices are also included in a somewhat different form from the micro-model specifications in chapters 6 and 7: the real assets (ASSETR) of the household include, among other items, both farm land and tractors, while MECHAGR represents a similar measure for the community; the education level of the members of the household represent education received, while EDUCSER measures education available in the community. The community-level indices thus capture supply effects not necessarily measured by the micro variables, as well as effects external to the household.

Table 10.5 presents the findings of these exploratory regressions. Total index of development (TINDEV) exerts a positive impact on

Table 10.5 Regressions with Community-Level Variables and Impacts of PDP

Eq. No.	Dep. Var.	Inter-cept	AGEW	AGEW2 [AGEW3]	AFM [AFM<16]	CD [CEB]	WE2	WE3	HE2	HE3	HE4	CS
			Independent Variables									
10.7	CEB	-5.03 (-8.42)	.60 (17.23)	-.0066 (-12.06)	-.22 (-17.04)	.90 (26.78)	.007 (.07)	.17 (.72)	.07 (.70)	.20 (1.14)	.20 (1.03)	
10.8	CD	1.14 (3.67)	-.086 (-6.61)	[.000024] [(6.57)]	[.20] [(3.50)]	[.35] [(27.28)]	.005 (.08)	-.009 (-.06)	-.08 (-1.21)	-.12 (-1.04)	-.16 (-1.30)	
10.9	DNC	3.69 (10.19)					-.24 (-1.48)	-.45 (-1.25)	-.10 (-.66)	-.44 (-1.61)	-.75 (-2.64)	
10.10	EUCM	-.02 (-.21)	.005 (2.28)				.06 (2.31)	.09 (1.51)	.08 (3.31)	.10 (2.35)	.15 (3.13)	.15 (8.14)
10.11	CUCM	-.08 (-1.19)	.003 (1.54)				.03 (1.57)	-.003 (-.06)	.06 (2.89)	.06 (1.72)	.08 (2.09)	.08 (5.12)

Eq. No.	Dep. Var.	AGEW·CS	ASSETP	ASSETR	ELEC	TIN-DEV	MECH-AGR	EDUC-SER	TRCSER [HTHSER]	PPRJ-PDP	DURA-TION	r^2
10.7	CEB		-.15 (-2.93)	.07 (1.93)	.25 (2.71)	.033 (4.40)	-.066 (-1.64)		-.108 (-3.72)	-.047 (-.34)	-.03 (-2.19)	.73
10.8	CD		.028 (.88)	.009 (.39)	-.08 (-1.36)	-.005 (-1.41)		-.065 (-2.54)	[.050] [(2.84)]	-.184 (-2.06)	.01 (1.38)	.50
10.9	DNC		-.06 (-.83)	.10 (1.79)	-.13 (-.89)	.04 (2.89)	-.14 (-2.23)	-.25 (-3.96)	.04 (.93)	-.79 (-3.67)	.002 (.08)	.07
10.10	EUCM	-.003 (-4.71)	.05 (3.76)	-.02 (-2.41)	.06 (2.61)	-.008 (-5.47)	.05 (5.59)	.04 (3.52)		.05 (1.56)	-.003 (-.76)	.23
10.11	CUCM	-.0013 (-2.98)	.03 (3.19)	-.02 (-2.56)	.01 (.63)	-.004 (-2.71)	.036 (4.79)	.02 (2.29)		.005 (.16)	.002 (.56)	.12

t values in parentheses.

CEB and a negative impact on contraceptive use. (TINDEV reveals no statistically significant impact on CD.) These results are consistent with each other and with the hypothesis that children are highly valued in rural Egyptian society. Indeed, as household income and prosperity rise, parents may elect to have larger families. Supported in the micro variable analysis, this interpretation is also confirmed by the community-level indices. The interpretation gains further support by the finding that fewer children are desired and contraceptives are utilized more extensively in communities where agricultural mechanization is relatively high. In these situations children are relatively less valuable on the farm. (However, MECHAGR is not statistically significant in the CEB equation.)

Transportation and communication services (TRCSER) exert a negative impact on CEB. This index may represent increased accessibility to urban attitudes and more employment opportunities for women. To the extent that these workforce opportunities are competitive with childrearing, one would expect a negative impact on CEB.

Health services (HTHSER) reveal a positive impact on CD; it is hoped that this is an implausible result! This finding may derive from reverse causation since health facilities may locate in areas of greatest need. Additional research is required on these relationships.

The most interesting finding relating to community-level indices pertains to the impact of education (EDUCSER). EDUCSER deters child deaths and increases contraceptive use. Moreover, fewer children are desired in villages that have relatively abundant educational facilities. In the micro-analysis presented in chapters 5 and 6, husbands' and wives' education did not exert a significant and direct short-run impact on CEB. But the impact may be indirect and take place in the intermediate-run. This may be explained by the existence of some Egyptian families who desire more surviving children than they are able to obtain. While increased education results in reduced family size desires, in absolute levels, the number of surviving children may still be deficient for these families, and thus increased education may not reduce CEB. Yet another explanation of the results rests on a recognition that the impact of education on CEB represents the *final* outcome of the impact of education on changing family size desires, child deaths, and contraceptive use.[19] We may be witnessing the *beginning* of these influences, which in the intermediate to long run may result in smaller numbers of children ever born. In the context of an analysis of the role of education, this timing interpretation is particularly appropriate. Education supplied today (as measured by EDUCSER) affects largely the cohorts receiving the education, but has little impact on mothers whose birth experience is being analyzed in the RFS. Consequently, we must be careful in concluding from the analysis of the micro-variables that education will not affect CEB. Indeed, the EDUCSER variable provides a dynamic element in the cross-sectional findings which may suggest that the static findings using the micro-data may change as the result of current educational programming. However, the overall findings are consistent with the hypothesis that the impact of providing increased educational services on CEB is likely to be relatively insignificant in the short run, and, possibly, even the intermediate run.

The overall impact of PDP, although premature to assess, is mixed in the various models:

1. for CEB, PDP projects' intensity has no impact, and duration deters births,
2. for CD, PDP projects' intensity reduces deaths, and duration shows no individually significant impact,
3. for contraceptive use, PDP projects' intensity and duration reveal no individually significant effects, and
4. for DNC, PDP projects' intensity reduces desired number of children.

Joint tests of the PDP effect have been made for the four models, showing that PDP is jointly significant at the 90 percent level for CEB and CD, but not for contraceptive use.

Overall, our preliminary exploration of the impact of community-level indices has been successful and encouraging. The results for the transportation, education, total development, and agricultural mechanization indices are plausible; they are also consistent with the analysis of the microeconomic relationships using the total RFS sample, and observed differences can be explained partially by changing variable definitions and coverage. As quantified by PPRJPDP and DURATION, the PDP does not appear as yet to exert a notable influence on children ever born, or contraceptive use, although it does appear to reduce child deaths and desired number of children. For three reasons these impacts must be considered as tentative. First, as noted above, each of the two PDP measures has a very small mean and variance; thus they may not capture the full PDP effect in an appropriate manner. Second, some of the other control variables represent the precise means through which PDP would exert its influence, and thus these control variables may mask some of the PDP effect. Third, it is not likely that the PDP with average duration of only ten months in the sampled thirty-two villages and an average project intensity of one project for each forty thousand persons will exert a quantitatively strong impact so soon. However, because PDP will in the long run exert its influence through such variables as socioeconomic development, mechanization and agricultural development, education, health services, and transporation and communication, to name a few, then examining the effects of these other variables may provide a preview of the ultimate impact of PDP.

Taking the results of this chapter as a whole, we can conclude that:

1. CEB may increase in the short run with socioeconomic development in general, and decrease with the provision of mechanized agricultural and urban transportation and communication services;
2. child deaths will decrease with socioeconomic development and the provision of educational services;
3. desired number of children will decrease with the provision of educational services and the expansion of mechanized agriculture; and
4. contraceptive use will increase with the provision of agricultural mechanization and educational services.

Thus, the direct impacts of PDP are somewhat unclear, since much depends on the *form* that the PDP expenditures take.

Policies designed to foster the socioeconomic development and welfare of rural Egyptians are to be strongly encouraged. However, a number of such policies are more likely than others to deter population growth. If population growth constitutes a relevant policy objective, then the identification of the impacts of alternative development policies on population growth is useful. In general, socioeconomic development policies that simultaneously raise the cost of (or reduce the benefits of) children to the household will reduce completed family size. Three examples of such policies are:

1. the provision of female workforce opportunities that are competitive with childrearing,
2. the encouragement of agricultural technologies and products where the contributions of children in production are relatively low,[20] and
3. the development of increased communication and transportation to increase the access of rural residents to the urban society.

At a somewhat more controversial and speculative level, one might consider a policy "package" of the following type. The government might promote the development of secondary and tertiary industries where education skills command a significant market premium, coupled with an increased provision of education services financed, in part, by the individuals receiving the benefits of that education. Thus, a mandatory education policy might be coupled with required expenditures by families in direct proportion to their size (e.g., nominal school fees, assessments for books and uniforms, etc.). Such a policy would raise the cost of children and encourage households to substitute "quality" for "quantity" in their decisions relating to completed family size.

These policies are neither exhaustive nor fully supported by all of the specific results of the current study. They are, however, consistent with the general results that have been obtained to date and are indications of the directions that mutually compatible family planning and development policies must take.[21] More specific policies, and greater confidence in those suggested, must await the availability of expanded data bases and, especially, those data sets which treat community-level variables in greater detail.

11. DEMOGRAPHIC RESEARCH IN EGYPT: WHERE FROM HERE?

11.1 SCOPE AND CONSTRAINTS

A variety of issues have been treated in this study of rural Egyptian demography, ranging from the determinants of fertility, mortality, age at first marriage, and workforce participation, to the nature of contraceptive knowledge, approval, and use. Moreover, community-level and household-level data have been combined in our search for findings relevant to the appraisal and formulation of population and development policies. Finally, the analysis has been carried out using a rather eclectic research strategy that has employed several different statistical techniques to evaluate hypotheses drawn from the disciplines of economics, demography, and sociology.

This research has been exploratory in four principal areas. First, it has been confined to a data set designed to yield broad descriptive results relating to Egyptian demography, but not specifically tailored to confront some of the questions examined in this study. This has resulted in "data compromises" which, at points, have been somewhat constraining. Second, a premium was placed on providing the findings in a prompt manner since their usefulness to policymakers would likely diminish with the passing of time. (Indeed, the second round of the Rural Fertility Survey began in the spring of 1982.) As a result, the most sophisticated statistical techniques (which are often the most time-consuming techniques to implement) were not always used, and only a limited amount of experimentation with alternative methods of estimation was undertaken. It was our judgment that for most of the questions we confronted, simplicity of exposition and timeliness of results outweighed the benefits of refined statistical analysis which, *a priori* may sharpen the findings, but would not alter the major conclusions. This is, of course, a testable hypothesis that merits examination. Third, given time and resource constraints, the analysis was confined to the cross-sectional data, and did not make use of the longitudinal (retrospective) information available on the data file. Fourth, in some instances research questions were bypassed that might have been considered even with the present cross-sectional data but which seemed less important for the present purposes.

However, in the process of completing our research, we have gained perspectives on some relevant questions that could and should be addressed in Egyptian demography. Many of these questions will require expanded data bases and/or more sophisticated modeling and estimating techniques although several could be confronted with the existing data.

It is appropriate to conclude with a brief discussion of some of these relatively "under-researched" questions in Egyptian demography, and of data requirements which would be fairly inexpensive to collect, but which could yield high returns in terms of socioeconomic-demographic research.

11.2 PRIORITY RESEARCH QUESTIONS: AN AGENDA

Nine areas of investigation (not necessarily listed in order of importance) appear to represent important themes to include on an agenda of future research in Egyptian demography.

1. *Infant and child mortality.* What determines infant and child mortality? Our research reveals that *household* attributes alone are relatively unimportant. Possibly community-level attributes (e.g., availability of pure water, medical services) represent the key. The identification of the sensitivity of death rates to these community-level variables (and possibly their interaction with household attributes) could be important to the formulation of public health policy.

2. *Fertility-mortality relationships.* How do infant and child deaths influence completed family size? If families "hoard" children in expectation of deaths, what specific factors influence this hoarding (community-level mortality experience versus, say, the mortality experience of the extended family)? What determines the

time lags between changing levels of community mortality, the recognition of this change, and the response to this change?

3. *Age at marriage.* What determines the age at first marriage (AFM)? No other variable appears to be more important in explaining completed family size than AFM, and yet there is a dearth of Egyptian research on the determinants of AFM.

4. *Workforce participation.* What are the determinants of workforce participation of children and wives? How is this workforce activity related to the characteristics of the household (e.g., number, age, and sex of children, level of wealth), the farm (e.g., farm technology, size of plot, type of crop), and the community (e.g., employment opportunities, prevalence of cottage industries)? Presumably the value of children on the farm, and the availability of employment opportunities for the wife, influence the benefits and costs of children.

5. *Schooling.* What determines the amount of education each child receives--sex, parity, family characteristics (e.g., parent's education, wealth, nature of farm production, and labor needs)? Again, the benefits and costs of children are related to their endowments of human capital, including education.

6. *Family planning.* What determines the decision to adopt, and the effectiveness of, modern contraceptives? What determines the decision to discontinue contraceptive use, or to switch to other contraceptive methods? To what extent are modern contraceptives used for the spacing of children versus the limiting of completed family size? What are the impacts of the use of modern contraceptives on the spacing of children and on completed family size? The statistical techniques and modeling necessary to answer this last question are quite complex.

7. *Sex preference.* What is the impact of sex preference for children, and the success in meeting this preference (e.g., two surviving sons), on completed family size? What determines sex preference--religious conservatism, income and wealth, land tenure arrangements, education, the role of women? From a policy perspective, the success of family planning programs is determined not only by the family size goal, but also by the nature and

strengths of sex preference.

8. *Benefits and costs of children.* What are the primary benefits and costs of children as perceived by their parents? What determines the size of these benefits and costs, and how do they vary with socioeconomic development?

9. *Status of women.* What are the different roles of women in rural Egyptian society? What causes these roles to change with socioeconomic development?

These questions are by no means exhaustive. However, our reading of the Egyptian demographic literature indicates that it is now time to move from descriptive accounts of large data sets to more rigorous hypothesis testing of issues such as those above.

11.3 DATA REQUIREMENTS

In addition to the types of data available in the Rural Fertility Survey and the Community Data Sheet, there are several modifications required in the existing data collected, and/or in additional categories of data that merit collection.

1. *Education.* Education data for each family member (including grandparents) should be gathered. This information should be in terms of years of schooling, not simply the broad classifications employed in the RFS. (The 1980 Contraceptive Prevalence Survey has collected information on years of schooling.)

2. *Wealth.* In addition to an inventory of major personal and real assets, information should be collected which provides rough estimates of the value of these assets (e.g., the size and nature of structures and equipment, the size of farm plots and the way in which they are used).

3. *Workforce participation.* More data are needed on the workforce participation of children and the mother so as to assess their role in the family's economic activities. Information is required on how much each family member works at various periods of time, and the specific activities of each member.

4. *Farm technology.* Data should be collected on the nature of farm production (list of specific crops and a description of land

use), and on the state of agricultural technology (use of tractors, use of powered pumps for irrigation, etc.).

5. *Family planning.* Data are required on the specifics of family planning services provided to the household. To what extent are the family planning services "actively" or "passively" supplied (i.e., visits by family planning personnel versus drop-in clinics). If house visits are made by family planning personnel, how frequent are those visits? Information is also required on the costs of obtaining family planning information and supplies: time costs, monetary costs, and "inconvenience" costs relating, for example, to the distance to a family planning clinic. (Some of these issues have been considered in the 1980 Contraceptive Prevalence Survey.)

6. *The community.* Community-level data are needed to facilitate research that provides results useful to the formulation of public policy. These community-level data may sometimes overlap with data collected at the household level, but the community-level variables may represent quite different interpretations (e.g., the supply of educational facilities versus the consumption of educational services). Community-level data should be gathered for the smallest administrative unit, viz., the village. In addition, these data should be collected for all villages, whether or not the village participates in a community-based program under study (e.g., the PDP).

11.4 MODELING AND STATISTICAL ANALYSIS

1. *Multivariate analysis.* Most of the analysis of Egyptian demographic data has relied on tabular techniques. (The exceptions are some academic studies, including Ph.D. dissertations.) By its very nature, tabular analysis is most suitable for exploratory and descriptive studies. This approach does not lend itself to rigorous hypothesis testing when there are many influences explaining a variable. On the one hand, most demographic research using tabular techniques suggests that many factors influence a given dependent variable (after all, the tables have several rows and columns). On the other hand, the analysis is typically undertaken only in terms of one or two variables at a time (and then with no, or only limited control for intervening influences). Such a procedure may be useful

for a guarded, "first pass" at the data; it is less useful for hypothesis testing. The time is ripe for increased application of multivariate statistical techniques (e.g., multiple regression analysis) to Egyptian demographic data.

2. *Multi-equation models of family behavior.* The models used in this study represent "reduced forms" of more complex family decision-making processes. The nature of this type of reduced-form analysis is illustrated in chapter 3, with reference to the complexity of identifying the impact of education on various aspects of household behavior. Presumably, multi-equation models of the household would be more appropriate to describe certain aspects of demographic and socioeconomic behavior. In some instances these sets of equations should be evaluated with simultaneous estimation procedures.

3. *Disequilibrium models.* As discussed in section 6.3, a potentially important area of Egyptian demographic research relates to rigorously specifying and quantifying household "disequilibrium" behavior. In terms of completed family size, many rural Egyptians have more or fewer children than they "desire." It is important to model explicitly the conditions for under- and overshooting desired, completed family size, and to estimate the magnitude and causes of disequilibrium outcomes. Such an inquiry may be particularly important in rural Egypt--and possibly in much of Africa--since supply constraints in attaining desired family size appear to be more relevant in these areas than elsewhere in the Third World.

11.5 CONCLUDING OBSERVATIONS

As this list of research questions and menu of data needs illustrates, much remains to be done in Egyptian demographic research. Our study represents an exploratory excursion into selected aspects of Egyptian demography. We are encouraged by the potential for demographic research in Egypt, especially given the large scope of, and the accessability to, sets of socioeconomic-demographic data, and also by the interest shown in demographic research by the academic community and by policymakers. The present climate is conducive not only to moving forward with this research, but also to expanding its dimensions, particularly if the data collected in the future provide increasingly useful information to ferret out results relevant to public policy. This research could assist the government in formulating policies that are based on firmer empirical grounds, and which may, in the long run, improve the condition of the Egyptian people.

APPENDIXES NOTES REFERENCES INDEX

Table A.1 Summary Statistics on Selected Household Attributes

		All Ever-Married Women			Women 35 and Over		
Variable Name	Mnemonic[a]	Upper	Lower	Total	Upper	Lower	Total
DEPENDENT							
Child. Ever Born	CEB	4.18	4.35	4.27	6.56	6.68	6.63
0		12.7	9.1	10.8	3.8	2.7	3.2
1		11.8	10.3	11.0	4.6	1.9	2.7
2		12.6	11.6	12.2	3.8	3.9	3.8
3		10.9	11.7	11.3	5.9	3.6	4.7
4		10.0	12.5	11.3	7.4	7.8	7.6
5		9.0	11.9	10.5	10.4	13.5	12.0
6		8.5	10.1	9.3	11.2	14.1	12.6
7		7.6	7.1	7.4	14.6	12.2	13.4
8		5.8	5.6	5.7	11.9	12.6	12.3
9		4.7	4.6	4.6	11.2	12.5	11.8
10		2.9	3.0	2.9	7.4	8.0	7.7
11		1.8	1.2	1.5	4.5	3.6	4.1
12+		1.8	1.3	1.5	4.5	3.7	4.1
Child Deaths	CD	1.16	0.90	1.02	2.00	1.57	1.78
0		49.9	54.8	52.5	28.9	33.1	31.1
1		20.5	22.1	21.3	19.9	24.5	22.3
2		12.6	11.3	12.0	17.3	17.1	17.2
3		7.6	6.5	7.0	13.3	12.6	12.9
4+		9.4	5.3	7.2	20.6	12.6	16.5
Death Ratio[b]	CD/CEB	0.23	0.17	0.20	0.28	0.21	0.24
Wife Ever Worked	WEW	13.0	28.4	21.1	13.0	28.0	20.6
Age at First Marriage	AFM	16.79	17.07	16.94	17.06	17.24	17.15
Currently Using Modern Contra.	CUCM	5.1	18.6	12.2	6.2	24.7	15.7
Ever Used Modern Contra.	EUCM	11.9	34.3	23.7	14.9	43.0	29.3
Desired Family Size[c]	DNC	4.95	3.76	4.31	5.15	4.04	4.58
Ideal Family Size[d]	IDEAL	4.40	3.34	3.78	4.56	3.50	3.97

[a] Numbers in rows with underlined mnemonics represent means. Other numbers represent percentages.

[b] Not defined for CEB = 0.

[c] Only numeric answers are used in calculations. The numbers for the six categories are 1719, 1952, 3671, 633, 674, and 1307, respectively.

Variable Name	Mnemonic[a]	All Ever-Married Women			Women 35 and Over		
		Upper	Lower	Total	Upper	Lower	Total
INDEPENDENT							
Wife's Age	AGEW	30.20	30.59	30.40	40.23	40.55	40.39
Wife's Age Sq.	AGEW2	991	1008	1000	1636	1663	1649
Wife's Age Cub.	AGEW3	34940	35553	35256	67291	68958	68145
Child. Surviving	CS	3.03	3.45	3.25	4.57	5.12	4.85
Interaction (AGEW,CS)	AGEW·CS	104.03	118.42	111.55	184.68	209.02	197.15
Death Ratio Sq.	$(CD/CEB)^2$	0.11	0.07	0.09	0.13	0.09	0.11
Age at First Marriage<16	AFM<16	38.7	32.1	35.4	41.6	35.4	38.4
AFM							
<15	AFM1	23.0	18.3	20.5	24.3	20.9	22.5
15	AFM2	15.7	13.8	14.7	17.3	14.5	15.9
16	AFM3	16.1	17.5	16.8	14.0	16.4	15.2
17	AFM4	10.4	12.4	11.4	7.3	9.5	8.4
18	AFM5	10.6	11.9	11.3	10.0	10.4	10.2
19	AFM6	6.0	6.6	6.3	3.6	4.3	4.0
20	AFM7	7.7	7.9	7.8	9.3	9.8	9.5
21+	AFM8	10.6	11.6	11.1	14.3	14.3	14.3
Husband's Educ.							
Illiterate[e]	HE1	67.7	57.9	62.7	75.8	67.7	71.7
No Cert.[e]	HE2	21.0	25.3	23.2	18.9	23.0	21.0
Prim. Cert.[e]	HE3	5.3	6.7	6.0	3.6	5.6	4.7
Prep. Cert.[e]+	HE4	6.1	10.0	8.1	1.7	3.6	2.7
Wife's Educ.							
Illiterate[e]	WE1	80.5	73.1	76.6	84.0	78.1	81.0
No Cert.[e]	WE2	16.4	22.0	19.4	14.5	19.8	17.2
Prim. Cert.[e]+	WE3	3.1	4.9	4.1	1.5	2.2	1.8
Electricity[e]	ELEC	32.6	52.7	43.1	28.2	55.0	41.9
Personal Assets[f]	ASSETP	0.69	1.16	0.94	0.64	1.13	0.89
Real Assets[f]	ASSETR	1.47	1.75	1.61	1.47	1.76	1.66
Pop. and Devel. Project	PDP	34.25	44.70	39.54	32.83	44.33	38.72
Number of Cases	N	1819	2011	3830	664	697	1361

[d] Only numeric answers are used in calculations. The numbers for the six categories are 1102, 1527, 2629, 385, 489, and 874, respectively.

[e] Coded 1 = yes; 0 = otherwise.

[f] This represents the average number of assets. Details on the asset composition are presented in table 6.1.

Table A.2 Regressions for CEB, CD and Death Ratio (Ever-married Women)

Eq. No.	Dependent Variable (Sample)[a]	Inter-cept	Independent Variables[b] AGEW	AGE2 [AGE3]	AFM	AFM<16 [AFM<18]	WE2	WE3
A.1	CEB	-7.33	.50	-.0052		.90	.02	-.18
		(-20.36)	(21.26)	(-14.15)		(15.45)	(.24)	(-1.17)
A.2	CEB	-8.48	.54	-.0058		[1.16]	.03	-.05
		(-23.43)	(23.43)	(-15.94)		[(20.09)]	(.37)	(-.35)
A.3	CEB	-9.61	.56	-.0060		c	.04	.05
		(-26.34)	(24.81)	(-16.97)			(.56)	(.37)
A.4	CEB (Age>40)	-6.97			-.14		.06	.30
		(-13.80)			(-5.55)		(.23)	(.36)
A.5	AFM	16.86					.05	1.96
		(271.73)					(.41)	(7.10)
A.6	CEB	-6.68	.48	-.0049			.034	-.29
		(-18.12)	(19.76)	(-12.94)			(.45)	(-1.88)
A.7	CEB (A>35;CEB>0)	7.41			-.15		-.03	-.13
		(21.72)			(-9.05)		(-.15)	(-.28)
A.8	CEB (A>40;CEB>0)	7.33			-.14		-.12	.15
		(14.97)			(-5.50)		(-.46)	(.19)
A.9	CEB	-4.51	.63	-.0060	-.28		.08	.03
		(-10.48)	(23.00)	(-13.92)	(-29.19)		(.90)	(.15)
A.10	CEB--CD ENDOG.	-4.50	.63	-.0059	-.28		.08	.030
		(-9.86)	(7.06)	(-13.31)	(-3.57)		(.85)	(.15)
A.11	CD--CEB ENDOG.	.63	-.04	[.000016]		-.03	.0081	-.004
		(2.94)	(-3.30)	[(5.81)]		(-.67)	(.18)	(-.04)
A.12	CEB (ex CEB=0)	-4.48	.59	-.0056	-.25		-.008	-.032
		(-9.53)	(20.19)	(-12.50)	(-25.36)		(-.09)	(-.18)
A.13	CEB (ex CEB=0)	-3.70	.51	-.0047	-.22		-.0038	-.031
		(-8.28)	(18.25)	(-10.94)	(-23.75)		(-.05)	(-.19)
A.14	CEB (ex CEB=0)	-4.25	.54	-.0056	-.19		.0039	-.012
		(-10.75)	(21.90)	(-14.89)	(-23.38)		(.06)	(-.08)
A.15	CD	1.21	-.08	[.00002]			.0028	.027
		(7.16)	(-9.33)	[(8.55)]			(.06)	(.30)
A.16	CD/CEB (ex CEB=0)	.17	-.0046	[.000001]		.011	.02	.003
		(4.05)	(-2.25)	[(1.87)]		(1.32)	(1.44)	(.13)
A.17	CEB (ex EUCM=1)	-3.84	.51	-.005	-.20		-.06	-.14
		(-10.13)	(20.77)	(-14.41)	(-22.25)		(-.68)	(-.79)

t values are in parentheses.

[a] Unless otherwise noted, the sample is the total RFS. In other cases it represents the total RFS excluding (ex) the items noted, or it represents constraints on the sample. The age (A) constraints apply to the wife.

[b] Definitions are provided in Appendix table A.1.

[c] The AFM binary variables for this equation are as follows: AFM1 = 2.28(22.76); AFM2 = 1.97(18.56); AFM3 = 1.88(18.14); AFM4 = 1.59(14.17);

HE2	HE3	HE4	ASSETP	ASSETR	ELEC	CD [CEB]	r^2	Obvs.	Eq. No.
.20	.10	.02	.0039	.09	.31	.95	.70	3830	A.1
(2.81)	(.85)	(.14)	(.13)	(3.95)	(5.16)	(45.25)			
.17	.14	.14	-.01	.08	.31	.93	.71	3830	A.2
(2.51)	(1.18)	(1.22)	(-.39)	(3.43)	(5.18)	(44.99)			
.18	.17	.22	-.01	.07	.28	.90	.73	3830	A.3
(2.65)	(1.50)	(1.99)	(-.39)	(3.15)	(4.89)	(44.27)			
.36	-.29	.11	.20	.18	.54	.90	.44	548	A.4
(1.34)	(-.64)	(-.18)	(2.14)	(2.10)	(2.52)	(17.81)			
							.01	3830	A.5
.18	.047	-.08	.0004	.09	.33	.99	.68	3830	A.6
(2.46)	(.38)	(-.68)	(.01)	(3.65)	(5.31)	(46.33)			
.19	.10	.10	.056	.22	.47	.86	.46	1016	A.7
(1.10)	(.32)	(.23)	(.84)	(3.65)	(3.30)	(24.24)			
.30	-.04	-.21	.22	.12	.41	.83	.42	533	A.8
(1.19)	(-.08)	(-.33)	(2.41)	(1.48)	(1.98)	(17.03)			
.13	.14	.08	-.01	.11	.25		.59	3830	A.9
(1.65)	(1.03)	(.58)	(-.41)	(3.98)	(3.52)				
.14	.14	.08	-.014	.11	.25	.01		3821	A.10
(1.53)	(1.03)	(.48)	(-.41)	(2.29)	(3.26)	(.01)			
-.07	-.05	-.12	-.0004	.01	-.10	[.27]		3821	A.11
(-1.58)	(-.66)	(-1.67)	(-.02)	(.66)	(-2.55)	[(11.34)]			
.16	.076	.03	.01	.11	.22	d	.60	3408	A.12
(2.03)	(.57)	(.24)	(.40)	(3.83)	(3.16)				
.16	.05	.01	.02	.09	.20	d	.64	3408	A.13
(2.05)	(.41)	(.11)	(.64)	(3.31)	(3.12)				
.19	.09	.10	.0047	.08	.23	.80	.71	3408	A.14
(2.76)	(.79)	(.86)	(.17)	(3.64)	(4.03)	(4.21)			
-.084	-.053	-.102	.0001	-.002	-.128	[.36]	.49	3830	A.15
(-1.94)	(-.71)	(-1.42)	(.01)	(-.10)	(-3.39)	[(45.37)]			
-.007	-.005	-.03	-.004	.003	-.02	[.027]	.10	3408	A.16
(-.76)	(-.27)	(-1.30)	(-1.04)	(.96)	(-2.46)	[(14.53)]			
.07	.03	.19	-.08	.09	.24	.96	.73	2918	A.17
(.87)	(.20)	(1.37)	(-2.18)	(3.47)	(3.65)	(41.70)			

AFM5 = 1.31(11.85); AFM6 = 1.07(8.17); AFM7 = .95(7.78). The AFM terms are statistically different from one another at the 90% level, except for the difference between AFM2 and AFM3, which is significant at the 65% level.

d The (CD/CEB) variable in equation A.12 is 1.94(14.21), and (CD/CEB) and $(CD/CEB)^2$ variables in equation A.13 are 7.89(24.21) and -8.76(-19.89), respectively.

Table A.3 Regressions for CEB, CD, WEW, EUCM, CUCM, and DNC (Intact Marriages, PDP Effects)

Eq. No.	Dep. Var.	Inter cept	Independent Variables[a]						
			AGEW	AGE2	WE2	WE3	HE2	HE3	HE4
A.18[b]	CEB	-4.36	.58	-.0059	.079	.064	.13	.053	.15
		(-12.12)	(26.42)	(-17.20)	(1.15)	(.46)	(2.02)	(.49)	(1.37)
A.19[c]	CEB	-4.40	.58	-.0059	.065	.063	.12	.052	.16
		(-12.94)	(26.40)	(-17.16)	(.94)	(.46)	(1.88)	(.47)	(1.53)
A.20[d]	CD	1.39	-.088		-.18	.023	-.076	-.036	-.025
		(7.41)	(-9.34)		(-.36)	(.23)	(-1.61)	(-.47)	(-1.00)
A.21[e]	CD	1.41	-.087		-.0061	.024	-.069	-.035	-.089
		(7.63)	(-9.35)		(-.12)	(.24)	(-1.56)	(-.45)	(-1.19)
A.22	WEW	.05	.013	-.00021	-.0067	.12	-.035	-.079	-.092
		(.56)	(2.11)	(-2.26)	(-.36)	(3.23)	(-1.99)	(-2.68)	(-3.36)
A.23	WEW	.043	.012	-.00021	-.0089	.12	-.036	-.079	-.090
		(.49)	(2.09)	(-2.23)	(-.48)	(3.23)	(-2.06)	(-2.69)	(-3.27)
A.24	EUCM	-.23	.005		.095	.099	.068	.11	.14
		(-5.28)	(3.29)		(5.25)	(2.72)	(3.99)	(3.89)	(5.12)
A.25	EUCM	-.24	.0052		.091	.099	.066	.11	.15
		(-5.68)	(3.40)		(5.00)	(2.71)	(3.89)	(3.88)	(5.32)
A.26	CUCM	-.15	.0037		.055	.0065	.032	.073	.10
		(-4.34)	(2.92)		(3.70)	(.22)	(2.28)	(3.05)	(4.40)
A.27	CUCM	-.16	.0037		.053	.0063	.031	.072	.10
		(-14.58)	(2.98)		(3.54)	(.21)	(2.18)	(3.04)	(4.51)
A.28	DNC	4.71			-.56	-.61	-.28	-.21	-.70
		(52.00)			(-4.67)	(-2.55)	(-2.44)	(-1.08)	(-3.85)
A.29	DNC	4.79			-.54	-.61	-.26	-.20	-.73
		(50.53)			(-4.45)	(-2.54)	(-2.29)	(-1.05)	(-3.99)

t values are in parentheses.

[a] Definitions are provided in appendix table A.1.

[b] Equation A.18 additionally contains a term for AFM: -.24(-29.23).

[c] Equation A.19 additionally contains a term for AFM: -.24(-29.27).

ASSETP	ASSETR	ELEC	CD	CS	AGEW·CS	PDP	r^2	Obvs.	Eq. No.
-.042 (-1.56)	.063 (2.82)	.26 (4.57)	.82 (40.82)				.77	3330	A.18
-.042 (-1.56)	.056 (2.51)	.26 (4.61)	.82 (40.96)			.16 (3.02)	.77	3329	A.19
.0012 (.061)	.0041 (.26)	-.15 (-3.69)					.49	3330	A.20
.0013 (.067)	.0095 (.59)	-.15 (-3.74)				-.13 (-3.47)	.50	3329	A.21
							.01	3308	A.22
						.022 (1.56)	.01	3307	A.23
.065 (9.03)	-.016 (-2.76)	.054 (3.63)		.13 (10.56)	-.0021 (-5.62)		.21	3332	A.24
.65 (9.04)	-.018 (-3.10)	.055 (3.69)		.13 (10.40)	-.0021 (-5.56)	.05 (3.61)	.12	3331	A.25
.047 (8.01)	-.015 (-3.13)	.021 (1.69)		.083 (7.89)	-.0014 (-4.70)		.12	3332	A.26
.047 (8.00)	-.016 (-3.34)	.021 (1.73)		.82 (7.82)	-.0014 (-4.67)	.026 (2.24)	.12	3331	A.27
-.11 (-2.23)	.04 (1.03)	-.048 (-.48)					.03	3197	A.28
-.11 (-2.24)	.05 (1.31)	-.052 (-.52)				-.27 (-2.93)	.03	3196	A.29

[d] Equation A.20 additionally contains terms for AGE3, AFM<16 and CEB, respectively: .000021(7.61), .39(41.73) and -.11(2.74).

[e] Equation A.21 additionally contains terms for AGE3, AFM<16, and CEB, respectively: .000021(7.56), .39(41.86) and -.11(-2.81).

Table A.4 Regressions for CEB, CD, WEW, EUCM, CUCM, and DNC (Upper and Lower Egypt)

Eq. No.	Dep. Var.[b]	Inter- cept	Independent Variables[a]					
			AGEW	AGE2	WE2	WE3	HE2	HE3
A.30[c]	CEB	-4.6	.58	-.0061	.074	.059	.13	.074
	LE	(-9.13)	(18.37)	(-12.53)	(.81)	(.33)	(1.46)	(.51)
A.31[d]	CEB	-3.92	.52	-.0055	-.007	-.041	.18	.24
	UE	(-8.03)	(16.42)	(-11.02)	(-.065)	(-.17)	(1.83)	(1.37)
A.32[e]	CEB	-4.32	.54	-.0057	.04	.027	.16	.15
	U-L/B	(-12.40)	(24.49)	(-16.50)	(.62)	(.19)	(2.42)	(1.34)
A.33[f]	CD	1.07	-.073		.009	-.016	-.065	-.083
	LE	(4.49)	(-6.22)		(.16)	(-.15)	(-1.17)	(-.90)
A.34[g]	CD	1.30	-.083		.026	.032	-.099	-.021
	UE	(5.20)	(-6.71)		(.36)	(.20)	(-1.48)	(-.18)
A.35[h]	CD	1.31	-.077		.015	.011	-.078	-.055
	U-L/B	(7.56)	(-8.98)		(.34)	(.12)	(-1.81)	(-.74)
A.36	WEW	.27	.0048	-.000085	-.059	.10	-.07	-.15
	LE	(2.00)	(.54)	(-.61)	(-2.29)	(2.04)	(-2.86)	(-3.62)
A.37	WEW	.03	.0067	-.00011	.025	.078	.0034	-.046
	UE	(.31)	(1.04)	(-1.05)	(1.11)	(1.56)	(.17)	(-1.28)
A.38	WEW	.08	.0053	-.00009	-.026	.095	-.037	-1.04
	U-L/B	(.95)	(.96)	(-1.04)	(-1.49)	(2.68)	(-2.23)	(-3.96)
A.39	EUCM	-.23	.007		.047	.084	.092	.16
	LE	(-3.74)	(3.29)		(1.94)	(1.77)	(3.86)	(3.94)
A.40	EUCM	-.098	.00092		.12	.072	.013	.057
	UE	(-2.35)	(.65)		(5.93)	(1.64)	(.72)	(1.71)
A.41	EUCM	-.22	.0033		.085	.089	.058	.11
	U-L/B	(-5.94)	(2.58)		(5.22)	(2.69)	(3.32)	(4.17)
A.42	CUCM	-.16	.0044		.06	.0017	.019	.104
	LE	(-2.97)	(2.39)		(2.84)	(.041)	(.93)	(3.04)
A.43	CUCM	-.078	.0016		.036	-.021	.029	.036
	UE	(-2.67)	(1.57)		(2.53)	(-.69)	(2.21)	(1.54)
A.44	CUCM	-.15	.0026		.053	-.0041	.025	.075
	U-L/B	(-5.02)	(2.48)		(3.94)	(-.15)	(1.97)	(3.44)
A.45	DNC	3.69			-.31	-.68	-.25	-.34
	LE	(37.69)			(-2.76)	(-3.07)	(-2.28)	(-1.85)
A.46	DNC	5.12			-.67	-.35	-.20	-.034
	UE	(39.53)			(-3.26)	(-.80)	(-1.05)	(-.10)
A.47	DNC	4.99			-.45	-.57	-.23	-.23
	U-L/B	(57.95)			(-4.07)	(-2.54)	(-2.20)	(-1.25)

t values are in parentheses.

[a] The sample is all eligible women. Definitions are in appendix table A.1.

[b] Designations for the regressions and samples are: UE = Upper Egypt sample; LE = Lower Egypt sample; U-L/B = Upper Egypt - Lower Egypt binary.

[c] Equation A.30 additionally contains a term for AFM: -31 (-19.49).

[d] Equation A.31 additionally contains a term for AFM: -.21 (-19.65).

[e] Equation A.32 additionally contains a term for AFM: -.21 (-26.40).

HE4	ASSETP	ASSETR	ELEC	CS[CD]	AGEW·CS	LE=1[i]	r^2	Obvs.	Eq. No.
.075 (.54)	-.028 (-.81)	.035 (1.16)	.25 (3.25)	[.87] [(28.60)]			.72	1992	A.30
.32 (1.78)	-.033 (-.702)	.097 (2.77)	.21 (2.34)	[.93] [(33.86)]			.74	1801	A.31
.17 (1.52)	-.03 (-1.00)	.063 (2.78)	.24 (4.16)	[.90] [(44.40)]		.28 (5.08)	.73	3805	A.32
-.11 (-1.25)	.011 (.49)	.019 (1.01)	-.026 (-.55)				.45	1992	A.33
-.16 (-1.28)	.029 (.93)	-.0071 (-.30)	-.13 (-2.11)				.55	1801	A.34
-.11 (-1.54)	.014 (1.05)	.0085 (.57)	-.088 (-2.33)			-.30 (-8.51)	.50	3805	A.35
-.16 (-4.23)							.02	1980	A.36
-.035 (-.98)							.03	1798	A.37
-.11 (-4.22)						.16 (12.25)	.05	3785	A.38
.16 (4.38)	.05 (5.40)	-.034 (-4.17)	.053 (2.54)	.17 (9.56)	-.0028 (-5.34)		.22	1997	A.39
.17 (5.10)	.051 (5.80)	-.0015 (-.23)	.0081 (.49)	.068 (4.80)	-.00086 (-2.13)		.15	1807	A.40
.15 (5.98)	.051 (7.80)	-.021 (-3.92)	.038 (2.81)	.12 (10.06)	-.0017 (-5.06)	.15 (13.0)	.23	3815	A.41
.087 (2.71)	.045 (5.52)	-.023 (-3.21)	.016 (.88)	.11 (6.85)	-.0018 (-4.05)		.12	1997	A.42
.13 (5.72)	.034 (5.59)	-.0061 (-1.34)	-.0093 (-.81)	.046 (4.61)	-.00086 (-3.05)		.09	1807	A.43
.102 (4.86)	.041 (7.59)	-.017 (-3.84)	.0086 (.78)	.075 (7.77)	-.0012 (-4.56)	.094 (9.15)	.14	3815	A.44
-.47 (-2.81)	-.027 (-.61)	.13 (3.36)	.22 (2.33)				.03	1943	A.45
-1.11 (-3.37)	-.029 (-.33)	.075 (1.13)	-.10 (-.62)				.02	1710	A.46
-.70 (-4.14)	-.023 (-.52)	.095 (2.63)	.078 (.85)			-1.14 (-13.44)	.07	3661	A.47

f Equation A.33 additionally contains a term for AGE3, AFM<16, and CEB, respectively: .000018 (5.8), -.14 (-2.82) and .32 (29.44).

g Equation A.34 additionally contains terms for AGE3, AFM<16 and CEB, respectively: .000022 (6.03), -.082 (-1.47) and .41 (34.63).

h Equation A.35 additionally contains terms for AGE3, AFM<16, and CEB, respectively: .00002 (6.03), -.11 (-2.85) and .37 (45.58).

i Binary variable where Lower Egypt = 1; Upper Egypt is in the intercept.

Table A.5 Regressions for CEB, CD, WEW, EUCM, CUCM, and DNC (Upper and Lower Egypt, PDP Effects)

Eq. No.	Dep. Var.[b]	Inter-cept	Independent Variables[a]						
			AGEW	AGE2	WE2	WE3	HE2	HE3	HE4
A.48[c]	CEB	-4.01	.52	-.006	-.01	-.039	.18	.26	.37
	UE	(-8.22)	(16.49)	(-11.06)	(-.11)	(-.17)	(1.82)	(1.46)	(2.04)
A.49[d]	CEB	-4.59	.58	-.0061	.079	.054	.13	.076	.072
	LE	(-9.08)	(18.37)	(-12.53)	(.86)	(.33)	(1.49)	(.51)	(.52)
A.50[e]	CD	1.34	-.084		.028	.032	-.99	-.026	-.17
	UE	(5.32)	(-6.77)		(.39)	(.20)	(-1.48)	(-.22)	(-1.40)
A.51[f]	CD	1.12	-.072		.023	-.019	-.055	-.078	-.12
	LE	(4.67)	(-6.16)		(.42)	(-.17)	(-.99)	(-.85)	(-1.37)
A.52	WEW	-.047	.0073	-.00011	.014	.077	-.0016	-.035	-.0083
	UE	(-.50)	(1.16)	(-1.11)	(.66)	(1.62)	(-.082)	(-.99)	(-.24)
A.53	WEW	.32	.0053	-.000095	-.074	.10	-.064	-.15	-.17
	LE	(2.30)	(.60)	(-.69)	(-1.81)	(2.00)	(-2.56)	(-3.57)	(-4.55)
A.54	EUCM	-.094	.00088		.12	.072	.013	.056	.17
	UE	(-2.25)	(.62)		(5.94)	(1.64)	(.72)	(1.69)	(5.03)
A.55	EUCM	-.26	.007		.041	.085	.088	.15	.17
	LE	(-4.12)	(3.00)		(1.67)	(1.79)	(3.67)	(3.89)	(4.50)
A.56	CUCM	-.077	.0016		.036	-.021	.029	.036	.13
	UE	(-2.61)	(1.55)		(2.54)	(-.69)	(2.21)	(1.53)	(5.67)
A.57	CUCM	-.17	.0044		.058	.0019	.018	.10	.089
	LE	(-3.12)	(2.40)		(2.71)	(.047)	(.85)	(3.01)	(2.35)
A.58	DNC	5.08			-.067	-.34	-.20	-.029	-1.08
	UE	(37.91)			(-3.29)	(-.79)	(-1.06)	(-.085)	(-3.28)
A.59	DNC	3.83			-.28	-.68	-.23	-.33	-.49
	LE	(36.32)			(-2.44)	(-3.08)	(-2.04)	(-1.79)	(-2.93)

t values are in parentheses.

[a] The sample is all eligible women. Definitions are in appendix table A.1.

[b] Designations for the regressions and samples are: UE = Upper Egypt sample; LE = Lower Egypt sample; U-L/B = Upper Egypt - Lower Egypt binary.

[c] Equation A.48 additionally contains a term for AFM: -.21 (-17.72).

ASSETP	ASSETR	ELEC	CD	CS	AGEW·CS	PDP	r^2	Obvs.	Eq. No.
-.035	.071	.23	.93			.28	.75	1800	A.48
(-.74)	(1.97)	(2.55)	(33.90)			(3.41)			
-.029	.035	.25	.86			-.037	.72	1991	A.49
(-.84)	(1.15)	(3.25)	(28.47)			(-.52)			
.03	.00054	-.13				-.083	.55	1800	A.50
(.94)	(.02)	(-2.20)				(-1.49)			
.0077	.018	-.025				-.126	.45	1991	A.51
(.36)	(.97)	(-.52)				(-2.82)			
						.19	.07	1797	A.52
						(11.61)			
						-.11	.04	1979	A.53
						(-5.42)			
.051	-.00046	.007		.067	-.00086	-.011	.15	1806	A.54
(5.81)	(-.069)	(.45)		(4.81)	(-2.14)	(-.70)			
.052	-.033	.052		.17	-.0028	.056	.22	1996	A.55
(5.54)	(-4.12)	(2.53)		(9.56)	(-5.33)	(2.93)			
.034	-.0057	-.0096		.046	-.00086	-.0044	.09	1806	A.56
(5.59)	(-1.22)	(-.83)		(4.62)	(-3.05)	(-.41)			
.045	-.02	.016		.11	-.0019	.021	.12	1996	A.57
(5.57)	(-3.19)	(.87)		(6.89)	(-4.04)	(1.29)			
-.030	.058	-.091				.18	.02	1709	A.58
(-.34)	(.86)	(-.55)				(1.13)			
-.034	.12	.22				-.31	.04	1942	A.59
(-.78)	(3.30)	(2.34)				(-3.99)			

[d] Equation A.49 additionally contains a term for AFM: -.21 (-19.49).
[e] Equation A.50 additionally contains terms for AGE3, AFM<16, and CEB, respectively: .00002 (6.04), -.085 (-1.54) and .41 (34.65).
[f] Equation A.51 additionally contains terms for AGE3, AFM<16, and CEB, respectively: .000019 (5.75), -.14 (-2.87) and .32 (29.30).

Table A.6 Regressions for Excess Demand and Supply of Children

Eq. No.	Dependent Variable	Intercept	Independent Variables								r^2	Obvs.
			WE2	WE3	HE2	HE3	HE4	ASSETP	ASSETR	ELEC		
A.60	Excess DD Rural Total	.40 (16.42)	-.06 (-1.99)	-.11 (-1.16)	-.05 (-1.60)	-.08 (-1.37)	-.14 (-1.79)	-.009 (-.71)	-.016 (-1.47)	-.08 (-3.04)	.03	1351
A.61	Excess DD Upper Egypt	.50 (14.67)	-.12 (-2.11)	-.08 (-.47)	-.03 (-.61)	-.17 (-1.55)	-.25 (-1.60)	.02 (.80)	-.04 (-2.11)	-.07 (-1.63)	.04	655
A.62	Excess DD Lower Egypt	.21 (6.11)	-.02 (-.45)	-.10 (-.93)	-.06 (-1.47)	-.03 (-.36)	-.09 (-1.02)	-.01 (-.41)	.02 (1.30)	-.02 (-.73)	.01	687
A.63	Equilibrium Rural Total	.31 (12.86)	-.02 (-.47)	-.06 (-.66)	-.002 (-.06)	.01 (.16)	.07 (.94)	-.01 (-.39)	-.01 (-.71)	-.05 (-1.87)	.01	1351
A.64	Equilibrium Upper Egypt	.27 (8.73)	-.05 (-.96)	.09 (.63)	-.002 (-.04)	.21 (2.16)	-.002 (-.01)	-.02 (-.81)	.005 (.32)	.01 (.21)	.01	655
A.65	Equilibrium Lower Egypt	.38 (9.84)	.02 (.38)	-.17 (-1.41)	-.01 (-.15)	-.14 (-1.83)	.09 (.96)	-.001 (-.03)	-.03 (-1.71)	-.11 (-3.04)	.03	687
A.66	Excess SS Rural Total	.30 (11.28)	.09 (2.27)	.17 (1.68)	.06 (1.54)	.07 (1.13)	.07 (.81)	.01 (1.02)	.02 (2.01)	.13 (4.53)	.05	1351
A.67	Excess SS Upper Egypt	.24 (7.27)	.17 (3.11)	-.02 (-.11)	.03 (.67)	-.05 (-.45)	.25 (1.68)	-.001 (-.06)	.03 (1.89)	.07 (1.49)	.04	655
A.68	Excess SS Lower Egypt	.41 (9.55)	.002 (.03)	.27 (2.01)	.07 (1.33)	.16 (1.92)	-.003 (-.03)	.01 (.37)	.01 (.46)	.13 (3.30)	.04	687

t values in parentheses.
The sample is ever-married women 35 years and older. See appendix table A.1 for definitions.

Table A.7 Duration of Breastfeeding by Selected Attributes

Characteristics[a]	Current Age Groups 15-	20-	25-	30-	35-	40-	45-49	Total	N
Age at 1st Marriage									
<15	15.0	18.0	18.3	19.5	19.6	20.8	19.6	19.0	675
15-17	13.5	15.7	16.8	20.2	20.0	21.4	20.1	18.6	1271
18-19	-	16.0	17.8	19.7	19.6	21.4	20.7	18.9	488
20-21	-	9.2	14.4	16.6	20.1	20.7	20.5	17.6	313
22-23	-	*	12.7	16.4	17.1	20.2	20.6	17.0	79
24+	-	-	*	14.9	17.9	16.9	20.6	17.1	97
Surviving Children									
<3	14.8	15.4	15.0	16.3	18.2	20.0	19.4	16.0	758
3-5	*	17.6	17.7	19.5	19.8	22.1	20.8	19.3	1513
6+	-	-	19.4	20.5	19.6	20.0	19.7	19.9	658
Wife's Education									
Illiterate	15.8	16.8	17.7	19.4	19.8	20.9	20.7	19.1	2247
No. Cert.	11.8	14.6	14.6	19.2	19.1	20.7	18.1	17.1	577
Prim. Cert.+	-	14.2	14.3	16.9	16.5	*	*	16.0	105
Husband's Education									
Illiterate	18.3	17.5	17.8	20.2	20.3	21.2	20.4	19.6	1849
No Cert.	8.0	15.3	16.9	17.8	18.2	20.4	19.7	17.5	680
Prim. Cert.	*	12.2	15.1	17.1	17.8	19.8	21.3	16.4	173
Prep. Cert.+	*	15.4	16.8	19.6	18.8	22.0	22.9	18.8	536
Wife's Employment									
Not Working	13.9	16.3	16.9	19.1	19.8	20.7	19.6	18.5	2389
Working	*	15.4	16.8	19.6	18.8	22.0	22.9	18.8	536
Husband's Occupation									
Agric.	15.7	16.9	17.7	19.6	19.7	20.7	20.8	19.1	1699
Nonagric.	12.1	15.1	15.9	18.7	19.4	21.2	19.3	17.8	1230
Electricity									
Yes	13.0	15.9	15.8	19.0	18.4	20.3	19.2	17.8	1313
No	16.3	16.3	18.0	19.4	20.5	21.3	21.0	19.3	1601

Table A.7 (continued)

Characteristics[a]	15	20-	25-	30-	35-	40-	45-49	Total	N
	Current Age Groups								
Real Assets									
0	*	16.7	16.8	18.7	18.7	21.2	20.1	18.4	512
1	12.9	15.0	16.7	18.6	20.2	22.2	20.0	18.5	997
2	*	16.9	16.2	19.3	19.4	20.5	20.2	18.5	673
3+	13.0	16.2	17.8	20.3	19.5	19.5	20.3	18.8	746
Personal Assets									
0	20.3	16.7	16.9	20.0	20.7	22.5	21.2	19.4	1150
1	12.6	16.3	17.3	19.1	19.3	19.8	19.9	18.4	1209
2	*	15.0	17.3	19.0	16.4	20.0	18.4	17.3	349
3+	*	13.2	13.7	17.4	20.1	19.1	19.5	17.0	220
Total									
Mean	14.5	16.1	16.9	19.2	19.6	20.9	20.2	18.6	-
Number	46	443	643	548	506	395	348	-	2929

* Less than 10 cases.

a For women with at least two CEB with known duration. The data, in months, are for the child before the last.

INTRODUCTION TO APPENDIX B

Communities in general, and villages in particular, reveal different structural environments that may cause individuals to respond differently to the same program. These different responses may occur even though individual characteristics are the same. Consequently, population policies and programs in recent years "have emerged which advocate community-based development programs [the PDP is an example of one such project], ...and international agencies...[which] emphasize the strengthening and development of community contexts."[1]

The UNFPA expert group on demographic transition and socioeconomic development reported that "one area of needed research on the determinants of fertility is the focus on structural constraints, i.e., the type of structure of the parents' community and/or immediate environment that limits their decisions and choices, how this social context changes under various regimes of social and economic development, and the impact of such changes on reproductive norms and behavior."[2]

R. Ridker argues that once the rural infrastructure for socioeconomic development exists, the institution of community-level fertility control programs involving and insuring community participation becomes more relevant and practical.[3] One approach to represent this orientation empirically is to create village-level measures or attributes which utilize individual data aggregated across each village. Another approach is to collect data that pertain to each village through a community-level survey. Because of the lack of such data, the first approach is employed in this study, although the ultimate unit of analysis is still the individual.

Accordingly, nine socioeconomic measures and a general level of development (a summary index) have been calculated for each village. Although these measures are continuous in nature, they are categorized for presentation in tabular form. Thus, villages were classified according to each measure into low, middle, and high levels. The cutoff points were chosen in order to be meaningful and to ensure the inclusion of about one-third of the villages in each level. Table B.1 shows these boundaries for all aggregated measures. Considering these socioeconomic measures as independent variables, different fertility and family planning dependent variables were calculated for those individuals in each level as shown in tables B.1 and B.2.

While the tables are self-explanatory, a description of how to interpret one panel in table B.1, say the percentage of literate wives, may be helpful. First, it is important to note that aggregated socioeconomic measures are village-level measures. Thus, for those villages where the percentage of literate wives is below 15 percent (low category), the children ever born (CEB), age at first marriage, number of surviving children, and child loss for those 1,457 women. are 4.21 children, 17 years, 3.21 and 0.69 children, respectively. Similar figures may be obtained for the middle category (for women in villages where the percentage of literate wives is in the 15 percent - 29 percent range) and the high category (for women in villages where the percentage of literate wives is over 30 percent), as shown in table B.1. The same interpretation applies to the remaining variables in table B.1.

Most of the relationships found in tables B.1 and B.2 are similar to those obtained in the analysis of the individual data in the text. However, we felt that providing these aggregated measures would add a dimension to the analysis that supplements our findings in the text. Moreover, this approach is in accordance with the emphasis by policymakers, as well as by researchers, on more aggregated units of analysis, and the relationships of these units to individual behavior.

Table B.1 CEB, AFM, CS, and CD by Socioeconomic Aggregated Village Measures

Socioeconomic Measures	Village Level Boundaries	CEB	Age at First Marriage	Surviving Children	Child Loss	Total Number of Cases
% Literate Wives	L:<15	4.21	17.00	3.21	.69	1457
	M:15-	4.11	16.99	3.12	.99	1153
	H:30+	4.50	16.83	3.43	1.07	1220
% Educated Wives (At least primary certificate)	L:0	4.20	17.08	3.29	.92	1215
	M:0-	4.18	16.89	3.08	1.11	1423
	H:5+	4.45	16.85	3.42	1.03	1192
% Literate Husbands	L:<30	4.28	16.99	3.24	1.08	1477
	M:30-	4.25	16.80	3.22	1.04	1356
	H:50+	4.29	17.06	3.31	.95	997
% Educated Husbands (At least preparatory certificate)	L:<5	4.16	16.96	3.19	.58	1500
	M:5-	4.31	16.84	3.23	1.09	1009
	H:10+	4.36	17.00	3.33	1.03	1321
% Wives Working Outside Home	L:<5	4.18	16.89	3.14	1.04	1137
	M:5-	4.26	16.90	3.26	1.01	1698
	H:20+	4.38	17.07	3.37	1.02	995
% Husbands Working in Nonagriculture	L:<30	4.15	16.95	3.20	.96	1165
	M:30-	4.18	16.90	3.13	1.04	1532
	H:50+	4.32	17.00	3.47	1.05	1132
% Households with Electricity	L:<10	4.07	16.94	3.09	.98	1111
	M:10-	4.07	17.25	3.02	1.04	1076
	H:50+	4.54	16.74	3.51	1.03	1643
Proportion of Personal Assets	L:<.1	4.23	16.87	3.13	1.10	1566
	M:.10-	4.14	17.02	3.17	.98	1277
	H:.15+	4.50	16.95	3.55	.95	987
Proportion of Real Assets	L:<.25	4.27	16.88	3.25	1.02	1164
	M:.25-	4.22	17.04	3.22	1.00	1282
	H:.35+	4.32	16.91	3.28	1.03	1384
General Level of Development	L	4.08	16.96	3.05	1.08	1144
	M	4.22	16.97	3.24	.98	1460
	H	4.51	16.89	3.45	1.06	1226

Table B.2 Family Planning Approval, Family Size Desires, and Ideal Spacing by Socioeconomic Aggregated Village Measures

Socioeconomic Measures	Village Level Boundaries	%Wives Approving of F.P.	%Husbands Approving of F.P.	%Wives Wanting No More Children	Ideal Spacing (years)	Ideal Family Size	Desired Family Size
% Literate Wives	L	49.97	39.46	42.97	2.36	4.10	4.65
	M	56.46	45.28	45.19	2.49	3.77	4.21
	H	67.05	57.29	54.51	2.55	3.45	4.02
% Educated Wives	L	53.17	41.57	45.02	2.40	3.92	4.47
	M	53.41	43.50	42.73	2.44	3.98	5.00
	H	66.36	56.37	55.12	2.55	3.46	3.95
% Literate Husbands	L	49.83	38.86	49.13	2.39	4.14	4.64
	M	58.63	48.16	45.95	2.45	3.72	4.25
	H	66.81	57.07	48.15	2.59	3.42	3.92
% Educated Husbands	L	54.00	42.33	44.60	2.42	3.84	4.44
	M	49.75	39.34	42.61	2.43	4.14	4.62
	H	66.99	57.82	53.98	2.54	3.50	3.96
% Wives Working Outside Home	L	46.97	34.49	40.19	2.44	4.09	4.66
	M	62.01	53.71	50.88	2.49	3.64	4.07
	H	61.30	49.55	49.34	2.43	3.77	4.34
% Husbands in Nonagriculture	L	50.52	39.45	42.80	2.40	3.91	4.46
	M	57.12	46.41	46.15	2.42	3.94	4.33
	H	64.76	55.22	53.53	2.58	3.50	4.14
% Households with Electricity	L	54.19	40.87	42.03	2.43	4.02	4.52
	M	46.94	37.45	40.61	2.43	4.03	4.48
	H	66.34	57.15	55.26	2.50	3.51	4.06
Proportion of Personal Assets	L	47.77	35.44	39.91	2.44	4.18	4.71
	M	56.97	45.89	46.36	2.40	3.81	4.28
	H	75.69	66.36	60.29	2.58	3.27	3.76
Proportion of Real Assets	L	54.21	42.70	46.57	2.54	3.93	4.41
	M	57.41	45.40	44.31	2.45	3.86	4.31
	H	59.97	51.81	50.72	2.41	3.63	4.24
General Level of Development	L	48.25	36.02	60.91	2.45	3.89	4.36
	M	57.74	46.44	45.76	2.49	3.98	4.47
	H	65.42	57.58	55.14	2.43	3.55	4.09

Table C.1 Village Councils by Governorates and PDP

Governorate	PDP					Non-PDP	Total
	Before Sept. 78	Oct. 78- Sept. 79	Oct. 79- Sept. 80	Oct. 80	Total		
Lower Egypt							
1. Sharkia	19	10	1	25	55	18	73
2. Behera	10	10	5	30	55	13	68
3. Dakahlia	10	10	11	24	55	21	76
4. Gharbia	10	10	33	-	53	-	53
5. K. El-Sheikh	13	12	-	14	39	-	39
6. Damietta	24	-	-	-	24	-	24
7. Kalubia	-	20	-	17	37	-	37
8. Ismalia	-	-	-	-	-	7	7
9. Menufia	-	-	-	-	-	122	122
Subtotal	87	72	49	110	318	181	499
Upper Egypt							
1. Giza	24	12	3	-	39	-	39
2. Beni-Suef	15	10	-	13	38	-	38
3. Fayoum	24	3	10	-	37	-	37
4. Menya	10	10	10	15	45	21	66
5. Assuit	10	10	10	18	48	-	48
6. Souhag	-	-	-	-	-	96	96
7. Aswan	-	-	-	-	-	33	33
8. Kena	-	-	-	-	-	71	71
Subtotal	83	45	33	46	207	221	428
Total	170	117	82	156	525	402	927

Source: Special Tabulations from 1976 census prepared by the Monitoring and Evaluation Office, PFPB.

Table C.2 Villages by Governorates and PDP

Governorate	PDP						
	Before Sept. 78	Oct. 78- Sept. 79	Oct. 79- Sept. 80	Oct. 80	Total	Non-PDP	Total
Lower Egypt							
1. Sharkia	122	72	4	192	390	70	460
2. Behera	65	75	29	199	368	80	448
3. Dakahlia	59	58	73	148	338	77	415
4. Gharbia	61	49	200	-	310	-	310
5. K. El-Sheikh	58	54	-	62	174	-	174
6. Damietta	56	-	-	-	56	-	56
7. Kalubia	-	111	-	70	181	-	181
8. Ismalia	-	-	-	-	-	19	19
9. Menufia	-	-	-	-	-	298	298
Subtotal	421	419	306	671	1817	544	2361
Upper Egypt							
1. Giza	90	50	12	-	152	-	152
2. Beni-Suef	89	55	-	70	214	-	214
3. Fayoum	102	12	38	-	152	-	152
4. Menya	51	61	52	112	276	60	336
5. Assuit	54	51	45	87	237	-	237
6. Souhag	-	-	-	-	-	264	264
7. Aswan	-	-	-	-	-	76	76
8. Kena	-	-	-	-	-	194	194
Subtotal	386	229	147	269	1031	594	1625
Total	807	648	453	940	2848	1138	3986

Source: See note to table C.1.

Table C.3 Rural Population by Governorates and PDP

	PDP						
Governorate	Before Sept. 78	Oct. 78 - Sept. 79	Oct. 79 - Sept. 80	Oct. 80	Total	Non-PDP	Total
Lower Egypt							
1. Sharkia	557,838	339,188	24,000	792,886	1,713,912	371,888	2,085,800
2. Behera	266,505	290,092	127,693	874,230	1,558,520	269,285	1,827,805
3. Dakahlia	332,692	241,608	348,471	693,908	1,616,679	429,841	2,046,520
4. Gharbia	325,028	268,707	910,736	-	1,504,471	-	1,504,471
5. K. El-Sheikha	290,995	282,384	-	359,604	932,983	-	932,983
6. Damietta	391,388	-	-	-	391,388	-	391,388
7. Kalubia	-	587,725	-	384,843	972,568	-	972,568
8. Ismalia	-	-	-	-	-	182,655	182,655
9. Menufia	-	-	-	-	-	1,475,399	1,475,399
Subtotal	2,164,446	2,009,704	1,410,900	3,105,471	8,690,521	2,729,068	11,419,589
Upper Egypt							
1. Giza	587,894	374,770	74,316	-	1,036,980	-	1,036,980
2. Beni-Suef	347,716	214,994	-	250,665	813,375	-	813,375
3. Fayoum	546,082	37,091	235,134	-	818,307	-	818,307
4. Menya	280,430	288,923	267,793	505,080	1,342,226	269,108	1,611,334
5. Assuit	322,545	262,105	243,726	399,775	1,228,151	-	1,228,151
6. Souhag	-	-	-	-	-	1,501,578	1,501,578
7. Aswan	-	-	-	-	-	360,803	360,803
8. Kena	-	-	-	-	-	1,317,137	1,317,137
Subtotal	2,084,667	1,177,883	820,969	1,155,520	5,239,039	3,448,626	8,687,665
Total	4,249,113	3,187,587	2,231,869	4,260,991	13,929,560	6,177,694	20,107,254

Source: See note to table C.1.

Table C.4 Availability of Community Data Sheets by Governorates

Governorates[a]	No. of Villages	First CDS	Second CDS	Total
Sharkia	30	31[b]	29	60
Behera	25	25	20	45
Dakahlia	31	20	20	40
Gharbia	53	20	20	46
Kafr El-Sheikh	25	20	20	46
Damietta	26	24	20	66
Kalubia	26	20	19	39
Giza	39	39	34	73
Beni-Suef	25	25	25	50
Fayoum	37	37	26	63
Menya	30	20	18	38
Assuit	30	30	20	50
Total	369	311	271	582

[a] Data as of April 1980 for first and second data sheets.
[b] One mother village was declared a town and thus eliminated from the areas covered in the PDP.

Notes

CHAPTER 1

1. A. R. Omran and M. N. El-Khorazaty (1977), in analyzing aggregate data from 85 countries, conclude that development and family planning "should go hand-in-hand to accomplish the necessary faster reduction in fertility. ...Family planning can help reduce fertility during the period when socio-economic development is still at an early stage and its effects [on fertility] are not yet realized. ...therefore, [family planning] can maximize the achievements of development by reducing the pace of population growth so that it does not surpass and/or impede development. On the other hand, development, in the long run, will tend to reinforce the effects of family planning" (p. 9).

2. See the first descriptive report by A. M. Khalifa, H. A. Sayed, and M. N. El-Khorazaty (1981b).

3. Our misgivings concerning the Upper Egypt and Lower Egypt classifications derive from the heterogeneity of these areas. For example, Giza Governorate is classified as Upper Egypt, but in terms of the analysis at hand, this area might be more appropriately included with Lower Egypt.

4. While it would have been desirable to "weight" assets according to their value, this was not possible given available data, and even rough guesses of the value of real assets, in particular, could have been wide of the mark.

5. The issue of child sex preference and its relation to completed family size constitutes an important research question not addressed in the present study.

6. Our view of "rationality" here emphasizes benefit-cost maximizing behavior. If a broader perspective is taken (e.g., psychological and religious), then leaving family size "up to God" could well reflect rational behavior.

7. A. Bindary (1978), Chairman of the Population and Family Planning Board, has observed that "...the problems of family planning in Egypt are not due to shortages of resources as much as they reflect the need for the better deployment of the already available resources" (p. 29).

8. The theoretical framework is presented in chapter 3.

9. The RFS defines employment activities as those inside or outside the

home, which are not traditionally undertaken by the wife. Examples include cottage industry activities, working in the village enterprises, and the like.

10. See above, section 1.2.3.

11. These results are consistent with the analysis above which shows that "development" may, in the short run, increase population growth. Real asset accumulation is only one component of "development"; other components, such as personal asset accumulation, education, use of electricity, as well as community-level services, all contribute to development.

12. W. S. Thompson (1929), A. M. Carr-Saunders (1936), F. W. Notestein et al. (1944), D. Kirk (1971), S. E. Beaver (1975), J. C. Caldwell (1976).

13. Using a somewhat different argument and employing aggregate data, D. Kirk has shown that not only may such a threshold exist (a grouping of development preconditions which vary from country to country), but that the rate of decline from this threshold will be greater the higher the growth-rate plateau in stage II. His empirical generalization may fit the rural Egyptian situation as well. D. Kirk (1971).

14. This "compositional effect" applies equally to the weight of the population between urban and rural areas. However, rural-urban differences are outside the scope of the present inquiry.

15. The microeconomic basis of this "switching point," associated with the research of R. A. Easterlin, is explored in chapter 3.

16. Using community-level data merged with the RFS for PDP areas, one finds that per 10,000 persons, the availability in Upper and Lower rural Egypt, respectively, of family planning extension workers is 1.67 and 1.96; of family planning doctors is .96 and .88; and of family planning centers is 1.01 and .84. While the levels of these resources may be affected by the particular sample (PDP), there is no reason to believe that the variation by region will be notably different for the rural area as a whole.

17. A. Bindary (1980b).

18. The positive impact of development on fertility is frequently documented, especially where contraceptive prevalence rates are low. A. R. Omran and M. N. El-Khorazaty (1977) evince that "developing countries will not achieve their ambitious fertility reduction targets...without an effective family planning effort. ...[Otherwise,] development may increase rather than decrease fertility [especially at early stages of development]" (p. 9). This is consistent with the results in comparing Lower and Upper Egypt where prevalence rates, while still modest, are higher in Lower Egypt, possibly offsetting the positive effect of development on fertility. In contrast, Upper Egypt prevalence rates are low and development is still in its early stages. See also M. Nag (1979) for a similar argument.

19. This is consistent with the observation concerning the very poor and illiterate: Upper Egypt is poorer and has a higher illiteracy rate than Lower Egypt. A recent study by the National Academy of Sciences (1981) supports

this result, where for the period between 1960 and 1976 the analysis showed that "in Lower Egypt the decline in marital fertility was about 5 percent, and in Upper Egypt there was a negligible rise of 1.3 percent" (p. 18).

20. National Academy of Sciences (1981).

CHAPTER 2

1. National Academy of Sciences (1981, Table 3, p. 12).

2. CAPMAS (1981b).

3. The "demographic transition" represents an empirical pattern of birth and death rate trends which occurs with regularity across many countries during modernization. See section 1.2.5.

4. National Academy of Sciences (1981, p. 1).

5. S. Abdel-Hakim (1981).

6. CAPMAS (1981b).

7. A. M. Khalifa (1978).

8. M. A. El-Badry (1956) and M. S. A. Issa (1971).

9. National Academy of Sciences (1981, p. 2).

10. Aspects of socioeconomic conditions in Egypt in general, and in rural areas in particular, are described in C. Issawi (1949, 1963), D. C. Mead (1967), H. Fakhouri (1972), M. Abdel-Fadil (1975), and CAPMAS (1978a).

11. While more recent data are available on Egyptian economic change, it is convenient to use the World Bank compilations since they provide data which permit a comparison of Egypt's performance with that of other Third World nations.

12. This section is based on W. Cleland (1936), K. Mazhar (1970, 1973), W. H. Kamel et al. (1971), A. Bindary (1972, 1973a,b, 1978), A. R. Omran and M. M. El-Nomrosey (1973), H. Shanawany (1973), P. Caldwell (1977), and Population and Family Planning Board (1979).

13. This section is based on S. M. Gadalla (1978), M. Al-Kordy (1979), P. Gupte (1979), A. Bindary (1980a,b), Supreme Council for Population and Family Planning (1980), and M. Gabr (1981).

14. A. Bindary (1978, 1980b).

15. Supreme Council for Population and Family Planning (1973).

16. Supreme Council for Population and Family Planning (1980, p. 8).

17. Supreme Council for Population and Family Planning (1980, pp. 12-13).

CHAPTER 3

1. L. Henry (1961, p. 2).

2. R. A. Easterlin (1978, p. 73). For more detailed discussions of natural fertility and its determinants, consult J. Bourgeois-Pichat (1965); C. Clark (1967); A. Sauvy (1969); G. Hawthorn (1970); T. J. Trussell (1979); J. Bongaarts (1980); J. A. Menken, T. J. Trussell, and S. Watkins (1981).

3. For a discussion of this evidence, consult R. A. Easterlin (1978, pp.

71-71).

4. R. Frisch (1975, 1978); S. L. Huffman, A. K. M. Chowdhury, and W. H. Mosley (1978); T. J. Trussell (1978); J. Bongaarts and H. Delagado (1979); J. Bongaarts (1980); J. A. Menken, T. J. Trussell, and S. Watkins (1981).

5. Some of the cultural-economic linkages to natural fertility are summarized and documented in R. A. Easterlin (1978, pp. 72-79).

6. H. Leibenstein (1957, p. 161).

7. The early seminal article was by G. S. Becker (1960). The best collection of papers in this new home economic tradition, as well as a useful bibliography, is found in T. W. Schultz (1974a).

8. J. A. Banks (1954); P. Neher (1971); J. Simon (1974); A. C. Kelley (1976); P. H. Lindert (1978).

9. G. E. Johnson and W. E. Whitelaw (1974); H. Rempel and R. A. Lobdell (1978); A. C. Kelley and C. Swartz (1979); J. C. Knowles and R. Anker (1981).

10. R. Blandy and A. Woodfield (1976).

11. R. Blandy and A. Woodfield (1976, p. 2).

12. R. Blandy and A. Woodfield (1976, p. 4).

13. R. Blandy and A. Woodfield (1976, p. 6).

14. R. Blandy and A. Woodfield (1976, p. 21).

15. B. L. Boulier and N. G. Mankiw (1980, p. 1).

16. While this is the thrust of the theoretical developments to date, limited attempts have been undertaken to represent children as producer durables. See, for example, D. N. DeTray (1972). In a recent exposition of the new home economics framework, G. S. Becker treats income from children as a reduction in the price of children. "The net cost of children is reduced if they contribute to family income by performing household chores, working in the family business, or working in the market place. Then an increase in the 'earning' potential of children should increase the demand for children. Indeed...farm families have had more children mainly because children have been considerably more productive on farms than in cities." G. S. Becker (1978, p. 5).

17. Formal treatments of these aspects of the model are found in Y. Ben-Porath (1973), and R. J. Willis (1973).

18. A discussion of this utility formulation is found in G. Becker (1965), K. Lancaster (1966), and R. Muth (1966).

19. For the mathematics, see R. J. Willis (1973) and Y. Ben-Porath (1973).

20. W. C. Sanderson (1976) has nicely summarized the role of tastes and preference formation in the Becker and the Easterlin schools.

21. R. J. Willis (1973) has a production function homogenous of degree one in the inputs to allow explicitly for differential effects of income on the number versus the quality of children. That is, child quality is itself produced with the time of the mother and father and intermediate inputs, and

is subject to a full wealth constraint.

22. G. Becker and H. G. Lewis (1973).

23. W. C. Sanderson (1973, pp. 471-472).

24. See, for example, H. Leibenstein (1957).

25. For a review of some of this literature, consult N. S. Scrimshaw (1978). The most extreme version of controlling child quality relates to consciously altering the child survival rate. According to Schrimshaw, "at least some of this mortality occurs when an infant is relatively unwanted whether because of its high birth order, close spacing of births, the number of living children already in the family, or the sex composition of the family in relation to that child's sex and to sex preference for children, or occasionally because the infant is 'difficult,' physically unattractive, or otherwise less acceptable" (p. 392).

26. The criticisms have proceeded on several fronts, only three of which will be mentioned here. First, it is noted that societal "norms" are relatively important. In commenting on Becker's (1960) seminal paper, J. S. Duesenberry (1960) observed: "the difference between economics and sociology is very simple. Economics is all about how people make choices. Sociology is all about why they don't have any choices to make" (p. 233). Over a decade later, N. B. Ryder (1960) struck the same theme in commenting on R. J. Willis' (1973) paper: "society intervenes, in obvious and in subtle ways, to insure that the outcome...makes sense on the society's behalf. These constraints on choice are what sociologists call norms" (p. 77). Economists do not deny the existence or importance of norms, but they are uneasy about the absence of a well-articulated theory of norm creation which has substantial empirical content and predictive power.

A second criticism of the economic model concerns the way in which family decisions are made. N. B. Ryder (1960) notes that "Willis presents a model within a framework of economic theory of the family, but he proceeds about this important task by systematically destroying the idea of the family" (p. 77).

A third criticism of the economic paradigm questions the ability of households to make "rational" family size decisions, especially since such a complex calculus applies to persons in the low-income setting. This criticism has been softened by the existence of abundant anthropological evidence illustrating the capacity of families to control family size, and by an even larger economics literature which demonstrates the acuteness of even peasants in low-income societies to efficiently manage their economic affairs.

The economic model is a powerful one, but that is not to deny its many limitations. In fact, the literature which best defines these limitations is found in the writings of economists, some of whom are the most active contributers to the new home economics paradigm. One need only consult R. J. Willis' list of seven "characteristics of fertility behavior which make it difficult to analyze with a choice-theoretic framework" (p. 27), or read carefully T. W. Schultz' (1974a) excellent synthesis of the new home economics literature, to appreciate that while powerful, the economic paradigm is only one element in explaining family size behavior. Schultz' appraisal merits quoting in detail: "Turning to fertility behavior in the low-income countries, the household model as it now stands has not been developed to treat the particular classes of circumstances that constrain the household in these countries. These are countries in which illiteracy abounds, human time is cheap, and the income opportunities that women have outside the home are mainly not jobs in the labor market. Furthermore, infant mortality is high, life expectancy at birth is low, debilitation during the adult years is substantial for reasons of inadequate nutrition and endemic diseases, and the availability of modern contraceptive techniques, including information about them, is, in general, wanting. These classes of circumstances are not as yet at home in the household model" (p. 20).

27. Many relationships, for example, may be nonlinear, an attribute which cannot be captured well where variables are categorized with very broad ranges.

28. W. P. McGreevey and N. Birdsall (1974).

29. K. O. Mason et al. (1971).

30. J. Simon (1974).

31. S. H. Cochrane (1979, p. 9).

32. T. W. Schultz (1974a, p. 10).

33. This section draws on a useful exposition of these problems in T. P. Schultz (1981, pp. 125-130).

34. For example, the supply equation might incorporate variables such as the availability of clean water, refrigeration, or medical facilities; the demand equation might include costs or availability of family planning. Yet another way to approach this problem would be to develop a disequilibrium model. See, for example, G. S. Madalla and F. D. Nelson (1974).

35. Each of the equations as specified incorporates "unexplained" factors, i.e., unaccounted for variables that influence demand or supply, and errors in measurement. These unexplained factors are denoted as the "error term" in multiple regression equations. If the error terms in the supply and demand equations are unassociated, and if the basic models are "identified" as noted above, then techniques for simultaneously estimating the two equations will result in reliable estimates of each equation.

CHAPTER 4

1. The figures and definitions are found in the 1976 census in which labor force is defined to include self-employed farm workers as well as unemployed, whether previously employed or looking for a job.

2. National Academy of Sciences (1981, table 5, p. 16).

3. S. F. Loza and M. N. El-Khorazaty (1979).
4. CAPMAS (1978c).
5. Detailed information on number of dwellings selected, number reached, number interviewed, number of eligible women in them, number of eligible women interviewed, and the rates of nonaccessibility and nonresponse by governorate are given in A. M. Khalifa, H. A. Sayed, and M. N. El-Khorazaty (1981b).

CHAPTER 5

1. H. S. Shryock et al. (1973, p. 511).
2. Scc H. S. Shryock et al. (1973) for further discussion.
3. Using the 1974/75 Egyptian National Fertility Survey data, H. A. Sayed and M. N. El-Khorazaty (1980) showed that for rural areas, memory lapse accounts for an underestimation of over one child on average for women aged 45-49.
4. The censoring effect refers to "the sample design's exclusion of any women who were not married by the date of the interview. To correct for this pattern of systematic exclusion, one must restrict attention to subsamples that are homogeneous in their exposure to the risk of marriage. This will be achieved by selecting some pivotal age A and excluding, or blocking out, all women who (1) have not reached age A, or (2) were married after age A " WFS (1977, p. 47).
5. Due to high marital stability and the high proportion of those who are currently married as compared to all ever-married women, the same patterns and levels are found when only currently married women are considered. Current age and duration of marriage are positively correlated to number of children ever born.
6. In comparing measures (means or rates) for different populations, categories, or subgroups (education, employment or assets, for example), extraneous sources of variation should be controlled for since attributes (births, deaths, etc.) are so highly correlated with factors such as age. Different methods have been used to provide this control in the demographic literature. The technique of adjusting for age, usually referred to as standardization, gives summary measures that, to some extent, hold constant the influence of such factors as age. Using the age distribution of a standard population (all ever-married women in our case), overall rates (or means) obtained are often called the age-adjusted rate (mean) obtained by *direct standardization.* These rates (means) are helpful in making comparisons, but are somewhat arbitrary, because they depend on the choice of the standard population. Actual subgroups are not likely to have such a distribution. In contrast, another method is available, an *indirect standardization,* which uses the actual distribution of the subgroups and the rates (means) of the standard population (frequently used to minimize strange results in the case where some cells are sparsely populated). For details, see H. S. Shryock et al.

(1973), J. L. Fleiss (1973), R. C. Elandt-Johnson and N. L. Johnson (1980).

7. See note 4 above for a discussion of the censoring effect.

8. As W. Brass (1975) has noted, data on child deaths suffer from several deficiencies: (1) surviving mothers (those interviewed) may not constitute a representative sample of the total population; (2) there may be under-reporting of child deaths by age; and (3) some stillbirths are reported in both the CEB and CD figures.

9. It would be more appropriate to use pregnancy history data--not available to us at the time this study was undertaken--since for any given mother's age, children born to women who married earlier have longer exposure to the risk of death.

10. These results are examined in detail in chapters 6 and 9.

CHAPTER 6

1. It should be noted that the desired population impacts of an agricultural mechanization program may be outweighed by the adverse employment and urban-growth effects.

2. While these variables may be interactive, our statistical analysis, which is exploratory in nature, will focus on single equation models. (One interactive model is reported in appendix A.) All of the regressions presented in chapters 6 and 8 use the entire Rural Fertility Survey sample of eligible women. However, the key models have also been estimated with the RFS sample of intact marriages. These models are presented as appendix table A.3. The results for the intact marriage sample are broadly the same as those for the entire RFS, and thus the intact marriage regressions are not analyzed separately, but are reported for reference only.

3. Studies of Egyptian fertility include: M. A. El-Badry (1956), A. M. Zikry (1963), M. A. El-Badry and H. Rizk (1967), T. P. Schultz (1970), H. Abou-Gamrah and M. A. Mamish (1971), S. Hassan (1971), S. Hassan, A. Sallam and A. M. Ahmed (1971), M. S. A. Issa (1971), A. M. Khalifa (1971, 1973a, 1973b, 1976), H. Fakhouri (1972), A. Bindary, C. B. Baxter and T. H. Hollingsworth (1973), A. R. Omran (1973b), S. F. Loza and M. N. El-Khorazaty (1979), H. A. Sayed and M. N. El-Khorazaty (1980), A. M. Khalifa and M. Abdel-Kader (1981a), and A. M. Khalifa, H. A. Sayed, and M. N. El-Khorazaty (1981b).

4. Some theoretical and empirical contributions in this literature include: H. Leibenstein (1957, 1974), G. S. Becker (1960), J. Blake (1968), T. P. Schultz (1969, 1970, 1972, 1973), J. S. DaVanzo (1972), G. S. Becker and H. G. Lewis (1973), R. J. Willis (1973), J. P. Encarnacion (1974), J. C. Caldwell (1975, 1976, 1977, 1978), H. Cochrane (1975, 1979), J. C. Knowles and R. Anker (1975), B. Turchi (1975), R. Blandy and A. Woodfield (1976), M. R. Rosenzweig (1976a, 1976b), D. N. De Tray (1977, 1978), R. A. Easterlin (1978), A. C. Kelley (1980), B. L. Boulier and N. G. Mankiw (1980), R. A. Easterlin et al. (1980), and A. C. Kelley and L. M. da Silva (1980).

5. The r^2 with age alone (both the linear and the squared terms) is .49; the r^2 with the age and the age at first marriage terms alone is .59. Thus, with the final r^2 of .73, we have been able to explain a considerably greater portion of CEB with the use of additional variables. An r^2 of .73 is reasonably high for this type of data set and for this variable.

6. While alternative functional forms which provide an estimate of an asymptote for CEB would be theoretically better, the quadratic used here appears to provide a reasonable representation of the relationship.

7. See, for example, L. Bumpass (1969), J. Palmore and M. Ariffin (1969), M. H. El-Guindy (1971a), D. Yaukey and T. Thorsen (1972), M. Davidson (1973), K. Maurer et al. (1973), D. P. Mazur (1973), J. P. Encarnacion (1974), W. P. McGreevey and N. Birdsall (1974), A. Hill (1975), and M. Kim (1977).

8. Some experimentation has been undertaken to reveal the nonlinear way in which age at first marriage affects CEB. These results are presented in appendix equations A.1 and A.3. These alternative models reveal that the remaining parameters are largely uninfluenced by the nonlinear specification. As a result, we have elected to present and analyze the simpler specifications, where age at first marriage enters as a continuous variable.

9. The regression is presented as appendix equation A.4.

10. While many empirical studies reveal a negative relationship between wife's education and fertility (and to a lesser extent husband's education and fertility), S. H. Cochrane (1979) has concluded: "The evidence seems to indicate that education may increase or decrease individual fertility. The decrease is greater for the education of women than of men and in urban than in rural areas. But education is more likely to increase fertility in countries with the lowest level of female literacy " (p. 9). Examples of studies which, taken in their entirety, reveal this mixed pattern include: M. A. El-Badry and H. Rizk (1967), S. Iutaka et al. (1971), M. Davidson (1973), A. M. Khalifa (1973b, 1976), J. Encarnacion (1974), E. Kogut (1974), M. A. Khan and I. Sirageldin (1975), J. C. Knowles and R. Anker (1975), D. Chernichovsky (1976), J. McCabe and M. Rosenzweig (1976), S. H. Cochrane et al. (1977), J. E. Kocher (1977), A. C. Kelley (1980), and R. Anker and J. C. Knowles (1981). Speculations on the impact of education on fertility are provided by CAPMAS (1978a) where it is concluded "...the higher the rate of education the less the level of fertility and vice versa. Thus, the State in its fight against the increase in population in the Republic has to pay special care to the generalization of education in all its stages and to concentrate all its effort in order to spread education in the rural areas in particular " (p. 233).

11. 2,933 of the women are classified as illiterate; 740 are classified as attending school, but not obtaining a primary school certificate; 156 are classified as having obtained at least a primary school certificate.

12. CAPMAS (1978a, pp. 237-238).

13. The next section considers the determinants of female workforce

participation. The results are broadly consistent with the interpretations provided here. In an attempt to ascertain the impact of working on CEB, equation 6.1 was run with WEW (=1 for workforce participation, 0 otherwise). The results indicate that working has no statistically significant impact on CEB. In particular:

$$\begin{aligned} CEB = & -4.37 + .55AGEW - .0058AGEW2 - .21AFM + .06WE2 + .02WE3 \\ & (-12.39)\quad (24.56)\quad (-16.60)\quad (-26.20)\quad (.86)\quad (.14) \\ & + .16HE2 + .15HE3 + .16HE4 - .01ASSETP + .07ASSETR \\ & \quad (2.36)\quad (1.31)\quad (1.47)\quad (-.45)\quad (3.24) \\ & + .28ELEC + .89CD + .05WEW. \\ & \quad (4.85)\quad (43.80)\quad (.75) \end{aligned}$$

$r^2 = .73$
t values in parentheses

14. Studies showing the impacts of female workforce participation on fertility are abundant. See, for example, A. J. Jaffe and K. Azumi (1960), J. D. Kasarda (1971), J. S. DaVanzo (1972), S. Goldstein (1972), A. M. Khalifa (1973b), K. Maurer et al. (1973), J. Abbott (1974), P. Peek (1975), N. Birdsall (1976), J. L. McCabe and M. Rosenzweig (1976), S. Kupinsky (1977), A. C. Kelley and L. M. da Silva (1980), and H. A. Sayed and M. N. El-Khorazaty (1980).

15. The education-age at first marriage relationship is also analyzed for Egypt by CAPMAS (1978a, pp. 76-77).

16. This negative WE3 effect is quantitatively large but statistically weak.

17. In chapters 5 and 9 there is some evidence of a "humped" or nonlinear relationship between CEB and WE; that is, CEB is higher for WE2 (some education) than for WE1 (illiterate women) and WE3 (primary certificate +). In an attempt to reconcile these findings with those in the present chapter, regressions have been run for CEB and age, and age at first marriage, using the *same* groupings for AGEW and AFM as were employed in chapter 9. When such control is made, the nonlinear relationship vanishes. Moreover, when additional variables are added--and especially ASSETP and HE--the relationship changes significantly. Thus, the tabular results must be viewed with some care since what is observed in chapter 9 as a nonlinear relationship is not statistically significant.

18. This interpretation must be guarded since AFM itself may be endogenous, and education may therefore affect AFM through "tastes" and through the opportunity cost of time.

19. The literature reveals mixed results on the impact of husband's education on fertility (S. H. Cochrane, 1979). For a negative relation see, for example, E. Kogut (1974), D. Chernichovsky (1976), and J. Kocher (1977);

for a positive relation see, S. Iutaka et al. (1971), S. DaVanzo (1972), M. Davidson (1973), M. A. Khan and I. Sirageldin (1975), M. Rosenzweig (1976a), S. H. Cochrane et al. (1977), and A. C. Kelley (1980).

20. A two-tailed test reveals that only category 2 (school, no primary certificate) is individually significant, although a one-tailed test would be appropriate here. If that were used, the significance level of each term exceeds 90 percent. A joint test of categories 2, 3, and 4 show husband's education to be significant at the 90 percent level.

21. The wealth-income effect on fertility is mixed in the literature. For a positive relationship, see I. Adelman (1963), B. Russet et al. (1964), D. M. Heer and E. S. Turner (1965), M. Nerlove and T. P. Schultz (1970), J. Encarnacion (1974), A. Bhattacharyya (1975), J. C. Caldwell (1975, 1977), J. C. Knowles and R. Anker (1975), D. Chernichovsky (1976), J. McCabe and M. Rosenzweig (1976), A. Aghajanian (1978), T. W. Merrick (1978), A. C. Kelley (1980). A useful review of the literature is found in J. Simon (1974). For a negative relationship, see S. Friedlander and M. Silver (1967), S. Iutaka et al. (1971), M. Davidson (1973), E. L. Kogut (1974), M. Rosenzweig (1976a), and S. H. Cochrane et al. (1977).

22. Joint tests show assets to be significant at the 99 percent level. The literature typically reveals that real assets (especially land holdings) have a positive impact on fertility. For example, see W. Stys (1957), P. Demeny (1968), R. A. Easterlin (1971), D. S. Kleinman (1973), W. W. Hicks (1974), S. E. Beaver (1975), I. Ajami (1976), M. Gerosvitz (1976), F. Arnold and C. Perjaranonda (1977), A. DeVany and N. Sanchez (1977), A. Latif and A. Chowdhury (1977), A. Aghajanian (1978), P. H. Lindert (1978), T. W. Merrick (1978). Exceptions to this relationship are found in J. Stoeckel and A. K. M. Chowdhury (1969), and M. Rosenzweig (1977).

23. In chapter 5 there was some evidence that the CEB-ASSETP relationship may be nonlinear. We therefore incorporated such a functional form in the regression and found that in two ranges of the CEB-ASSETP curve there are effects of different sign (positive for 0 - 2 assets range; negative for 3 or more assets), but that these effects are not statistically different from one another. As a result, the CEB-ASSETP in equation 6.1 is taken to be linear.

24. T. P. Schultz (1969, 1978), A. D. Williams (1977), and R. Olsen (1980).

25. B. L. Boulier (1979).

26. The technique involves modeling the various ways in which a household could obtain an observed combination of deaths and births and, then, constructing a general likelihood function which (1) makes assumptions on the occurrence of these events using assumed probability distributions, and (2) constructs an unobservable (latent) variable denoted as the number of children which would have been born to the family in the absence of experience of child deaths. The likelihood function parameters are estimated

using nonlinear techniques. For a detailed discussion of this procedure, consult J. A. Mauskopf (1981).

27. Average CEB for the 35+ and 40+ women are 6.6 and 7.3, respectively.

28. We are grateful to J. A. Mauskopf for permitting us to use her computer program developed to estimate the generalized maximum likelihood function.

29. While Boulier's technique uses model life tables, the essence of his computations is to transform the CD variable as follows:
$CDN = (CD_{family} - MR \cdot CEB_{family})$ where MR is the average mortality rate of the population being considered. In this case the replacement rate is $\hat{\beta}/(1 + \hat{\beta}MR)$ where $\hat{\beta}$ is the estimated coefficient of CDN.

30. If in fact households do not replace expected child deaths on a one-for-one basis, then the Boulier estimates are biased. The importance of such a bias is unclear.

31. S. H. Preston (1978).

32. D. N. DeTray (1978) has argued that a test of the importance of supply constraints can be made by comparing the impact of the education variable on CEB for the complete sample with the noncontracepting portion of the sample. If the effect of education on CEB is more negative for the contracepting population, then supply constraints may be relatively important. Appendix equation A.17 presents the basic CEB equation for the non-contracepting population. While comparing equations 6.1 and A.17 does reveal that the impact of education is more negative in the noncontracepting population, in neither regression is the education variable statistically different from zero. The DeTray test is therefore inconclusive as regards the Egyptian data set.

33. T. D. Wallace (1979).

34. J. A. Mauskopf (1981).

35. A comment is in order on the quadratic death ratio model. D. N. DeTray and Z. Khan (1977) have shown that even if there were no *behavioral* link between mortality and fertility, there is reason to expect a quadratic relationship between these variables. This is explained simply on the basis of the relative probabilities of the infant mortality variable. They conclude: "while there are reasonable arguments to support the contention that the relationship between mortality and fertility is nonlinear, it would be virtually impossible to test that hypothesis" with the data typically available for this type of analysis. D. N. DeTray and Z. Khan (1977, p. 323).

36. M. S. Issa (1981), using the 1974/75 National Fertility Survey found that mean parities, standardized by age and marriage duration, show lower values for rural Upper Egypt compared to rural Lower Egypt. He concluded that "Rural areas of Upper Egypt...show a relatively depressed level of fertility due to lower levels of natural fertility determinants" (p. 39).

37. B. Boulier and M. Rosenzweig (1978).

38. Consistency of the results, shown in our CEB model represented by equation 6.1, may be depicted by standardizing years since first marriage by age-specific natural fertility. This is done by dividing CEB by the number of children a woman would have if she had reproduced according to a natural fertility schedule from her AFM to her age on the survey date (AGEW). The resulting measure, denoted as the duration ratio (DRAT), is the one suggested by B. Boulier and M. Rosenzweig (1978). The DRAT was computed for the RFS data employing the same natural fertility schedule used by Boulier and Rosenzweig. On average, the DRAT value for the rural woman is .72. The regression model for the same independent variables in equation 6.1, excluding the AGEW and AFM variables, is

$$\begin{aligned} DRAT = {} & \underset{(14.09)}{.58} + \underset{(2.63)}{.14WE2} + \underset{(.58)}{.06WE3} - \underset{(-.40)}{.02HE2} + \underset{(.05)}{.004HE3} + \underset{(.29)}{.02HE4} \\ & - \underset{(-1.39)}{.03ASSETP} + \underset{(.10)}{.002ASSETR} + \underset{(2.37)}{.10ELEC} + \underset{(7.29)}{.10CD}\,. \end{aligned}$$

$r^2 = .02$

t values in parentheses

The main conclusion that education fails to reveal a negative influence on CEB is maintained, although with DRAT, WE2 shows a positive impact while the influence of HE3 vanishes. The largest difference in the results is the insignificant influence of ASSETR on DRAT. This is somewhat surprising given the highly consistent impact of ASSETR on several measures in our study.

39. See section 5.3, chapter 5, for a discussion of the definition of "workforce participation."

40. The low r^2 is partly the result of the definition of the dependent variable. A probit transformation where the dependent variable is constrained to lie between zero and unity represents a more appropriate statistical model for WEW. We have fitted such a model and the resulting estimated t-values are virtually the same as those obtained for the simple OLS model. Consequently, for expositional simplicity we present here only the OLS estimates.

41. As described in note 40, the Upper and Lower Egypt data were fitted with a probit transformation, and the results were basically the same as the OLS estimates.

42. While throughout this section reference is made to "child deaths," it should be noted that technically these are "offspring deaths." Mortality refers to all offspring of the eligible woman, irrespective of the offspring's age.

43. For Egypt, consult A. E. Sarhan (1967), M. H. El-Guindy (1971a), V. G. Valaoras (1972), A. H. Mousa and S. Mohamed (1973), A. R. Omran (1973c).

See also W. Ascoli et al. (1967), N. S. Scrimshaw (1970), S. Chandrasekhar (1972), L. Mata et al. (1972), S. H. Preston et al. (1972), K. E. Vaidyanathan (1972), K. V. Bailey (1975), S. H. Preston (1976, 1978), T. P. Schultz (1976), D. Friedlander (1977), and H. Ware (1977).

44. Appendix equations A.33 - A.35 reveal that the determinants of CD are broadly the same between Upper and Lower Egypt, although on average, other things equal, mortality is higher in Upper Egypt.

45. A joint one-tailed test of the negative impact reveals the husband's education to be significant at the 90 percent level.

46. For example, see W. Ascoli et al., (1967), N. S. Scrimshaw (1970), L. Mata et al., (1972), K. E. Vaidyanathan (1972), K. V. Bailey (1975), and S. H. Preston (1976).

47. A joint test reveals assets to be significant at the 95 percent level.

48. See T. P. Schultz (1976) and D. N. De Tray and Z. Khan (1977).

49. B. L. Boulier and N. G. Mankiw (1980); J. A. Mauskopf (1981).

CHAPTER 7

1. J. Bongaarts (1978). For an early analysis of this framework, consult K. Davis and J. Blake (1956).

2. M. Nag (1979) showed that from the empirical point of view "there is no evidence that modernization [socioeconomic changes] has affected the following variables significantly in any direction, positive or negative: frequency of intercourse, divorce/separation, and involuntary abstinence" (p. 40).

3. S. F. Loza and M. N. El-Khorazaty (1979, p. 18).

4. It is worth mentioning that 85.4 percent of ever-married women have breastfed their last child, and this statistic reaches 95.7 percent among women who have already had at least one live birth. The important point here is to recognize it as a contraceptive method.

5. CAPMAS (1981a, 1981b).

6. A. M. Khalifa, H. A. Sayed, and M. N. El-Khorazaty (1981b).

7. While most of the results in table 7.4 are invariant to an adjustment for age, a cohort effect is clearly evident in the breastfeeding-education relationships. For example, for wife's education, the unadjusted figures range from 5.8 to 7.7; the adjusted ones from 5.8 to 10.0. The adjustment, then, serves to strengthen the general relationships model in the text.

8. M. Nag (1979, p. 38).

9. M. Nag (1979, p. 11).

10. J. Bongaarts (1979).

11. Data on improper (inefficient) use of modern contraceptives and discontinuation rates are to be collected in the second round of the RFS scheduled in March 1982.

12. M. Nag (1979, pp. 40-41). For a recent case study, see A. Romaniuk (1981). M. N. El-Khorazaty (1978) discusses the effect of different family planning strategies with different prevalence and discontinuation rates on future fertility and population figures in Egypt. Higher rates of dis-

continuation and improper use of modern methods with lower prevalence rates will result in an increase in fertility rates in Egypt.

13. These respondents are excluded from the tabulations.

CHAPTER 8

1. This speculation is to be examined in detail in the second round of the RFS, to be conducted in 1982.

2. The following analysis combines the results of chapter 7 with a preview of some of the major findings in chapter 10.

3. A discussion of this index is found in chapter 4, section 4.3.3.

4. B. F. Johnston and W. C. Clark (1982) have emphasized that the *composition* of production activities and household consumption constitutes a critical dimension to developing an integrated rural development policy that increases wealth while simultaneously diminishing family size (chapters 3 and 4).

5. Several socioeconomic determinants of fertility control in Egypt are examined in M. Abdel-Kader (1971), A. Thavarajah and M. M. Farag (1971), M. El-Rafei (1973), Z. A. Marzouk (1973), and S. M. Gadalla (1978).

6. For reference, the regression models considered in this chapter have been re-estimated using the sample of intact marriages. These results are presented in appendix table A.3. Since the findings are largely invariant to the sample used, we have elected to analyze in the text only the results of the total RFS sample.

7. A probit transformation where the dependent variable is constrained to lie between zero and unity represents a more appropriate statistical model for CUCM and EUCM. We have fitted such a model, and the resulting estimated t-values are virtually the same as those obtained for the simple OLS model. Consequently, for expositional simplicity we present here only the OLS estimates.

8. The positive impact of education on contraceptive use is a fairly pervasive empirical finding. See S. H. Cochrane (1979, ch. 5); also, for example, J. C. Caldwell (1968), J. Palmore (1969), CELADE (1972), B. Chung et al. (1972), J. Knodel and P. Pitakepsombati (1973), A. Speare et al. (1973), A. Sear (1975), and A. M. Khalifa (1976).

9. The impact of wife's education on contraceptive use does not appear to work through the impact of education on workforce participation. Indeed, WEW is statistically insignificant when introduced into equations 8.1 and 8.2; moreover, the estimated parameter on WE2 and WE3 is uninfluenced by the inclusion or exclusion of WEW. Considering only the result for EUCM, we find:

$$\underset{}{\text{EUCM}} = \underset{(-4.79)}{-.19} + \underset{(10.87)}{.13\text{CS}} - \underset{(-5.62)}{.002\text{AGEW}\cdot\text{CS}} + \underset{(2.56)}{.003\text{AGE}} + \underset{(5.03)}{.09\text{WE2}} + \underset{(2.67)}{.09\text{WE3}}$$

$$+ .06HE2 + .11HE3 + .14HE4 + .06ASSETP - .02ASSETR$$
$$(3.92) \quad (3.92) \quad (5.40) \quad (9.16) \quad (-2.68)$$

$$+ .06ELEC - .0006WEW.$$
$$(4.19) \quad (-.04)$$

$r^2 = .21$

t values in parentheses

10. The estimates of CS may be biased downward if women who use contraception are able to attain smaller family sizes.

11. See above, note 7.

12. See D. Kirk (1966). M. S. A. Issa (1981), in his detailed analysis of Egyptian fertility using the 1974-75 National Fertility Survey, concludes: "Southern Egypt, both the rural and urban areas, is still the most traditional society in Egypt. Current fertility there is at a high level and is in a natural regime, particularly in rural areas. ...Cultural institutions, values and attitudes such as strong kin ties, strong son preference, large family size norms, endogenous marriages, extended family, polygamy, low levels of female's education and participation in the labor force, are holding very strongly in Upper Egypt " (p. 14). For different arguments, see O. Schieffelin (1967), A. El-Sharabasy (1969), S. Ewies (1971), and L. S. El-Hamamsy (1972).

13. To explore in greater detail the impact of contraceptive use by age, the sample was also divided into three cohorts: <25, 25-34, and 35+. For each age group, contraceptive use reveals a statistically significant positive "impact" on CEB.

14. Some of the statistical and methodological issues involved in measuring the impact of family planning are discussed by A. I. Hermalin (1973).

15. Earlier studies on the impact of contraceptive use on fertility in Egypt assumed proper use of modern contraceptives to estimate the number of births averted to show the reduction in birthrates as a result of contraceptive use. See M. M. El-Nomrosey (1971), B. M. Ibrahim (1974), and M. N. El-Khorazaty (1978).

16. Operationally this would apply to women who have completed their childbearing, and for whom there are no supply constraints.

17. The negative impact of education on desired family size is widely found in the empirical literature. See, for example, J. Caldwell (1968), J. Palmore et al. (1969), D. Pool (1970), CELADE (1972), A. Speare et al. (1973), R. Freedman et al. (1974), A. Paydarfar (1975), W. Weekes-Vaglioni (1976), H. Rizk (1977), and S. H. Cochrane (1979, ch. 4).

18. See R. A. Easterlin and E. Crimmins (1981).

19. M. S. A. Issa (1981, pp. 212-239).

20. M. S. A. Issa (1981, p. 24). See also pp. 212-239.

21. As an experiment, wife's workforce status was introduced into equation

8.5. WEW was found to have a statistically significant deterring impact on DNC. In particular, we found:

$$\underset{}{DNC} = \underset{(54.31)}{4.70} - \underset{(-4.33)}{.49WE2} - \underset{(-2.08)}{.48WE3} - \underset{(-2.53)}{.27HE2} - \underset{(-1.46)}{.27HE3} - \underset{(-4.22)}{.73HE4}$$

$$- \underset{(-2.18)}{.10ASSETP} + \underset{(1.69)}{.06ASSETR} - \underset{(-1.20)}{.11ELEC} - \underset{(-3.82)}{.39WEW}.$$

$r^2 = .029$

t values in parentheses

22. M. S. A. Issa (1981) concludes that rural Egypt in general, and Upper Egypt in particular, can be described as being largely in the natural fertility regime: "Rural areas in Upper Egypt...show a relatively depressed level of fertility due to lower levels of natural fertility determinants... " (p. 39).

23. A probit transformation where the dependent variable is constrained to lie between zero and unity represents a more appropriate statistical model. We have fitted such a model and the resulting estimated t-values are virtually the same as the OLS regressions in appendix table A.6. Consequently, for expositional simplicity we present only the OLS estimates.

24. The probit results are generally confirmed by some separate regressions which use the degree of excess demand (DNC-CS) as the dependent variable. For women 35+ in rural Egypt, one such regression is as follows:

$$(DNC\text{-}CS) = \underset{(-1.84)}{-.38} - \underset{(-2.07)}{.49WE2} - \underset{(-.93)}{.59WE3} - \underset{(-1.82)}{.41HE2} - \underset{(-1.52)}{.62HE3} - \underset{(-.76)}{.41HE4}$$

$$+ \underset{(.27)}{.02ASSETP} - \underset{(-.75)}{.06ASSETR} - \underset{(-3.06)}{.58ELEC} + \underset{(7.83)}{1.38UPPER}.$$

$r^2 = .09$

t values in parentheses

25. An examination of the determinants of surviving children for the 35+ sample reveals that the net supply of children increases with wealth (electricity, real assets), but not with education.

$$CS = \underset{(34.07)}{4.51} + \underset{(.03)}{.007WE2} + \underset{(.01)}{.008WE3} + \underset{(1.34)}{.22HE2} - \underset{(-.48)}{.15HE3} + \underset{(.09)}{.04HE4}$$

$$+ \underset{(.49)}{.03ASSETP} + \underset{(4.00)}{.22ASSETR} + \underset{(4.63)}{.63ELEC}.$$

$r^2 = .04$

t values in parentheses

26. For an integrated development strategy that combines policies in the areas of nutrition, health, and family planning, see B. F. Johnston and W. C.

Clark (1982). P. Mauldin and B. Berelson (1978) have provided a convincing statistical statement which supports the view of the mutually reinforcing effects of family planning programs and development as a strategy for population policy in developing countries.

CHAPTER 9

1. T. W. Schultz (1974b, p. 10).
2. S. H. Cochrane (1979, p. 42).
3. J. M. Stycos (1968).
4. S. H. Cochrane (1979, p. 39).
5. S. Timur (1977, p. 472).
6. A. M. Khalifa (1971a,b, 1973a); S. M. Gadalla (1978); H. A. Sayed and M. N. El-Khorazaty (1980); M. S. A. Issa (1981).
7. A recent review of some of these relationships is found in S. H. Cochrane et al. (1980).
8. United Nations (1980, p. 231).
9. This particular group was selected to restrict attention to women who are homogenous in their exposure to the risk of marriage. This minimizes the "censoring effect." (See chapter 5, note 4, for the definition of the censoring effect.)
10. See note 6 above.
11. See A. K. Jain (1981) for a discussion of this index.
12. A. K. Jain (1981).
13. The relationship between education and mortality is complex and determined in part by the age at marriage. Child mortality and pregnancy loss are sensitive to age at marriage, and the latter, in turn, is influenced by education. These relationships are explored in greater detail in chapter 6.
14. M. Nag (1979).
15. See A. K. Jain (1981) for a similar relationship observed in Indonesia and Malaysia.
16. A. K. Jain (1981, p. 589).
17. There is also more to female education than its relationship to the number of children ever born. A. K. Jain (1981) emphasizes that education of women increases "exposure to the information and ideas disseminated through printed material. This brings changes in their general behavior involving breastfeeding, use of contraception, and fertility. In addition, staying longer in schools increases the age at marriage " (p. 594).
18. It is also necessary to obtain information on years of schooling, not simply the broad educational categories available in the present study.

CHAPTER 10

1. Aspects of the PDP are described in A. S. Hassan (1977), N. Iskander

and I. Omar (1979), A. A. Fattah (1979, 1980), A. Bindary (1980), UNFPA (1980, 1981a), H. Shanawany (1980), and A. M. Khalifa, H. A. Sayed, and M. N. El-Khorazaty (1981b).

2. UNFPA (1981a, p. 62).

3. For details by governorates, see appendix tables C.1-C.3.

4. UNFPA (1981b, p. 36).

5. An incentive income payment system has been established for the PDP staff at all levels, in which a standard amount of income incentives, either monthly or quarterly, is determined for each level. Each staff member is evaluated by his/her immediate supervisor according to a standard evaluation sheet to determine his/her performance level. Activities to be evaluated are different for each level according to responsibilities. Factors to be considered are comprehension of job responsibilities, job performance, training acquired or provided, attendance at or scheduling of meetings, visits made, and services provided (especially family planning), IEC (information, education and communication) activities conducted or provided, family planning practice in the community, accuracy of records, etc. Each staff member is paid an income incentive according to his/her level of performance as a percentage of the standard amount of incentives. No incentive is paid when the level of performance is below 60 percent.

6. UNFPA (1979, p. 1).

7. UNFPA (1981a, p. 22).

8. B. F. Johnston and W. C. Clark (1982) review a limited number of other case studies of integrated rural development policies which emphasize aspects of population control.

9. Currently there are three circulating, unpublished reports which evaluate selected aspects of the PDP. These include J. M. Stycos and R. Avery (1980), A. M. Khalifa, H. A. Sayed, and M. N. El-Khorazaty (1981b), and A. M. Khalifa and A. Way (1981c). The results of these studies will be compared with those of the present study at the conclusion of this chapter.

10. For real assets, the greater prosperity of PDP villages is unequivocal. A larger proportion of non-PDP households possess no assets at all, and for PDP and non-PDP households with real assets, the number per household is 2.24 and 1.75, respectively. In terms of personal assets, there is again a greater prevalence of households with no assets in the non-PDP sample. On the other hand, assets per household are fewer in number in the PDP versus the non-PDP samples (1.42 versus 1.62).

11. Each of the basic equations has been also fitted on the PDP and non-PDP samples, which allows all the parameters to be influenced by "PDP effects." While statistical tests have not been performed, an examination of the results indicates that the slope coefficients are broadly invariant to the PDP effect. Thus, the simple binary specification appears to provide a useful

representation of the PDP effect.

12. Since the PDP programs were in operation for only ten months, on average, recent measures of fertility and mortality which refer to the period since the program's introduction should be used. However, these data, contained in the pregnancy history file, were not available to us at the time of this study.

13. A. M. Khalifa and A. Way (1981c).

14. See A. M. Khalifa and A. Way (1981c, pp. 13, 17).

15. It is of considerable interest to note that while the estimated parameters on CD, EUCM, CUCM, and DNC are not statistically significant from zero in Upper Egypt, the signs of each of these parameters are broadly consistent with the supply constraint hypothesis, and also with the possibility that CEB may increase with economic development (or the PDP).

16. See above, note 9.

17. A more detailed discussion of these indices is provided in chapter 4, section 4.3.2.

18. A measure of non-PDP programming is also available in the data file, and the correlation between PDP and non-PDP programming (.38) is relatively high.

19. Here we adopt the interpretation that increased contraceptive use will reduce CEB.

20. Note that this policy may be inconsistent with employment policies, and with other objectives and constraints.

21. For a discussion of various rural development policy packages, and strategies for implementing these integrated development schemes, see B. F. Johnston and W. C. Clark (1982).

APPENDIX B

1. M. Nizamuddin (1980, p. 3). See also B. Berelson (1976), R. Freedman (1974), J. E. Kocher (1973), G. McNicoll (1975), United Nations (1978), and UNFPA (1979) for similar arguments.

2. United Nations (1978, p. 61).

3. R. Ridker (1976).

References

Abbott, J. 1974. "The Employment of Women and the Reduction of Fertility: Implications for Development." *World Development* 2:23-26.

Abdel-Fadil, M. 1975. "Development, Income Distribution and Social Change in Rural Egypt (1952-70)." Occasional Paper No. 45, Department of Applied Economics, Cambridge University.

Abdel-Hakim, S. 1981. *Population Density and Distribution in Egypt.* A paper presented to panel on Population Growth in Egypt, June 4-7, Cairo.

Abdel-Kader, M. 1971. "Summary Factors Determining Husband's Attitudes Towards Family Planning." *Egyptian Population and Family Planning Review* 4,1 (June):73-78.

Abou-Gamrah, H. 1977. *A Path to Stationary Population in Egypt and Its Family Planning Targets.* Mimeographed paper. Cairo: American University in Cairo.

Abou-Gamrah, H., and Mamish, M. A. 1971. "Socio-Economic Fertility Differentials in Arab Countries." *Fertility Trends and Differentials in Arab Countries,* Part II, Research Monograph Series. Cairo: Cairo Demographic Centre 2:211-240.

Abul Nil, M. 1978. "Difference in Attitudes Between Husbands and Wives in Upper and Lower Egypt Towards Family Planning." *Population Studies* (Cairo) 45:3-70. (Arabic)

Adelman, I. 1963. "An Econometric Analysis of Population Growth." *American Economic Review* 53 (June):314-339.

Aghajanian, A. 1978. "Fertility and Family Economy in the Iranian Rural Communities." *Journal of Comparative Family Studies* 9 (Spring):119-127.

Ajami, I. 1976. "Differential Fertility in Peasant Communities: A Study of Six Iranian Villages." *Population Studies* 30:453-463.

Al-Kordy, M. 1979. "The Population Matter Between Family Planning and Development Projects in Egypt." *Population Studies* (Cairo) 51 (October /December):1-70. (Arabic)

Anker, R., and Knowles, J. C. 1981. *Fertility in Kenya.* Belgium: Ordina Press.

Arnold, F., and Perjaranonda, C. 1977. "Economic Factors in Family Size Decisions in Thailand." *Report No. 2, World Fertility Study.* Bangkok, Thailand.

Ascoli, W., Guzman, M. A., Scrimshaw, N. S., and Gordon, J. E. 1967.

"Nutrition and Infection Field Study in Guatemalan Villages, 1959-1964. IV. Death of Infants and Preschool Children." *Archives of Environmental Health* 15 (October):439-449.

Badran, H. 1974. "The Cost of a Child; the Decision to Have a Big Family Depends on the More or Less Conscious Evaluation of the Cost/Benefit Ratio." *Ceres* 7,4:25-30.

Bailey, K. V. 1975. "Malnutrition in the African Region." *Chronicle of the World Health Organization* 29:354-364.

Banks, J. A. 1954. *Prosperity and Parenthood.* London: Routledge and Kegan Paul.

Basu, D. N. 1978. "Impact of Agricultural Development on Demographic Behavior with Particular Reference to Fertility." In *Population Change and Rural Development in India*, ed. J. R. Rele and M. K. Kain. Bombay: International Institute for Population Studies.

Beaver, S. E. 1975. *Demographic Transition Theory Reinterpreted: An Application to Recent Natality Trends in Latin America.* Lexington, Mass.: D. C. Heath and Co.

Becker, G. S. 1960. "An Economic Analysis of Fertility." In *Demographic and Economic Changes in Developed Countries.* Princeton, N.J.: Princeton University Press.

Becker, G. S. 1965. "A Theory of the Allocation of Time." *Economic Journal* 75 (September):493-517.

Becker, G. S. 1978. *The Demand for Children.* Mimeographed paper. Chicago: University of Chicago, Workshop in Applications of Economics.

Becker, G. S., and Lewis, H. G. 1973. "On the Interaction Between the Quantity and Quality of Children." *Journal of Political Economy* 81, part 2 (March/April):S279-88.

Ben-Porath, Y. 1973. "Economic Analysis of Fertility in Israel." In *Economics of Family: Marriage, Children and Human Capital*, ed. T. W. Schultz. Chicago: University of Chicago Press for the NBER.

Ben-Porath, Y. 1980. "Child Mortality and Fertility: Issues in the Demographic Transition of a Migrant Population." In *Population and Economic Change in Developing Countries*, ed. R. A. Easterlin. Chicago: University of Chicago Press.

Berelson, B. 1976. "Social Science Research on Population: A Review." *Population and Development Review* 2:219-266.

Bhattacharyya, A. K. 1975. "Income Inequality and Fertility: A Comparative View." *Population Studies* 29,1:5-20.

Bindary, A. 1972. *Family Welfare-A Suggested System for Social Security.* Mimeographed paper. Cairo: The Supreme Council for Family Planning, Executive Board.

Bindary, A. 1973a. *Family Plannning.* Mimeographed paper. Cairo: The Supreme Council for Family Planning, Executive Board.

Bindary, A. 1973b. "Some Research Needs of the National Planning Program." In *Egypt: Population Problems and Prospects*, ed. by A. R. Omran. Chapel Hill, N. C.: Carolina Population Center, University of North Carolina.

Bindary, A. 1978. "Situation Analysis." In *1979/80 Project Document submitted to the UNFPA*, by Population and Family Planning Board. Cairo: The Supreme Council for Population and Family Planning.

Bindary, A. 1980a. "National Population and Family Planning Policy." *Population Studies* (Cairo) 53 (April/June):1-23. (Arabic)

Bindary, A. 1980b. *Population and Rural Development.* Paper presented to Cairo University Development Research and Technological Planning Center and Secretariat General of Local Government's Workshop on Local Government and Regional Development, January 6-10, Cairo.

Bindary, A., Baxter, C. B., and Hollingsworth, T. H. 1973. "Urban Rural Differences in the Relationship Between Women's Employment and Fertility: A Preliminary Study." *Journal of Biosocial Science* 5,2 (April): 159-167.

Birdsall, N. 1976. "Women and Population Studies." *Signs* 1:699-712.

Blake, J. 1968. "Are Babies Consumer Durables? Critique of the Economic Theory of Reproductive Motivation." *Population Studies* 22:5-25.

Blandy, R., and Woodfield, A. 1976. *Towards a Characteristics Asset-Portfolio Theory of Fertility.* Mimeographed paper. Australia: University of Adelaide, Department of Economics.

Bongaarts, J. 1978. "A Framework for Analyzing the Proximate Determinants of Fertility." *Population and Development Review* 4,1:105-132.

Bongaarts, J. 1979. "The Fertility impact of Traditional and Changing Childspacing Practices in Tropical Africa." Center for Policy Studies, Working Paper No. 42. New York: The Population Council.

Bongaarts, J. 1980. "Does Nutrition Affect Fecundity? A Summary of the Evidence." *Science* 208:564-569.

Bongaarts, J., and Delgado, H. 1979. "Effects of Nutritional Status on Fertility in Rural Guatemala." In *Natural Fertility*, ed. J. A. Menken and H. Leridon. Leige, Belgium: Ordina Editions.

Boulier, B. L. 1979. Letter to T. Dudley Wallace.

Boulier, B. L., and Mankiw, N. G. 1980. "An Econometric Model of the Demand, Supply and Regulation of Fertility." Mimeographed paper. Princeton, N.J.: Princeton University.

Boulier, B. L., and Rosenzweig, M. R. 1980. "Age, Biological Factors, and Socioeconomic Determinants of Fertility: A New Measure of Cumulative Fertility for Use in the Socioeconomic Analysis of Family Size." *Demography* 15,4:487-497.

Bourgeois-Pichat, J. 1965. "Les Facteurs de la Fecondite non Dirigee." *Population* 20:383-424.

Brackett, J. W., Ravenholt, R. T., and Chao, J. C. 1978. "The Role of Family Planning in Recent Rapid Declines in Fertility in Developing Countries: Some Findings From the World Fertility Survey." *Studies in Family Planning* 9,12:314-323.

Brass, W. 1975. *Methods of Estimating Fertility and Mortality from Limited and Defective Data.* An Occasional Publication, International Program of Laboratories for Population Statistics, University of North Carolina at Chapel Hill.

Brass, W., and Barrett, J. C. 1978. "Measurement Problems in the Analysis of Linkages Between Fertility and Child Mortality." In *The Effects of Infant and Child Mortality on Fertility*, ed. S. H. Preston. New York: Academic Press.

Bumpass, L. L. 1969. "Age at Marriage as a Variable in Socio-Economic Differentials in Fertility." *Demography* 6:45-54.

Cain, M. T. 1977. "The Economic Activities of Children in a Village in Bangladesh." *Population and Development Review* 3,3:201-228.

Caldwell, J. C. 1968. "The Control of Family Size in Tropical Africa." *Demography* 5:589-619.

Caldwell, J. C. 1975. *Population Growth and Socioeconomic Change in West Africa.* New York: Columbia University Press.

Caldwell, J. C. 1976. "Toward a Restatement of Demographic Transition Theory." *Population and Development Review* 2,3-4:321-366.

Caldwell, J. C. 1977. "The Economic Rationality of High Fertility: An Investigation Illustrated with Nigerian Survey Data." *Population Studies* 31:5-27.

Caldwell, J. C. 1978. "A Theory of Fertility: From High Plateau to Destabilization." *Population and Development Review* 4,4 (December):553-577.

Caldwell, P. 1977. "Egypt and the Arabic and Islamic World." In *The Persistence of High Fertility*, Volume II, ed. J. C. Caldwell. Canberra: Department of Demography, Australian National University.

CAPMAS. *Statistical Yearbook.* Cairo: Central Agency for Public Mobilization and Statistics. Selected Years.

CAPMAS. 1978a. *Population and Development: A Study on the Population Increases and Its Challenge to Development in Egypt.* Cairo: Central Agency for Public Mobilization and Statistics. (Arabic)

CAPMAS. 1978b. *1976 Population and Housing Census: Detailed Results (Total Republic).* Cairo: Central Agency for Public Mobilization and Statistics, Ref. No. 1978-15111-93. (Arabic)

CAPMAS. 1978c. *Reproduction Behavior of Egyptian Women and Their Attitudes Towards Family Planning According to the National Fertility Survey: 1974/1975.* Cairo: Central Agency for Public Mobilization and Statistics, Ref. No. 1R/78. (Arabic)

CAPMAS. 1981a. *Egyptian Fertility Survey 1980.* Cairo: Central Agency for Public Mobilization and Statistics, Ref. No. 95-22000-81.

CAPMAS. 1981b. *A Statement on the Population of the Arab Republic of Egypt.* Cairo: Central Agency for Public Mobilization and Statistics.

Carr-Saunders, A. M. 1936. *World Population.* Oxford: The Clarendon Press.

CELADE (United Nations Center for Demographic Training and Research in Latin America) and CFSC (Community and Family Study Center). 1972. *Fertility and Family Planning in Metropolitan Latin America.* Chicago: University of Chicago Press.

Chandrasekhar, S. 1972. *Infant Mortality, Population Growth and Family Planning in India.* Chapel Hill, N.C.: University of North Carolina Press.

Chaudhury, R. H. 1977. "Relative Income and Fertility." *Demography* 14,2:179-195.

Chernichovsky, D. 1976. *Fertility Behavior in Developing Economies: An Investment Approach.* Paper Presented at IUSSP Seminar on Household Models of Economic-Demographic Decision-Making, (November) Mexico City.

Chowdhury, A. K. M., Khan, A. R., and Chen, L. C. 1976. "The Effect of Child Mortality Experience on Subsequent Fertility in Pakistan and

Bangladesh." *Population Studies* 30:249-261.

Chung, B. M., et al. 1972. *Psychological Perspectives: Family Planning in Korea*. Seoul: Hollym Corporation.

Clark, C. 1967. *Population Growth and Land Use*. New York: St. Martin's Press.

Cleland, W. 1936. *The Population Problem in Egypt*. Lancaster: The Science Press.

Cochrane, S. H. 1975. "Children as By-Products, Investment Goods, and Consumer Goods: A Review of Some Micro-Economic Models of Fertility." *Population Studies* 29:373-390.

Cochrane, S. H. 1979. *Fertility and Education. What Do We Really Know?* World Bank Staff Occasional Papers, No. 26. Baltimore: Johns Hopkins University Press.

Cochrane, S. H., Baidya, B. G., and Hay, J. 1977. "Memo of Fertility in the Parsa Pretest in Rural Nepal." World Bank: Division on Population and Human Resources.

Cochrane, S. H., O'Hara, D. J., and Leslie, J. 1980. *The Effects of Education on Health*. Mimeographed paper. World Bank Staff Working Paper 405, pp. 96.

Cuca, R., and Pierce, C. S. 1977. *Experiments in Family Planning*. Baltimore: Johns Hopkins University Press.

DaVanzo, J. S. 1972. *The Determinants of Family Formation in Chile, 1960: An Econometric Study of Female Labor Force Participation, Marriage, and Fertility Decisions*. Mimeographed paper. Santa Monica, Calif.: The Rand Corporation, R-830-AID.

Davidson, M. 1973. "A Comparative Study of Fertility in Mexico City and Caracas." *Social Biology* 20 (December):460-496.

Davis, K., and Blake, J. 1956. "Social Structure and Fertility: An Analytical Framework." *Economic Development and Cultural Change* 4,3 (April): 211-235.

De Tray, D. N. 1972. *The Interaction Between Parent Investment in Children and Family Size: An Economic Analysis*. Mimeographed paper. Santa Monica, Calif.: The Rand Corporation, R-1003-RF.

De Tray, D. N. 1977. "Age at Marriage and Fertility: A Policy Review." *Pakistan Development Review* 16,1 (Spring).

De Tray, D. N. 1978. *The Demand for Children in a 'Natural Fertility' Population*. Mimeographed paper. Santa Monica, Calif.: The Rand Corporation.

De Tray, D. N., and Khan, Z. 1977. "On the Care and Handling of Regression Specifications in Fertility Research." *Pakistan Development Review* (August):309-324.

Demeny, P. 1968. "Early Fertility Decline in Austria-Hungary: A Lesson in Demographic Transition." *Daedulus* 97 (Spring):502-522.

DeVany, A., and Sanchez, N. 1977. "Property Rights, Uncertainty and Fertility: An Analysis of the Effect of Land Reform on Fertility in Rural Mexico." *Review of World Economics* 113:741-764.

Duesenberry, J. S. 1960. Comment on "An Economic Analysis of Fertility" by G. S. Becker. In *Demographic and Economic Change in Developed Countries*. Universities-National Bureau Conference Series, No. 11. Princeton, N.J.: Princeton University Press.

Easterlin, R. A. 1971. "Does Human Fertility Adjust to the Environment?" *American Economic Review: Papers and Proceedings* 61:399-407.

Easterlin, R. A. 1975. "An Economic Framework for Fertility Analysis." *Studies in Family Planning* 6:54-63.

Easterlin, R. A. 1978. "The Economics and Sociology of Fertility: A Synthesis." In *Historical Studies of Changing Fertility*, ed. C. Tilly. Princeton, N.J.: Princeton University Press.

Easterlin, R. A. 1980. "Fertility and Development." *Population Bulletin of ECWA* 18 (June):1-40.

Easterlin, R. A., and Crimmins, E. M. 1981. *An Exploratory Study of the Synthesis Framework of Fertility Determination with WFS Core Questionnaire Data*. Mimeographed paper. Philadelphia: University of Pennsylvania.

Easterlin, R. A., Pollack, R. A., and Wachter, M. L. 1980. "Toward a More General Economic Model of Fertility Determination: Endogenous Preference and Natural Fertility." In *Population and Economic Change in Developing Countries*, ed. R. A. Easterlin. Chicago: University of Chicago Press.

Elandt-Johnson, R. C., and Johnson, N. L. 1980. *Survival Models and Data Analysis*. New York: John Wiley and Sons.

El-Badry, M. A. 1956. "Some Aspects of Fertility in Egypt." *The Milbank Memorial Fund Quarterly* 34,1:22-43.

El-Badry, M. A., and Rizk, H. 1967. "Regional Fertility Differences Among Socio-Economic Groups in the United Arab Republic." *World Population Conference, 1965*. Vol. 6. New York: United Nations.

El-Guindy, M. H. 1971a. "Trends of Infant Mortality Rates by Sex and Age, Urban and Rural Arab Republic of Egypt 1950-1969." *Population Researches and Studies* 1 (October):13-49.

El-Guindy, M. H. 1971b. "Age at Marriage in Relation to Fertility in Egypt." *Fertility Trends and Differentials in Arab Countries*, Research Monograph Series. Cairo: Cairo Demographic Centre 2:107-115.

El-Hamamsy, L. S. 1972. "Belief Systems and Family Planning in Peasant Societies." In *Are Our Descendants Doomed? Technological Change and Population Growth*, ed. H. Brown and E. Hutchings, Jr. New York: The Viking Press.

El-Hinnawy, H. 1978. "Cost-Benefit Analysis of the Family Planning Programme." *Population Studies* (Cairo) 46 (July/September):6-15.

El-Khorazaty, M. N. 1978. "Family Planning Practice and Population Projections." Workshop Publication Series, No. W/2, Demographic Projection Analysis. Cairo: Computer Center, American University in Cairo.

El-Nomrosey, M. M. 1971. "The Impact of Contraceptive Use on Fertility Levels: An Analytical Study." Cairo: The Supreme Council for Family Planning.

El-Rafei, M. 1973. "Determinants of Family Planning Acceptance in a Low Socio-Economic Group of Women." *Egyptian Population and Family Planning Review* 6,1 (June):15-24.

El-Sharabasy, A. 1969. *Islam and Family Planning*. Cairo: The Egyptian Family Planning Association.

Encarnacion, J. P. 1974. "Fertility and Labor Force Participation: Philippines, 1968." *Philippine Review of Economics and Business* 11:113-

141.

Ewies, S. 1971. "The Impact of Islamic Ideology Upon the Egyptian Family." Cairo: National Centre for Sociological and Criminological Research.

Fakhouri, H. 1972. *Kafr El-Elow: An Egyptian Village in Transition.* New York: Holt, Rinehart and Winston.

Farah, N. R., and Eid, S. 1979. *On the Interaction Between Socio-Economic Indicators of Development and Some Population Measures.* Cairo: Population and Family Planning Board.

Fattah, A. A. 1979. "Population and Development Project." *Population Studies* (Cairo) 49:20-35. (Arabic)

Fattah, A. A. 1980. "Population and Development Project Achievements 1978/1979." *Population Studies* (Cairo) 53 (April/June):31-45. (Arabic)

Fergany, N. 1975. *The Relationship Between Fertility Level and Societal Development and Implications for Planning to Reduce Fertility.* Cairo: Population and Family Planning Board.

Fleiss, J. L. 1973. *Statistical Methods for Rates and Proportions.* New York: John Wiley and Sons.

Frederiksen, H. 1966. "Determinants and Consequences of Mortality and Fertility Trends." *Public Health Reports* 81,8 (August):715-727.

Freedman, R. 1974. "Community Level Data in Fertility Surveys." World Fertility Survey. Occasional Paper No. 8, The Hague: International Statistical Institute.

Freedman, R., Coombs, L., Chang, M., and Sun, T. H. 1974. "Trends in Fertility, Family Size Preferences and Practices of Family Planning: Taiwan, 1965- 1973." *Studies in Family Planning* 5 (September):270-288.

Friedlander, D. 1977. "The Effect of Child Mortality on Fertility. Theoretical Framework of the Relationship." Proceedings of the IUSSP Conference, Mexico. Liege, Belgium: International Union for the Scientific Study of Population.

Friedlander, S., and Silver, M. 1967. "A Quantitative Study of the Determinants of Fertility Behavior." *Demography* 4,1:30-70.

Frisch, R. 1975. "Demographic Implications of the Biological Determinants of Female Fecundity." *Social Biology* 22:17-22.

Frisch, R. 1978. "Population, Food Intake, and Fertility." *Science* 200 (1978):22-30.

Gabr, M. 1981. "Population Perspectives in Egypt, 1980." Statement to The Egypt Consultative Group Meeting in Aswan, Egypt, January 1981.

Gadalla, S. M. 1978. *Is There Hope? Fertility and Family Planning in a Rural Egyptian Community.* Cairo: American University in Cairo Press.

Gerosvitz, M. 1976. "Land Reform: Some Theoretical Considerations." *Journal of Development Studies* 13 (October):79-91.

Goldstein, S. 1972. "The Influence of Labor Force Participation and Education on Fertility in Thailand." *Population Studies* 26:419-436.

Gupte, P. 1979. "The World Watches Egypt's New Population Programme." *Populi* 6,1:3-7.

Hassan, A. S. 1977. "Definitions and Dimensions of Relating Population Targets to Local Development's Project." *Population Studies* (Cairo) 43:4-14. (Arabic)

Hassan, S. 1966. *The Influence of Child Mortality on Fertility.* Paper Presented at the Annual Meeting of the Population Association of America, New York City.

Hassan, S. 1971. "Effect of Religion and Child Mortality on Fertility." *Fertility Trends and Differentials in Arab Countries*, Part II, Research Monograph Series. Cairo: Cairo Demographic Centre 2:273 and Appendix.

Hassan, S. 1973. "Childhood Mortality Experience and Fertility Performance." In *Egypt: Population Problems and Prospects*, ed. A. R. Omran. Chapel Hill, N.C.: Carolina Population Center, University of North Carolina.

Hassan, S.; Sallam, A.; and Ahmed, A. M. 1971. "Factors Affecting Fertility in Rural Areas of Lower Egypt." *Fertility Trends and Differentials in Arab Countries*, Part II, Research Monograph Series. Cairo: Cairo Demographic Centre 2:241-266.

Hawthorn, G. 1970. *The Sociology of Fertility.* London: Collier-MacMillan Ltd.

Heer, D. M. 1966. "Economic Development and Fertility." *Demography* 3,2:423-444.

Heer, D. M., and Smith, D. O. 1968. "Mortality Level, Desired Family Size, and Population Increase." *Demography* 5,1:104-121.

Heer, D. M., and Turner, E. S. 1965. "Area Differences in Latin American Fertility." *Population Studies* 18:279-292.

Henry, L. 1961. "Some Data on Natural Fertility." *Eugenics Quarterly* 8:81-91.

Hermalin, A. I. 1973. "Regression Analysis of Aerial Data." In *Measuring the Effect of Family Planning Programs on Fertility*, ed. C. Chandrasekaran and A. I. Hermalin. Belgium: Ordina Editions.

Hicks, W. W. 1974. "Economic Development and Fertility Change in Mexico, 1950-1970." *Demography* 11:407-421.

Hill, A. 1975. "The Fertility of the Asian Community of East Africa." *Population Studies* 29:344-372.

Huffman, S. L., Chowdhury, A. K. M., and Mosley, W. H. 1978. "Postpartum Amenorrhea: How is it Affected by Maternal Nutritional Status?" *Science* 200,9:1155-1157.

Ibrahim, B. M. 1974. *The Population Averted in Egypt 1966-73.* Paper presented at the Tenth Conference on Statistics and Computer Science. Institute of Statistical Studies and Research, Cairo University, Cairo.

Isely, R., Zivetz, L., Norman, R., and Banatte, H. 1979a. "Determinants of Child Survival." *Relationships of Rural Development Strategies to Health and Nutritional Status: Consequences for Fertility.* Mimeographed paper. Research Triangle Park, N.C.: Research Triangle Institute.

Isely, R., Zivetz, L., Norman, R., and Banatte, H. 1979b. "Child Survival and Fertility." *Relationships of Rural Development Strategies to Health and Nutritional Status: Consequences for Fertility.* Mimeographed paper. Research Triangle Park, N.C.: Research Triangle Institute.

Iskander, N., and Omar, I. 1979. "Population and Development Project, Management Development, and Training of Coordinators." *Population Studies* (Cairo) 50:53-75.

Issa, M. S. A. 1971. "Recent Fertility Trends in Egypt." *Fertility Trends and Differentials in Arab Countries*, Part 1, Research Monograph Series. Cairo: Cairo Demographic Centre 2:151-162.

Issa, M. S. A. 1981. *Modernization and the Fertility Transition, Egypt: 1975*. Ph.D. dissertation, University of Pennsylvania.

Issawi, C. 1949. "Population and Wealth in Egypt." *Milbank Memorial Fund Quarterly* 27,1:98-115.

Issawi, C. 1963. *Egypt in Revolution: An Economic Analysis*. London: Oxford University Press.

Iutaka, S., Bock, E. W., and Varnes, W. G. 1971. "Factors Affecting Fertility of Natives and Migrants in Urban Brazil." *Population Studies* 25 (March):55-62.

Jaffe, A. J., and Azumi, K. 1960. "The Birth Rate and Cottage Industries in Underdeveloped Countries." *Economic Development and Cultural Change* 9:52-63.

Jain, A. K. 1981. "The Effect of Female Education on Fertility: A Simple Explanation." *Demography* 18,4:577-595.

Johnson, G. E., and Whitelaw, W. E. 1974. "Urban-rural Income Transfers in Kenya: An Estimated Remittance Function." *Economic Development and Cultural Change* 22,3:473-479.

Johnston, B. F., and Clark, W. C. 1982. *Redesigning Rural Development: A Strategic Perspective*. Baltimore: Johns Hopkins University Press.

Kamel, W. H., et al. 1971. "The Health Educative Role of the Nurse in Family Planning." *Egyptian Population and Family Planning Review* 4 (December):7-17.

Kasarda, J. D. 1971. "Economic Structure and Fertility: A Comparative Analysis." *Demography* 8:307-317.

Kelley, A. C. 1976. "Savings, Demographic Change, and Economic Development." *Economic Development and Cultural Change* 24 (July):683-694.

Kelley, A. C. 1980. "Interactions of Economic and Demographic Household Behavior." In *Population and Economic Change in Less Developed Countries*, ed. R. A. Easterlin. Chicago: University of Chicago Press for NBER.

Kelley, A. C., and Swartz, C. 1979. "The Impact of Family Structure on Household Decision Making in Developing Countries: A Case Study of Urban Kenya." In *Economic and Demographic Change: Issues for the 1980s*. Liege, Belgium: Ordina Editions for the IUSSP.

Kelley, A. C., and da Silva, L. M. 1980. "The Choice of Family Size and the Compatibility of Female Workforce Participation in the Low-Income Setting." *Revue Economique* 31,6 (November):1081-1104.

Khalifa, A. M. 1971a. *Differential Fertility in Egypt: A Multi-Variate Analysis*. Ph.D. Dissertation. Chapel Hill, N.C.: The University of North Carolina.

Khalifa, A. M. 1971b. "Economic Aspects of Fertility. An Appraisal." *Egyptian Population and Family Planning Review* 4,2 (December):17-31.

Khalifa, A. M. 1973a. "A Proposed Explanation of the Fertility Gap Differentials by Socio-Economic Status and Modernity: The Case of Egypt." *Population Studies* 27,3:431-442.

Khalifa, A. M. 1973b. *Status of Women in Relation to Fertility and Family*

Planning in Egypt. Cairo: National Centre for Sociological and Criminological Research.

Khalifa, A. M. 1976. "The Influence of Wife's Education on Fertility in Rural Egypt." *Journal of Biosocial Science* 68:53-60.

Khalifa, A. M. 1978. "Rural-Urban Fertility Differences and Trends in Rural Egypt, 1930-1970." In *Women's Status and Fertility in the Muslim World*, ed. J. Allman. New York: Praeger Publishers.

Khalifa, A. M., and Abdel-Kader, M. 1981a. *Modernity, Fertility and Contraceptive Behavior in Rural Egypt*. Cairo: National Centre for Sociological and Criminological Research.

Khalifa, A. M., Sayed, H. A.. and El-Khorazaty, M. N. 1981b. *Marriage, Fertility and Family Planning: A Study of the RFS 1979*. Cairo: Population and Family Planning Board. (Arabic)

Khalifa, A. M., and Way, A. 1981c. *An Evaluation of the Impact of the Population and Development Program (PDP), Based on Data from the 1980 Contraceptive Prevalance Survey*. Mimeographed paper. Columbia, Md.: Population and Family Planning Board and Westinghouse Health Systems.

Khan, M. A., and Sirageldin, I. 1975. *Education, Income and Fertility in Pakistan*. Paper presented at the Applied Research Institute, University of Karachi and Research Department of United Bank, Ltd. (September).

Khattab, H. 1978. "Practice and Non-Practice of Family Planning in Egypt." In *Social Sciences in Family Planning*, ed. A. Molnos. London: International Planned Parenthood Federation.

Kim, M. 1977. "Age at Marriage, Family Planning Practices and Other Variables as Correlates of Fertility in Korea." *Demography* 1 (November): 413-428.

Kirk, D. 1966. "Factors Affecting Moslem Natality." In *Family Planning and Population Programs: A Review of World Developments*, ed. B. Berelson et al. Chicago: University of Chicago Press.

Kirk, D. 1971. "A New Demographic Transition?" In *Rapid Population Growth: Consequences and Policy Implications*, National Academy of Sciences. Baltimore: Johns Hopkins University Press.

Kleinman, D. S. 1973. "Fertility Variation and Resources in Rural India." *Development and Cultural Change* 21:679-696.

Knodel, J., and Prachuabmoh, V. 1973. "Desired Family Size in Thailand: Are the Responses Meaningful?" *Demography* 10:619-637.

Knodel, J., and Pitakepsombati, P. 1973. "Thailand: Fertility and Family Planning among Rural and Urban Women." *Studies in Family Planning* 4 (September):229-255.

Knowles, J. C., and Anker, R. 1975. *Economic Determinants of Demographic Behavior in Kenya*. Mimeographed paper. World Employment Project. Geneva: International Labor Organization.

Knowles, J. C., and Anker, R. 1981. "An Analysis of Income Transfers in a Developing Country: The Case of Kenya." *Journal of Development Economics* 8 (July):205-226.

Kocher, J. E. 1973. *Rural Development, Income Distribution and Fertility Decline*. New York: The Population Council.

Kocher, J. E. 1977. *Rural Development and Fertility Change in North-East Tanzania*. Mimeographed. In the collected papers of The Population Association of America's Annual Meeting, St. Louis 5:378-398.

Kogut, E. L. 1974. "The Economic Analysis of Fertility: A Study of Brazil." *International Labor Organization (ILO) Population and Employment Working Paper* 7 (September).

Kupinsky, S. 1977. *The Fertility of Working Women: A Synthesis of International Research.* New York: Praeger Publishers.

Lancaster, K. 1966. "A New Approach to Consumer Theory." *Journal of Political Economy* 74 (April):132-157.

Latif, A., and Chowdhury, A. K. M. 1977. "Land Ownership and Fertility in Two Areas of Bangladesh." *Bangladesh Development Studies* 5:239-245.

Leibenstein, H. 1957. *Economic Backwardness and Economic Growth.* New York: John Wiley and Sons; London: Chapman and Hall.

Leibenstein, H. 1974. "An Interpretation of the Economic Theory of Fertility." *Journal of Economic Literature* 12,2 (June):457-79.

Lindert, P. H. 1978. *Fertility and Scarcity in America.* Princeton, N.J.: Princeton University Press.

Loza, S. F. 1979. "Differential Concern for Children's Education in Egypt and its Effect on Fertility." *Population Studies* (Cairo) 51 (October/December):9-29.

Loza, S. F., and El-Khorazaty, M. N. 1979. *Causes of Fertility Differences in Egypt: Intermediate Variable Analysis.* Paper presented at the 14th Annual Conference on Statistics, Computer Science and Operations Research, 10-12 March 1979. Institute of Statistical Studies and Research, Cairo University, Cairo.

Madalla, G. S., and Nelson, F. D. 1974. "Maximum Likelihood Methods for Models of Markets in Disequilibrium." *Econometrica* 42,6:1013-1030.

Marzouk, Z. A. 1973. "Social Studies on Fertility and Contraception in Alexandria." In *Egypt: Population Problems and Prospects*, ed. A. R. Omran. Chapel Hill, N.C.: Carolina Population Center, University of North Carolina.

Mason, K. O. et al. 1971. *Social and Economic Correlates of Family Fertility: A Survey of the Evidence.* Mimeographed paper. Research Triangle Park, N.C.: Research Triangle Institute.

Mata, L., et al. 1972. "Influence of Recurrent Infections on Nutrition and Growth of Children in Guatemala." *American Journal of Clinical Nutrition* 25 (November):1267-1275.

Mauldin, P., and Berelson, B. 1979. "Conditions of Fertility Decline in Developing Countries, 1965-75." In *Demographic Transition and Socioeconomic Development.* Proceedings of the United Nations/UNFPA Expert Group Meeting, Istanbul. New York: United Nations.

Maurer, K., Ratajczak, R., and Schultz, T. P. 1973. *Marriage, Fertility, and Labor Force Participation of Thai Women: an Econometric Study.* Mimeographed paper. Santa Monica, Calif.: The Rand Corporation, R-829-AID/RF.

Mauskopf, J. A. 1981. *Births, Deaths, and Replacement Births: Application of a Maximum Likelihood Model to Brazil.* Ph.D. Dissertation. Durham, N.C.: Duke University.

Mazhar, K. 1970. "Family Planning In Egypt." *Family Planning in Africa Programs and Constraints.* Proceedings of a Working Group Held at the

Development Centre, Paris.

Mazhar, K. 1973. "A Note on the Assets and Difficulties of Egypt's Family Planning Program." In *Egypt: Population Problems and Prospects*, ed. A. R. Omran. Chapel Hill, N.C.: Carolina Population Center, University of North Carolina.

Mazur, D. P. 1973. "Relation of Marriage and Education to Fertility in the USSR." *Population Studies* 27,1 (March):105-115.

McCabe, J. L., and Rosenzweig, M. R. 1976. "Female Employment Creation and Family Size." In *Population and Development: The Search for Selective Interventions*, ed. R. G. Ridker. Baltimore: Johns Hopkins University Press.

McGreevey, W. P., and Birdsall, N. 1974. *The Policy Relevance of Recent Social Research on Fertility*. Washington, D.C.: Interdisciplinary Communications Program, Smithsonian Institute.

McNicoll, G. 1975. "Community-Level Population Policy: An Exploration." *Population and Development Review* 1:1-21.

Mead, D. C. 1967. *Growth and Structural Change in the Egyptian Economy.* Homewood, Ill.: Richard D. Irwin.

Menken, J. A., Trussell, T. J., and Watkins, S. 1981. "The Nutrition Fertility Link: An Evaluation of the Evidence." *Journal of Interdisciplinary History* 11: 425-441.

Merrick, T. W. 1978. "Fertility and Land Availability in Rural Brazil." *Demography* 15:321-336.

Michael, R. T. 1973. "Education and the Derived Demand for Children." *Journal of Political Economy* 81, part 2 (March/April):S128-S164.

Mousa, A. H., and Mohamed, S. 1973. "Differential Death, Sex and Age Groups in Urban and Rural, Arab Republic of Egypt 1963-1970." *Population Researches and Studies* 5 (October):29-35.

Muth, R. 1966. "Household Production and Consumer Demand Functions." *Econometrica* 34 (July):699-708.

Nag, M. 1979. *How Modernization Can Also Increase Fertility.* New York: The Population Council.

Nag, M., Peet, R. C., and White, B. N. F. 1977. *Economic Value of Children in Two Peasant Societies.* International Union for the Scientific Study of Population, International Population Conference, Mexico. Liege, Belgium: IUSSP 1:123-139.

National Academy of Sciences. 1981. *The Estimation of Recent Trends in Fertility and Mortality in Egypt.* Report No. 9 by the Committee on Population and Demography. Washington, D. C.: National Academy Press.

Neher, P. 1971. "Peasants, Procreation and Pensions." *American Economic Review* 61 (June):380-399.

Nerlove, M., and Schultz, T. P. 1970. *Love and Life Between the Censuses: Model of Family Decision-Making in Puerto Rico, 1950-1960.* Mimeographed paper. Santa Monica, Calif.: The Rand Corporation, RM-6322-AID.

Nizamuddin, M. 1980. *Community and Program Variables and their Effects on Fertility Related Behavior of Rural Pakistani Women.* Background Paper No. 6 presented at the World Fertility Survey Conference, 7-11 July 1980, London.

Notestein, F. W., et al. 1944. *The Future Population of Europe and the Soviet Union.* Geneva: League of Nations.

O'Hara, D. J. 1972. "Mortality Risks, Sequential Decisions on Births and Population Growth." *Demography* 4,3 (August):285-298.

Olsen, R. J. 1980. "Estimating the Effect of Child Mortality on the Number of Births." *Demography* 17,4 (November):429-444.

Omran, A. R. 1973a. *Egypt: Population Problems and Prospects.* Chapel Hill, N.C.: Carolina Population Center, University of North Carolina.

Omran, A. R. 1973b. "The Population of Egypt, Past and Present." In *Egypt: Population Problems and Prospects*, ed. A. R. Omran. Chapel Hill, N.C.: Carolina Population Center, University of North Carolina.

Omran, A. R. 1973c. "The Mortality Profile." In *Egypt: Population Problems and Prospects*, ed. A. R. Omran. Chapel Hill, N.C.: Carolina Population Center, University of North Carolina.

Omran, A. R. 1973d. "The Fertility Profile." In *Egypt: Population Problems and Prospects*, ed. A. R. Omran. Chapel Hill, N.C.: Carolina Population Center, Univeristy of North Carolina.

Omran, A. R., and El-Khorazaty, M. N. 1977. *The Development Level Needed to Enhance Family Planning Programs.* A paper presented at the Annual Meeting of the Population Association of America, St. Louis.

Omran, A. R., and El-Nomrosey, M. M. 1973. "The Family Planning Efforts in Egypt." In *Egypt: Population Problems and Prospects*, ed. A. R. Omran. Chapel Hill, N.C.: Carolina Population Center, University of North Carolina.

Palmore, J. A. 1969. "The West Malaysian Family Survey, 1966-1967." *Studies in Family Planning* 40 (April):11-20.

Palmore, J. A., and Ariffin, M. 1969. "Marriage Patterns and Cumulative Fertility in West Malaysia: 1966-1967." *Demography* 6 (November):383-401.

Paydarfar, A. A. 1975. "Sociocultural Correlates of Fertility Among Tribal, Rural and Urban Populations in Iran." *Social Biology* 22 (Summer):151-166.

Peek, P. 1975. "Female Employment and Fertility: A Study Based on Chilean Data." *International Labor Review* 122:207-216.

Piatier, A., and Geraud, P. 1976. *Relationships Between Demography and Socioeconomic Development: An Attempt to Determine Some Variables for Planning Purposes.* Cairo: Population and Family Planning Board.

Plank, S. J., and Milanesi, M. L. 1973. "Infant Feeding and Infant Mortality in Rural Chile." *Bulletin of the World Health Organization* 48: 203-210.

Pool, D. I. 1970. "Social Change and Interest in Family Planning in Ghana: An Exploratory Analysis." *Canadian Journal of African Studies* 4 (Spring): 209-227.

Population and Family Planning Board. 1979. *Demographic Situation in Egypt.* Mimeographed paper. Paper submitted to the Chairman of the Supreme Council for Population and Family Planning. Cairo: Population and Family Planning Board.

The Population Council. 1974. *Arab Republic of Egypt: Country Prospects.* New York: The Population Council.

Preston, S. H. 1975a. Introduction. In *Seminar on Infant Mortality in*

Relation to the Level of Fertility. Paris: Committee for International Coordination of National Research in Demography.

Preston, S. H. 1975b. "Health Programs and Population Growth." *Population and Development Review* 1,2 (December):189-200.

Preston, S. H. 1976. *Mortality Patterns in National Populations with Special Reference to Recorded Causes of Death.* New York: Academic Press.

Preston, S. H., ed. 1978. *The Effects of Infant and Child Mortality on Fertility.* New York: Academic Press.

Preston, S. H., Keyfitz, N., and Schoen, R. 1972. *Causes of Death: Life Tables for National Populations.* New York: Seminar Press.

Rashad, H. 1974. "Implications of Alternative Patterns of Population Growth to Economic Development in Egypt." Technical Papers, Demographic Projection Analysis. Cairo: American University in Cairo.

Rempel, H., and Lobdell, R. A. 1978. "The Role of Urban-to-Rural Remittances in Rural Development." *Journal of Development Studies* 14,3.

Ridker, R. 1976. *Population and Development: The Search for Selective Intervention.* Baltimore: The Johns Hopkins University Press.

Rizk, H. 1977. "Trends in Fertility and Family Planning in Jordan." *Studies in Family Planning* 8 (April):91-99.

Rodgers, G. B. 1978. "Fertility and Desired Fertility: Longitudinal Evidence From Thailand." *Population Studies* 30:511-526.

Romaniuk, A. 1981. "Increase in Natural Fertility During the Early Stages of Modernization: Canadian Indians Case Study." *Demography* 18,2 (May):157-179.

Rosenzweig, M. R. 1976a. *Rural Wages, Labor Supply and Land Reform: A Theoretical and Empirical Analysis.* Discussion Paper No. 20. Research Program in Development Studies, Princeton University (December).

Rosenzweig, M. R. 1976b. "Female Work Experience, Employment Status, and Birth Expectations: Sequential Decision-Making in the Philippines." *Demography* 13:339-356.

Rosenzweig, M. R. 1977. "The Demand for Children in Farm Households." *Journal of Political Economy* 85:123-146.

Russet, B. B., et al. 1964. *World Handbook of Social and Political Indicators.* New Haven: Yale University Press.

Ryder, N. B. 1960. Comment in *Economics of the Family: Marriage, Children and Human Capital*, ed. T. W. Schultz. Chicago: University of Chicago Press for the NBER.

Sanderson, W. C. 1976. "On Two Schools of the Economics of Fertility." *Population and Development Review* 2,3-4(September and December):469-477.

Sarhan, A. E. 1967. "Mortality Trends in the U.A.R." *Fertility, Family Planning, Mortality.* World Population Conference, 1965. New York: United Nations 2:358-360.

Sauvy, A. 1969. *General Theory of Population.* New York: Basic Books.

Sayed, H. A., and El-Khorazaty, M. N. 1980. "Levels and Differentials of Fertility in Egypt." *Population Studies* (Cairo) 55 (October/December):11-38.

Sayed, Y., ed. 1978. *A Theoretical Framework for the Rural Development*

Project. Cairo: Population and Family Planning Board. (Arabic).

Schieffelin, O., ed. 1967. *Muslim Attitudes Toward Family Planning*. New York: The Population Council.

Schultz, T. P. 1969. "An Economic Model of Family Planning and Fertility." *Journal of Political Economy* 77 (March/April):153-180.

Schultz, T. P. 1970. *Fertility Patterns and their Determinants in the Arab Middle East; Research Program on Economic and Political Prospects of the Middle East*. Santa Monica, Calif.: The Rand Corporation Resources for the Future.

Schultz, T. P. 1972. "Fertility Patterns and Their Determinants in the Arab Middle East." In *Economic Development and Population Growth in the Middle East*, ed. C. Cooper and S. Alexander. New York: Elsevier.

Schultz, T. P. 1973. "Explanation of Birth Rate Changes Over Space and Time; A Study of Taiwan." *Journal of Political Economy* 81, part 2 (March/April):S238-74.

Schultz, T. P. 1978. "Fertility and Child Mortality Over the Life Cycle: Aggregate and Individual Experience." *American Economic Review* 68 (May):208-15.

Schultz, T. P. 1981. *Economics of Population*. Reading, Mass.: Addison-Wesley Publishing Company.

Schultz, T. W. 1974a. *Economics of the Family: Marriage, Children and Human Capital*, ed. T. W. Schultz. Chicago: University of Chicago Press for the NBER.

Schultz, T. W. 1974b. "Fertility and Economic Values." In *Economics of the Family: Marriage, Children, and Human Capital*, ed. T. W. Schultz. Chicago: University of Chicago Press for the NBER.

Scrimshaw, N. S. 1970. "Synergism of Malnutrition and Infection." *Journal of the American Medical Association* 212,10:1685-1692.

Scrimshaw, N. S. 1978. "Infant Mortality and Behavior in the Regulation of Family Size." *Population and Development Review* 4,3 (September): 383-403.

Sear, A. M. 1975. "Predictors of Contraceptive Practice for Low Income Women in Cali, Columbia." *Journal of Biosocial Science* 7:171-188.

Shanawany, H. 1973. "Stages in the Development of a Population Control Policy." In *Egypt: Population Problems and Prospects*, ed. A. R. Omran. Chapel Hill, N.C.: Carolina Population Center, University of North Carolina.

Shanawany, H. 1980. *Utilizing Research to Manage the Population and Development Project*. Paper presented at the Seminar on The Demographic Situation in Egypt. Institute of Statistical Studies and Research, Cairo University, Cairo.

Shapiro, S., Schlesinger, E. R., and Nesbit, R. E., Jr. 1968. *Infant, Perinatal, Maternal and Childhood Mortality in the United States*. Cambridge, Mass.: Harvard University Press.

Shryock, H. S., and Siegel, J. S. 1973. *The Methods and Materials of Demography*, Volumes 1 and 2. Washington, D.C.: U. S. Bureau of the Census.

Simon, J. L. 1974. *The Effects of Income on Fertility*. Chapel Hill, N.C.: Carolina Population Center, University of North Carolina.

Snyder, D. W. 1974. "Economic Determinants of Family Size in West

Africa." *Demography* 11:613-627.

Speare, A., Jr., et al. 1973. "Urbanization, Non-Familial Work, Education and Fertility in Taiwan." *Population Studies* 27 (July):323-334.

Stoeckel, J., and Chowdhury, A. K. M. 1969. "Differential Fertility in a Rural Area of East Pakistan." *Milbank Momorial Fund Quartorly* 47:189-198.

Stycos, J. M. 1968. *Human Fertility in Latin America.* Ithaca, N.Y.: Cornell University Press.

Stycos, J. M., and Avery, R. 1980. *Early Impact Measurement of the Egyptian Population and Development Program, Based on Data from the 1979 Rural Fertility Survey.* Mimeographed paper. Ithaca, N.Y.: International Population Program, Cornell University.

Stys, W. 1957. "The Influence of Economic Conditions on the Fertility of Peasant Women." *Population Studies* 11:136-148.

Supreme Council for Population and Family Planning. 1973. *National Policy of Population and Family Planning.* Cairo: The Supreme Council for Population and Family Planning.

Supreme Council for Population and Family Planning. 1980. *National Population, Human Resources Development and Family Planning Programme Strategy.* Cairo: The Supreme Council for Population and Family Planning.

Thavarajah, A., and Farag, M. M. 1971. "Demographic and Socio-Economic Characteristics of Women Seeking Fertility Control." *Fertility Trends and Differentials in Arab Countries*, Part III, Research Monograph Series. Cairo: Cairo Demographic Centre 2:311-344.

Thompson, W. S. 1929. "Population." *American Journal of Sociology* 34,6 (May):959-975.

Timur, S. 1977. "Demographic Correlates of Women's Education: Fertility, Age at Marriage and the Family." International Union for the Scientific Study of Population, International Population Conference, Mexico. Liege, Belgium: IUSSP.

Trussell, T. J. 1978. "Menarche and Fatness: Reexamination of the Critical Body Composition Hypothesis." *Science* 200 (1978):1506-1509.

Trussell, T. J. 1979. "Natural Fertility: Measurement and Use in Fertility Models." In *Natural Fertility*, ed. H. Leridon and J. Menken. Leige, Belgium: Ordina Editions.

Turchi, B. 1975. *The Demand for Children: The Economics of Fertility in the U.S.*. Cambridge, Mass.: Ballinger Publishing Company.

United Nations. 1978. "United Nations/UNFPA Expert Group Meeting on Demographic Transition and Socio-Economic Development." *Population Bulletin of the United Nations* 11:60-66.

United Nations. 1980. *World Population Trends and Policies: 1979 Monitoring Report.* Volume 1, ST/ESA/SER.A/70. New York: United Nations.

UNFPA. 1979. *On Integration of Family Planning with Rural Development.* Policy Development Studies, No. 1. New York: United Nations Fund for Population Activities.

UNFPA. 1980. *Donor Assistance to Family Planning Programmes in Egypt.* Mimeographed paper. New York: United Nations Fund for Population Activities.

UNFPA. 1981a. *Report of Mission on Needs Assessment for Population*

Assistance. Mimeographed paper. Report Number 37. New York: United Nations Fund for Population Activities.

UNFPA. 1981b. *1980 Report*. New York: United Nations Fund for Population Activities.

Vaidyanathan, K. E. 1972. "Some Indices of Differential Mortality in India." In *Studies on Mortality in India*, ed. K. E. Vaidyanathan. Gandhigram: Institute of Rural Health and Family Planning.

Valaoras, V. G. 1972. *Population Analysis of Egypt, 1935-1970: with Special Reference to Mortality*. Occasional Paper No.1. Cairo: Cairo Demographic Center.

Wallace, T. D. 1979. *Child Replacement and Fertility: Adjusting for Spurious Correlation*. Mimeographed paper. Durham, N.C.: Duke University.

Ware, H. 1977. "The Relationship Between Infant Mortality and Fertility: Replacement and Insurance Effects." Proceedings of the IUSSP Conference, Mexico City. Liege, Belgium: International Union for the Scientific Study of Population.

Weekes-Vaglioni, W. 1976. *Family Life and Structure in Southern Cameroon*. Paris: Development Centre of Office of Economic Cooperation and Development.

Weintraub, R. 1962. "The Birth Rate and Economic Development." *Econometrica* 30 (October):812-817.

WFS. 1977. *Basic Documentation: Guidelines for Country Report No. 1*. London: World Fertility Survey.

Williams, A. D. 1977. "Measuring the Impact of Child Mortality on Fertility: A Methodological Note." *Demography* 14:581-590.

Willis, R. J. 1973. "Economic Theory of Fertility Behavior." In *Economics of the Family: Marriage, Children, and Human Capital*, ed. T. W. Schultz. Chicago: University of Chicago Press.

World Bank. 1980. *World Tables 1980*. Baltimore: Johns Hopkins University Press for the World Bank.

Yaukey, D., and Thorsen, T. 1972. "Differential Female Days at First Marriage in Six Latin American Cities." *Journal of Marriage and the Family* (May):375-379.

Zikry, A. M. 1963. *Socio-Cultural Determinants of Human Fertility in Egypt*. Ph.D. Dissertation. Syracuse, N.Y.: Syracuse University.

Index

ABOUT THE AUTHORS

ALLEN C. KELLEY, Ph.D. Stanford University (1964), is James B. Duke Professor of Economics and Associate Director, Center for Demographic Studies, Duke University. Previously on the faculty of economics at the University of Wisconsin-Madison, Dr. Kelley has also held visiting positions at the Australian National University, Harvard University, Heriot-Watt University in Edinburgh, International Institute for Applied Systems Analysis in Vienna, and Stanford University. A specialist in economic demography, development and history, his collaborative books include *Dualistic Economic Development: Theory and History, Lessons from Japanese Development: An Analytical Economic History,* and *Disease and Economic Development.*

ATEF M. KHALIFA, Ph.D. University of North Carolina at Chapel Hill (1971), is Professor and Chairman of the Department of Population and Biostatistics, Cairo University. A sociologist by training, his research has highlighted the interrelationships between education and fertility, and has included extensive empirical analysis of demographic problems in the Arab region. As Director of the Department of Statistics of the Egyptian Population and Family Planning Board, Dr. Khalifa was responsible for the Rural Fertility Survey and the Contraceptive Prevalence Survey.

M. NABIL EL-KHORAZATY, Ph.D. University of North Carolina at Chapel Hill (1975), is Associate Professor in the Department of Statistics, Cairo University. An applied statistician by training, his research has focused on demographic problems, including an investigation of the determinants of family planning in Egypt, as well as the application of statistical models to demographic estimation and analysis. As Director of the Monitoring and Evaluation Office of the Egyptian Population and Family Planning Board, Dr. El-Khorazaty has carried out and supervised numerous research projects which delineate various aspects of population policy in Egypt, including an analysis of the Population and Development Project (PDP).

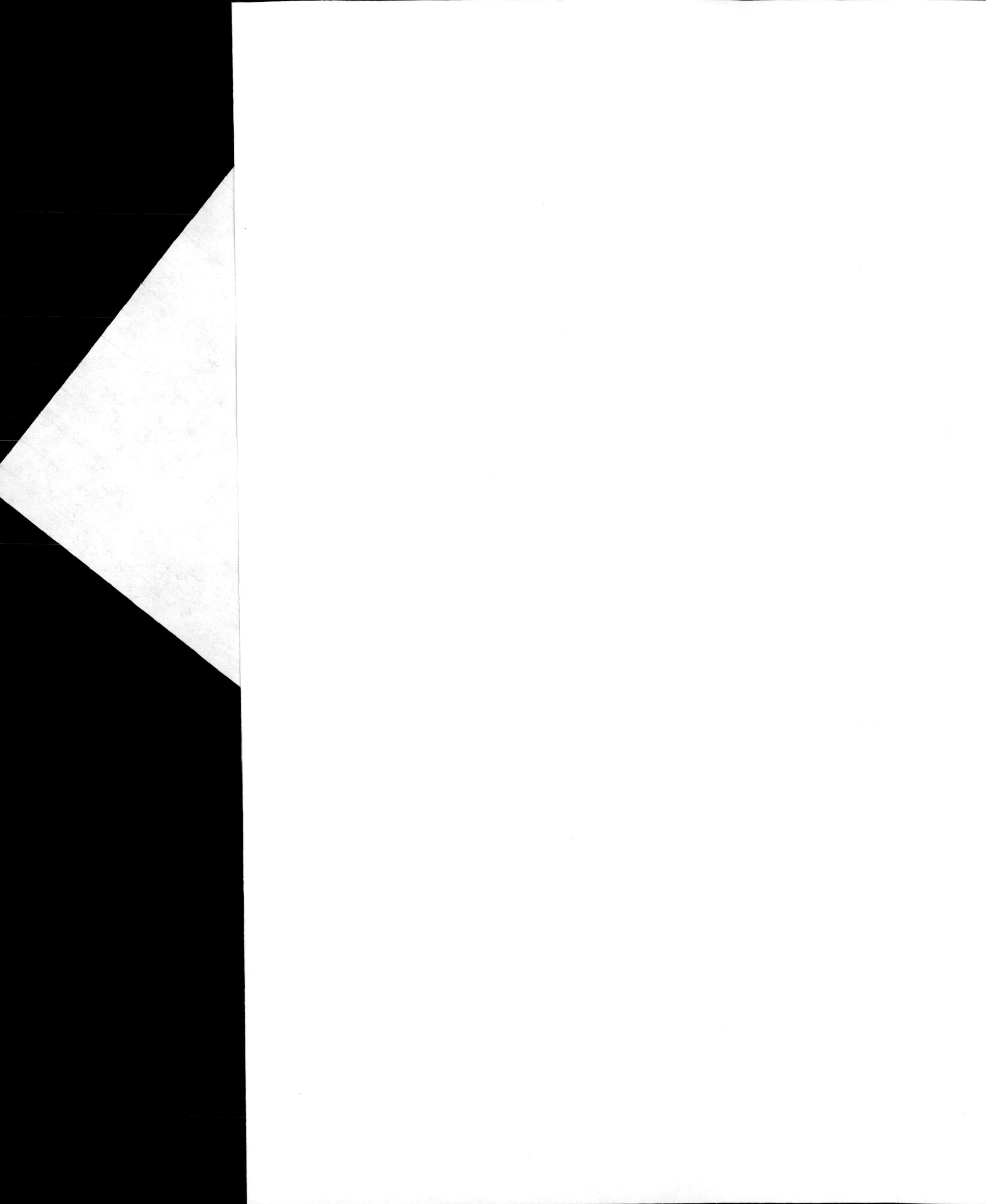

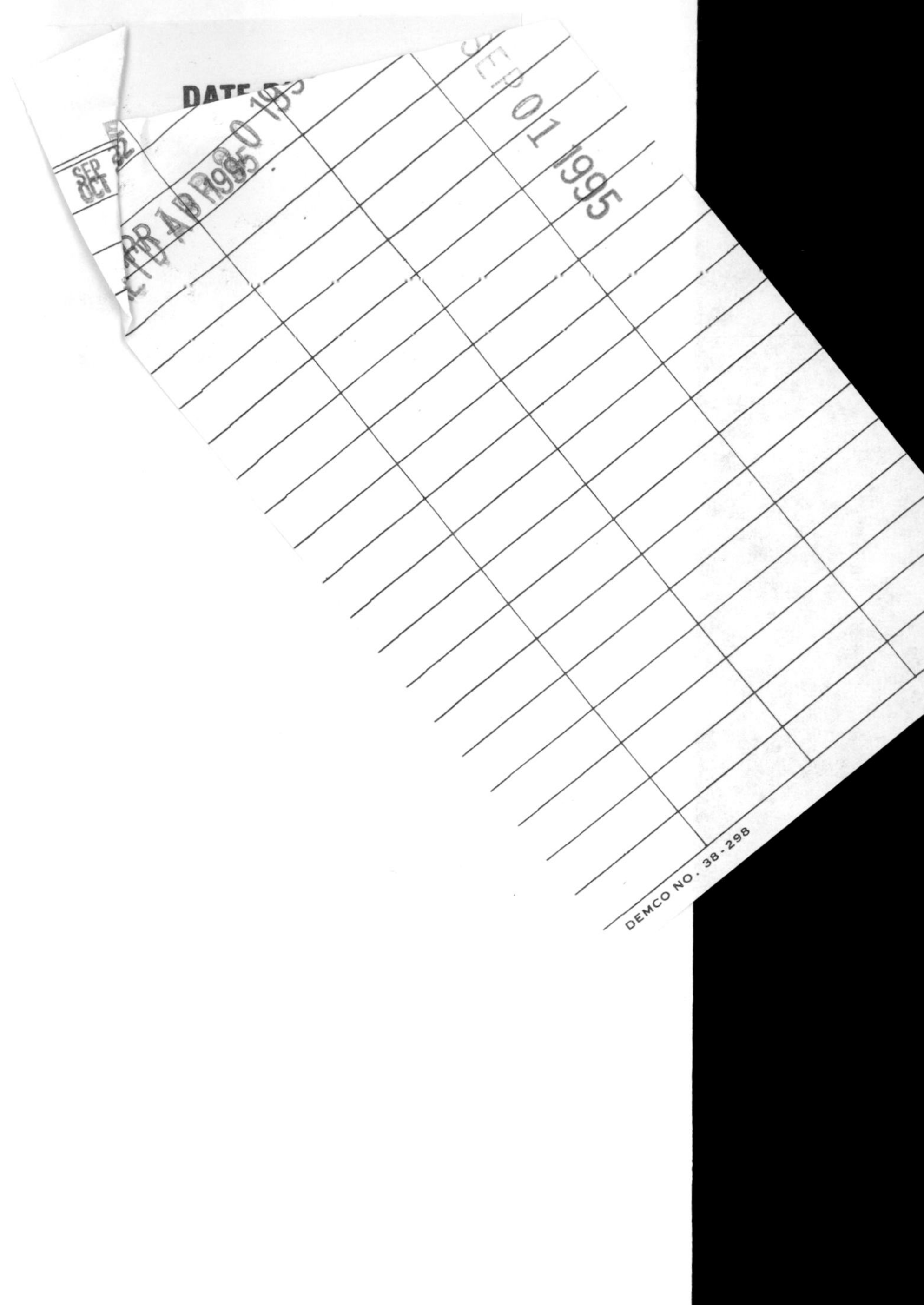
DATE D
SEP 01 1995
DEMCO NO. 38-298

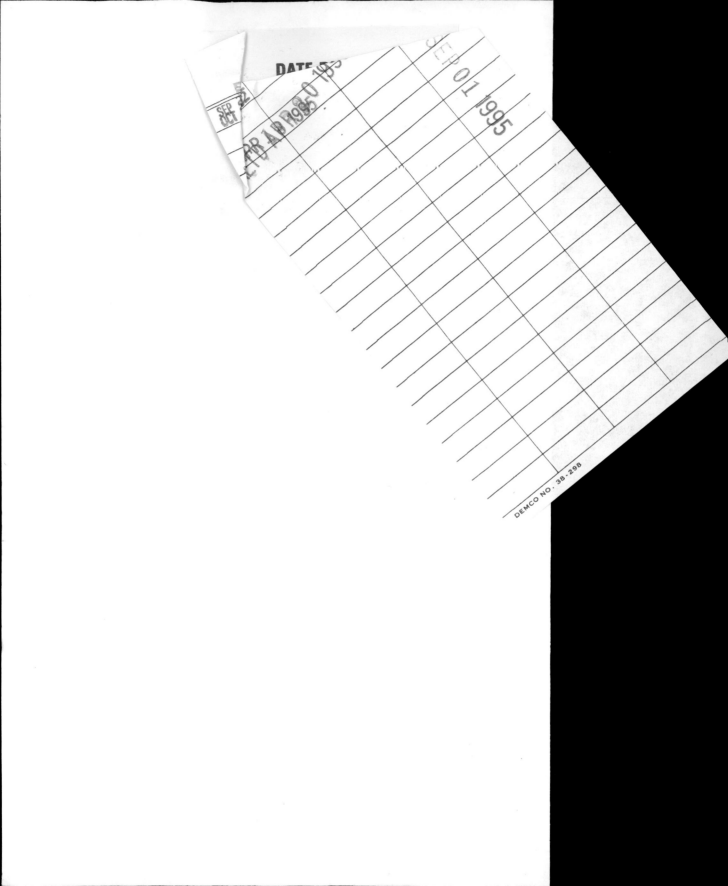